GOVERNANCE IN TRANSITION

PUBLIC
MANAGEMENT REFORMS
IN OECD COUNTRIES

ORGANISATION FOR ECONOMIC CO-OPERATION AND DEVELOPMENT

ORGANISATION FOR ECONOMIC CO-OPERATION AND DEVELOPMENT

Pursuant to Article 1 of the Convention signed in Paris on 14th December 1960, and which came into force on 30th September 1961, the Organisation for Economic Co-operation and Development (OECD) shall promote policies designed:

— to achieve the highest sustainable economic growth and employment and a rising standard of living in Member countries, while maintaining financial stability, and thus to contribute to the development of the world economy;

— to contribute to sound economic expansion in Member as well as non-member countries in the process of economic development; and

— to contribute to the expansion of world trade on a multilateral, non-discriminatory basis in accordance with international obligations.

The original Member countries of the OECD are Austria, Belgium, Canada, Denmark, France, Germany, Greece, Iceland, Ireland, Italy, Luxembourg, the Netherlands, Norway, Portugal, Spain, Sweden, Switzerland, Turkey, the United Kingdom and the United States. The following countries became Members subsequently through accession at the dates indicated hereafter: Japan (28th April 1964), Finland (28th January 1969), Australia (7th June 1971), New Zealand (29th May 1973) and Mexico (18th May 1994). The Commission of the European Communities takes part in the work of the OECD (Article 13 of the OECD Convention).

Publié en français sous le titre :

LA GESTION PUBLIQUE EN MUTATION
LES RÉFORMES DANS LES PAYS DE L'OCDE

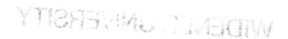

FOREWORD

The role of government is evolving in OECD countries in response to fundamental changes in economies and societies. In adjusting to these new demands and conditions, governments of OECD Member countries are reviewing and reforming systems of public management. They are reconsidering how government relates to citizens and enterprises, how best to ensure provision of public services, and how to define the inherent functions that governments must perform. In short, they are deeply concerned with maintaining the capacity to govern in the face of great change.

Although pressures for reform, national cultures, and phases of development differ widely, Member countries have increasingly come to pursue a common reform agenda driven by the need for fiscal consolidation, by the globalisation of the economy, and by the impossibility of meeting an apparently infinite set of demands on public resources.

The purpose of this report is to present an overview of these dynamic changes in strategies of governance, and to offer countries an opportunity to compare their own ideas and progress with those of other countries.

This report is also a synthesis of current and past work carried out in the Public Management Service (PUMA). During its first mandate, which ended in 1994, the Public Management Committee produced several general reports on public sector management developments and structures, and many reports on particular managerial issues and emerging trends. Based on this body of work, this report sets out the results of an effort by the Committee to analyse broad developments in public management. It takes stock of the various reform approaches being tried, highlights promising practices in selected areas, and points to issues still being faced.

The Public Management Committee has reviewed and discussed the report, and has agreed on a statement on public management reform. This statement is set out as **Conclusions of the Public Management Committee** in the first section of this book.

Although the report has been prepared with the active collaboration of Member countries, the views and conclusions in its main body may not be shared by national authorities. It is published under my responsibility.

Jean-Claude PAYE
Secretary General

TABLE OF CONTENTS

Part A

OVERALL ANALYSIS

Part B

SPECIFIC REFORM INITIATIVES

CONCLUSIONS OF THE OECD PUBLIC MANAGEMENT COMMITTEE

The demands placed upon governance in OECD countries are considerably more complex today than when the OECD was established thirty years ago. Governments in Member countries are still committed to promoting policies that achieve the highest sustainable economic growth and employment and that contribute to economic and social well-being. But today such efforts must be pursued in a different context. The world economy is increasingly dynamic, open, and internationally competitive. The importance of the public sector has grown considerably, such that its efficiency has a significant impact on total economic efficiency. More than ever, its activities affect the operating environment of the private sector. Good governance is critical to ensuring that challenges to society are dealt with adequately.

Unchanged governance structures and classic responses of "more of the same" are inappropriate to this intricate policy environment, since:

- maximising economic performance and ensuring social cohesion requires governments to adjust rapidly to changing circumstances, to create and exploit new opportunities and thus to deploy and redeploy resources more rapidly and flexibly;
- highly centralised, rule-bound, and inflexible organisations that emphasize process rather than results impede good performance;
- large government debts and fiscal imbalances exacerbated by recession – and their implications for interest rates, investment, and job creation – place limits on the size of the state and require governments to pursue greater cost-effectiveness in the allocation and management of public resources;
- extensive and unwieldy government regulations that affect the cost structures and thus the productivity of the private sector restrict the flexibility needed in an increasingly competitive international market-place;
- demographic changes and economic and social developments are adding to the services that the community expects from governments, while consumers are demanding a greater say in what governments do and how they do it; they expect value for money and are increasingly reluctant to pay higher taxes.

The challenge for governance at the end of the 20th century is one of institutional renewal. Setting appropriate frameworks for both public and private sector activity under conditions of increasing global interdependence, uncertainty, and accelerating change is a major challenge. It requires a reappraisal of the rationale for government intervention and a re-examination of the cost-effectiveness of public sector institutions, their programmes and regulatory activities. Governments must strive to do things better, with fewer resources, and, above all, differently. Outdated institutions and practices need to be redesigned or replaced with ones that better match the realities and demands of dynamic market economies with the objectives and responsibilities of democratic systems. If the public sector is to remain responsive to the needs of those it serves, governments must foster the development of organisations that perpetually adapt and reshape themselves to meet changing client needs, and that develop new ways to cope with the changing world. Governments must be willing and able to learn.

Reforming management

Responding adequately to this challenge demands radical change to the structures and processes for managing public action. Member countries have acknowledged the imperative for wide-ranging reinvention within their public sectors. Management structures have been analysed and innovations introduced, albeit at a differing pace and with differing emphases across countries. Some countries have set about reducing the size of the public sector. Others put greater emphasis on the key role of a vigorous public sector in economic and social development. The common agenda that has developed encompasses efforts to make governments at all levels more efficient and cost-effective, to increase the quality of public services, to enable the public sector to respond flexibly and more strategically to external changes, and to support and foster national economic performance.

A new paradigm for public management has emerged, aimed at fostering a performance-oriented culture in a less centralised public sector. It is characterised by:

- a closer focus on results in terms of efficiency, effectiveness and quality of service;
- the replacement of highly centralised, hierarchical organisational structures by decentralised management environments where decisions on resource allocation and service delivery are made closer to the point of delivery, and which provide scope for feedback from clients and other interest groups;
- the flexibility to explore alternatives to direct public provision and regulation that might yield more cost-effective policy outcomes;
- a greater focus on efficiency in the services provided directly by the public sector, involving the establishment of productivity targets and the creation of competitive environments within and among public sector organisations; and,
- the strengthening of strategic capacities at the centre to guide the evolution of the state and allow it to respond to external changes and diverse interests automatically, flexibly, and at least cost.

This fundamental change in outlook has engaged all Member countries in a difficult process of cultural change: Instead of thinking in terms of due process and rigid frameworks for service provision, institutions and individuals are encouraged to focus more on improving the results of public interventions, including exploring alternatives to direct public provision.

Increasing autonomy and flexibility in resource use is fundamental to developing a performance-oriented culture. The devolution of resource allocation decisions – from central management bodies to line departments and agencies; within line departments; from central to lower levels of government; and from the public sector to private sector subcontractors – has become a widespread practice among Member countries. Its purpose is to encourage managers to focus on results by providing them with flexibility and autonomy in the use of both financial and human resources. The quid pro quo for additional autonomy has been more stringent accountability for performance. This is being achieved through various contractual arrangements that define global, sometimes multi-year, funding levels; establish goals and objectives for programmes; and require the development of indicators for monitoring, reporting, and evaluating performance in results-oriented terms. The strategy has been described as a balanced effort both to let managers manage and to make managers manage.

Devolution, supported by more stringent performance requirements and enhanced accountability, has been largely successful. It allows departments to adopt practices best suited to their individual business and needs. It has served to increase the responsibility and accountability of managers, and has contributed toward a sharper focus on results and a better use of resources. Critical to its success has been a concomitant emphasis on the reform of human resource management to ensure the recruitment, retention, and development of a capable, motivated work-force.

Implementation is far from complete, however, and has raised a number of issues that countries will need to address if this strategy is to reach its full potential. For example:

- the pace and extent of devolution has been uneven; further work is necessary to ensure that the empowerment of managers filters downwards and outwards in organisations;
- fostering diversity of practice through greater managerial flexibility has raised concerns about an erosion of a service-wide perspective, the collective interest of government, and traditional public service values;
- efforts to link incentives for individuals to organisational performance through performance appraisal and performance pay have encountered significant difficulties;
- the processes of converting broad and sometimes conflicting government objectives into operational targets and measuring the extent of their achievement need to be further refined;
- increased managerial autonomy has implications for public accountability, requiring clarification of precisely who – elected representatives or officials – is responsible for which results in a decentralised management environment.

Making government more client-oriented is central to making it more performance-oriented. Successful early attempts have been made to change the culture of public service institutions from a concern with narrow self-interest to a customer service orientation emphasizing value for money.

Significant progress has been made in improving client access to services, increasing the transparency of operations and decision-making, providing remedies for unfair treatment, and reducing administrative burdens by cutting unnecessary red tape. Building flexibility, choice, and discretion into policy instruments and delegating decision-making authority to officials who deal directly with clients have also improved responsiveness. So, too, has the establishment of consultative mechanisms, which allow service design to better reflect client needs.

Despite the progress made, there remains a need to instil a client focus across the public sector and at all organisational levels, so that a concern with quality becomes second nature. A few countries set service standards that specify the quality of service that can be expected and against which performance is assessed; this practice should be applied more widely. In so doing, care needs to be taken to ensure that individual client interests are balanced against broader taxpayer interests in the trade-off between cost and quality, and that client responsiveness does not lead to client capture.

Public sector activities are more efficient when product markets are competitive or contestable. Although increasing competition may not always be possible or appropriate, greater recourse to market disciplines has been a key element of reform in most countries. Such changes reflect the growing realisation, brought about by a closer focus on results, that once it has been decided to provide a particular service, governments have a number of means of ensuring that it is delivered in a cost-effective way. Creating conditions in which public sector organisations must compete for business provides powerful incentives to improve quality, contain costs, and improve efficiency. Corporatisation and privatisation are important policy options in this context.

Successful experience with market-type mechanisms suggests scope for their adoption by a greater number of countries. Market-oriented arrangements, including user charging, internal markets, market testing, and contracting out, have, under certain conditions, served to ration demand, economise resource use, and produce substantial and well-documented efficiency savings. They have also contributed to enhanced quality of service and value for money. Demand generated under market disciplines has provided robust indicators of performance and thus supported the related objective of better performance measurement in the public sector. Although more monitoring is essential, alternative policy instruments such as property rights and vouchers seem promising. By creating conditions under which individual and State interests converge, they may help achieve desired policy outcomes more cost-effectively, without significant adverse distributional consequences.

Improving the management of regulation must become an increasingly important focus for government action. Regulation in its many forms remains a key policy instrument, and the quality of regulation is crucial to government effectiveness. But what originally seemed a relatively low-cost means of implementing public policies has become, when poorly managed, an impediment to good overall economic performance and a source of declining government credibility. The aggregate costs imposed on individuals and private firms by multiple regulations are a major cause for concern. The complexity and sheer number of regulations also raise concerns about consistency and cohesiveness among rules, legal clarity, accountability, openness and intrusion on private life.

Analysing the impact of regulatory systems as a whole and exploring cost-effective alternatives to regulation must become routine elements of the central management functions of government. Efforts by Member countries to reduce the quantity of regulation and to improve quality through the establishment of user, design, legal and analytical standards have yielded immediate gains. Many regulations that were outdated, unworkable, or anti-competitive have been eliminated or revised. In some countries, the growth in new regulations has been slowed. But efforts are only beginning in many countries and need to be accelerated. Likewise, attempts to explore alternatives to regulation, such as economic incentives and information disclosure, and to improve the management of the regulatory process through, for example, the use of regulatory checklists, are very recent. Internationalisation has added to the growing pressure for reform; the proliferation of multilateral and bilateral co-operative agreements has led to a pressing need to develop regulatory co-operation strategies enabling governments to adapt to this new environment.

Managing reform

Fostering a performance-oriented culture of continuous adjustment and improvement requires dynamic and flexible implementation strategies that can be adapted by many different individuals and institutions. They must be designed to allocate limited improvement resources to best effect. A ''selective radical'' strategy for implementing reform may be the preferred solution. Incrementalism is unlikely to succeed in bringing about fundamental change in behaviour and attitudes. Yet complete re-design of governance structures is impossible, given limited resources and capacities to absorb overwhelming change. An optimum reform strategy may be to select a number of high-profile changes that are restricted enough to be feasible, but radical enough to significantly affect behaviour and crucial governance capacities. The manner in which selective, radical change is introduced, *i.e.* whether undertaken ''voluntarily'' or ''imposed'' and whether it is introduced in a single comprehensive package or in multiple, staggered segments; as well as the pace and sequencing of changes must be determined by national conditions. In addition, all strategies must reflect the fact that reform is a journey rather than a destination.

Radical reform inevitably involves trade-offs and raises new issues. If not properly addressed, these issues may jeopardise the effectiveness of both individual and collective reform efforts. Among the crucial questions confronting reform strategists in this regard are:

– How to keep reforms coherent and consistent in conditions of substantial devolution of authority and greater separation of reponsibilities among policy-makers, funders, and providers of services. The centre of government must maintain and develop strategic capacities to ensure that reforms are designed and implemented in a mutually supportive way. Reforms must be designed to reinforce and not replace key public service values such as the fair and equitable treatment of individuals, probity, accountability, and respect for the law.

– How to ensure that organisations have the capacity to implement reforms. Central management bodies need to withdraw from detailed prescription of how line managers should do things and focus more on setting broad frameworks for activity. Yet they retain a key leadership role in improving management capacities by providing support and training, by disseminating information on best practice in programme and personnel management, and by assisting agencies to make their own decisions about the best way of proceeding.

– How to ensure reforms receive sustained, visible political support so as to promote reform and counter resistance to change. To be successful, reforms need support from the highest level. But this support may wane in the absence of clear indications of improved performance. Close monitoring and comprehensive evaluation of reform efforts are essential to winning and sustaining support and learning from experience. Yet, they have received attention from only a handful of countries to date. They are fundamental to the development of learning organisations that perpetually adapt to improve performance. In their absence, reforms are no more than articles of faith, and may engender resistance to further change.

– How to foster a more participative approach to governance. In a globalised system, combined with decentralised service provision and greater consumer sovereignty at the national level, governments can no longer ''impose'' solutions with certainty as to policy outcome. Developing strategies to involve different interests, whether they be national or supra-national, is an essential requirement for future action.

Priorities for future action

The quality and effectiveness of governance is crucial to national prosperity and well-being. The pressures to make public services more responsive and cost-effective will not abate. The costs of not pursuing public sector management reform are high, and will be reflected in declining international competitiveness and stagnating national economic and social prosperity. Creating environments in the public sector that promote a culture of continual improvement, foster innovation in pursuing public policy goals, and make individual and team performance count is an essential and ongoing task. But efforts must be woven into a framework where the central capacity to govern is retained, where a just balance is struck between centralised direction and local discretionary action, where democratic accountability is protected, and where traditional values of integrity and equity are meshed with new values of cost-effectiveness and quality of service.

In the decades to come, the well-performing public sector will be radically different in appearance and behaviour. Typically, it will:

– be less involved direct service provision;
– concentrate more on providing a flexible framework within which economic activity can take place;
– regulate better, with more complete information about likely impacts;
– continuously evaluate policy effectiveness;
– develop planning and leadership functions to respond to future economic and social challenges; and,
– take a more participative approach to governance.

The many structural and managerial changes made to the public sector in OECD countries are an important first step in this complex and evolutionary process. They will ensure that the nature of governance and the role of the state will continue to evolve. There is a widely held belief, supported by available evidence, that a results-oriented culture is emerging and that public sector performance has improved. However, reforms need to be pushed further.

Governance capacities in the future will depend increasingly upon the innovative ability and commitment of public sector personnel. Harnessing this energy will require effective leadership by both central management bodies and senior line managers, actively promoting the values of cost-effectiveness and continual improvement.

Local circumstances and national differences rule out any notion of a unique best reform model. Nevertheless, countries have much to learn from each other.

The emerging policy agenda will include the following broad programme of actions:

Government as policy-maker
– facilitating coherent and effective policies by improving the decision-making and rule-setting processes of government, especially as regards the flow of policy-relevant information and policy evaluation;

Government's performance
– further developing strategies, structures ,and systems to let and make managers manage; removing unnecessary constraints and providing appropriate incentives;
– providing effective ways to measure and monitor performance, strengthen accountability for performance, and engrain a focus on quality performance;
– developing and maintaining a motivated, skilled, and flexible public sector work-force committed to a set of common public service values;

Government's strategic capacity
– enhancing the capacity of the public sector to respond flexibly and automatically to future changes in its external environment;
– improving government's capacity to operate strategically, to ensure adaptation to emerging opportunities and threats, to guide the overall evolution of the public sector, and to harmonize the efforts of central management bodies;
– adopting a strategic approach to human resource management and industrial relations, and ensuring the sound discharge of the state's functions as employer;

Government as enabler
– setting a framework for the public, private, or mixed supply of goods and services; enhancing consumer choice and quality of service; introducing competition wherever practicable; and generally promoting an efficient and effective use of resources;
– identifying ways to improve interaction between the public and private sectors;

Government as reformer
– strategically managing the overall reform process; monitoring and evaluating experiences in implementing reforms so that public sector organisations can learn from one another, exchange information and compare performance.

Part A

OVERALL ANALYSIS

EXECUTIVE SUMMARY

Governance capacities are being challenged

Pressure to control public expenditure has long driven efforts to increase efficiency and economy. But several factors today combine to intensify pressure for reform of a fundamental nature.

OECD economies are undergoing profound structural change. An increasingly open international economy puts a premium on national competitiveness and highlights the mutual dependence of the public and private sectors. Citizen demand is more diversified and sophisticated, and, at the same time, the ability of governments to deal with stubborn societal problems is being questioned. The policy environment is marked by great turbulence, uncertainty and an accelerating pace of change. Meanwhile large public debt and fiscal imbalances limit governments' room for manoeuvre.

Traditional governance structures and managerial responses are increasingly ineffectual in this context. Radical change is required in order to protect the very capacity to govern and deliver services. This involves a rethinking of the rationale for government intervention and reworking incentives, strengthening decision-making and reassessing cost-effectiveness in the public sector. Flexibility to adapt to changing circumstances is crucial: organisations need to build a capacity to adapt continuously.

A major transition in governance is under way

Countries have responded to these challenges differently. Although there is no single best model of public sector management, common reform trends can be identified. Some have been inspired by best private sector practice, adapted to public sector needs. The objective is fundamental change, transforming behaviour and attitudes.

Two vital elements of public service reform strategies stand out: a closer focus on results in terms of efficiency, effectiveness, and quality of service, and replacement of highly centralised hierarchical structures with decentralised management environments.

Other key principles are flexibility to explore alternatives to direct public provision and regulation, enhancing choice; stimulation of competitive environments; and strengthening strategic capacities at the centre of government. Most countries have initiated significant structural change through policies of privatisation and corporatisation. Some have made reducing the core public service a key objective.

Devolving authority and providing flexibility in resource use are corner-stones of the new managerial approach being adopted to develop a performance-oriented culture. They are complemented by more stringent accountability for performance through contractual arrangements, target-setting and strengthened reporting. Letting and making managers manage sums up the strategy.

Effective human resources management is central. Priorities include the development of high-quality leadership and management, the introduction of personnel and labour practices that are more flexible and performance-oriented, accompanied by staff training.

Making government more client-oriented is crucial to making it more performance-oriented. Progress has been made in several areas, such as access to services, transparency, and provision of grievance procedures. Commitment to public standards of service appears promising in terms of providing a yardstick for judging performance and managing public expectations.

Increasing market disciplines in the public sector has shown that significant gains are possible under certain conditions. Competition provides powerful incentives to contain costs and to improve quality through innovation. Successful, albeit limited, experience with market-type mechanisms (such as user charges, internal markets, and contracting out) argues for their wider application.

Improving the quality of regulation has become an increasingly important focus of reform. Analysing the impact of regulatory systems and exploring cost-effective alternatives to regulation should increasingly become routine elements of government's central management functions.

The reforms involve trade-offs and raise new issues

There is a drawback to reform that may be too easily discounted. Greater local autonomy might weaken policy coherence and public accountability, and erode traditional public service values such as equity and integrity. Formal separation of policy-making and policy execution functions could lead to impoverished policy unless mechanisms for providing feedback from operations are strengthened.

Incentives may not work as planned: there is a need, in particular, to ensure that individual and organisational goals are consistent. More stringent accountability is contingent upon performance measurement techniques which are not yet fully developed. A balance must be struck between individual needs and the greater public interest.

Implementing reform is itself problematic. An optimum reform strategy may be to select a limited number of high-profile changes that are restricted enough to be feasible while radical enough to have significant impact. Building external support for the reforms (*e.g.* by mobilising citizen interests) is seen as crucial to overcoming resistance and sustaining vital political support.

The future agenda

The quality and effectiveness of governance is crucial to national prosperity. Reforms to date are an important first step. There are signs of improved performance and the emergence of a results-oriented culture. Current reforms need to be pushed further where they are most promising. The rate of take-up of reforms is uneven and the pace of implementation is slow.

Close monitoring and analysis are indispensable. It is too early to judge many of the changes. A major learning process is under way about the conditions under which instruments such as market-type mechanisms, performance-related pay, and contract-based employment best operate. The general scarcity of rigorous evaluation of reforms is regrettable.

Chapter 1

INTRODUCTION: STRUCTURE OF THE REPORT

Important changes are taking place in the way the public sector is managed in OECD countries. Administrative modernisation has been an ongoing process for decades. But the pace of change has picked up noticeably in recent years as governments react to pressures and prepare to deal with current and emerging challenges. In many countries, a fundamental shift is being attempted from a centralised, hierarchical, rule-driven administration to one characterised by devolved management and market orientation. Emphasis has shifted from mere compliance with procedures to concern for results. The changes are, in many cases, seen as both fundamental and irreversible. The objective of this report is to take stock of the reforms.

With its emphasis on review, the report complements other work by the Public Management (PUMA) Committee, notably the triennial *Survey of Public Management Developments* and its annual updates. It also builds on the Committee's 1991 report *Serving the Economy Better,* which set out views on public management reform in relation to structural adjustment.

The report cannot be very prescriptive since there is no single best model of public management and reforms must take account of national differences and local circumstances. Furthermore, the limited amount of analysis to date makes drawing firm conclusions more difficult. The report aims, rather, to improve understanding of the reforms, their positive and negative impacts, where they have been successful and where they have been disappointing, by learning from the diverse experiences of countries. Its focus is on the tools of public sector management rather than on the functions of the state. It is directed primarily at those who are responsible for designing, managing and implementing public management reform programmes. But the reforms affect a wider audience, ultimately the whole community, and rely on the involvement of many actors for success. The report is therefore addressed to decision-makers, parliamentarians, oversight bodies and public service managers, as well as businesses, trade unions and academics.

Part A of the report provides an overall assessment of the reforms. Chapter 2 looks at the context in which the reforms are taking place, examining the pressures for reform. Chapter 3 then describes the principal thrusts of reform, the main lines of response by Member countries. It gives an overview of reforms across a wide spectrum. Chapters 4-11 narrow the perspective and deepen the analysis. For the most significant reform initiatives, they examine objectives, impacts, benefits, costs and how successful the initiatives have been in really changing the situation on the ground. These chapters also discuss dilemmas facing reformers as they try to introduce new ideas without sacrificing the best of the old, and as they seek to balance sometimes conflicting objectives. Chapter 12 discusses the management of reform programmes. It addresses issues of pace of reform, capacity and responsibility, building support and overcoming resistance. Chapter 13 highlights key reform issues and suggests priorities for pursuing reform further. Part B examines in greater detail specific reform initiatives in key areas in which the PUMA Committee has carried out work.

Chapter 2

GOVERNANCE CAPACITIES CHALLENGED

SUMMARY

A variety of factors have come together to make reform a burning issue. Key among these are: the development of a global market-place, which highlighted the impact of government activities on national competitiveness; a perception that public sector performance was inferior to that of the private sector; concern that the public sector was squeezing out the private sector; limits to future growth of the public sector, given budget deficits and high levels of public debt; a lowering of expectations about government's ability to solve economic and societal problems by traditional remedies; citizen demands for improved responsiveness, choice and quality of service; and demands from public sector staff. Put together, these pressures have resulted in a reappraisal of the rationale for government intervention and a re-examination of public sector management and performance.

The public sector is large in all OECD countries (see Table 1). Public expenditure in 1991 ranged from 32 per cent of GDP in Japan and Switzerland, the lowest level among OECD countries, to 63 per cent of GDP in Sweden. Government employment accounted for 32 per cent of total employment in Norway and Sweden. The level of aggregate expenditures remains stubbornly high, despite efforts to reduce it in many countries. Very few countries show a lower expenditure share of GDP in 1991 than in 1980. No country for which internationally comparable data are available has been able to reduce its expenditure shares below the 1970 level. Expenditure per capita, measured in purchasing power parities, roughly doubled in the 1980s (see Figure 1). The doubling of expenditure per capita illustrated in Figure 1 occurred against a background of generally unimpressive GDP growth rates. These difficulties in downsizing reflect new and growing demands on the public sector, as well as political and managerial factors.

The importance of the public sector goes well beyond considerations of size. Acting on behalf of political authorities, the public sector affects every part of the economy and society. Its cost-effectiveness conditions economic development and sustains political and social cohesion. The role and efficiency of the public sector, including the regulatory framework, is a significant factor in the overall efficiency of the economy. Any inefficiency must be funded by higher charges or taxes or passed on as costs or hardships arising from poor service. Society as a whole ultimately bears the burden of higher taxes and related deadweight losses.

The rate of growth of the public sector in the 1970s and early 1980s set the scene for subsequent pressures for reform. In the first place, it became increasingly clear that economic and social objectives could not be achieved without the public sector making its full contribution. In particular, the magnitude of economic issues facing countries spurred a critical appraisal of its performance. Fundamental questions were raised about the affordability of the state sector and whether it provided value for money. Second, earlier expansion set clear limits to further growth. More and more, demands for new services and renewed expenditure pressures would have to be satisfied by offsetting reductions elsewhere. Third, there emerged a concern that the very size of the public sector was an impediment to its good management and its flexibility to adapt to new challenges. The convulsions of many large organisations in the private sector show that this is not just a public sector phenomenon. Fourth, there were also concerns about the crowding-out effects of the public sector on the private sector.

Table 1. **Total government outlays as percentage of GDP 1970-94**[1]

	1970	1975	1980	1985	1990	1991	1992	1993	1994 est.
Australia	–	31	32	37	35	37	38	34	38
Austria	38	45	48	51	49	50	50	53	52
Belgium	42	51	59	62	55	56	56	57	55
Canada	34	38	39	45	46	49	50	50	48
Denmark	41	48	56	59	59	59	61	63	63
Finland	30	38	38	44	45	54	59	61	59
France	39	43	46	52	50	51	52	55	55
Germany	38	48	48	47	45	48	47	48	49
Greece	24	29	31	44	47	46	46	48	49
Iceland	–	31	28	31	34	35	36	–	–
Ireland	–	–	49	52	41	42	43	43	43
Italy	33	42	42	51	53	54	54	56	56
Japan	19	27	32	32	32	31	32	34	35
Netherlands	41	51	55	56	54	54	55	56	55
Norway	40	45	48	45	54	55	57	57	57
Portugal	22	30	26	43	43	50	53	53	53
Spain	22	24	32	41	42	44	45	47	46
Sweden	43	48	60	63	59	61	67	72	67
Switzerland	32	39	40	43	43	43	–	–	–
Turkey	–	–	21	18	–	–	–	–	–
United Kingdom	37	44	43	44	40	41	43	44	43
United States	31	33	32	33	33	34	35	34	34

1. Total government outlays = current outlays + net capital outlays.
Source: OECD Analytical Database and *OECD Economic Outlook*, No. 56, December 1994, OECD, Paris.

Figure 1. **Evolution of government expenditure per capita in PPP's**
1980-91

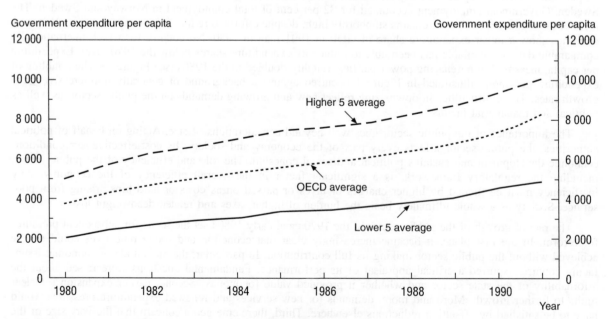

Note: Total outlays = current expenditure including transfers + capital expenditure.
Higher 5 = SWE, DNK, BEL, CAN and DEU; Lower 5 = JPN, GRC, IRL, ESP and PRT.
Source: OECD/PUMA Public Sector Database, and *National Accounts.*

A well-performing and effective public sector is an important factor in the international competitiveness of our economy and society. The public sector influences social development in manifold ways. In future, public sectors will compete over how effectively they create good conditions for viable and profitable business and industry. The public sector cost burden of the private sector must not endanger the latter's competitive capacity. The authorities must not set up obstacles to creativity and innovation for individuals and companies.

Public management reform must encourage an increase in overall productivity and social development according to democratically approved goals. This means not only making public management more efficient, but also and primarily, developing a critical approach to what the public sector does, and by what means.

(Finnish Ministry of Finance, 1992)

The external environment of the public sector has changed dramatically. A global market-place has developed. Deregulation and internationalisation are key features. There are now fewer restrictions on transactions in goods and services. Capital resources and key groups of highly skilled labour have become very mobile. Multinational businesses have flourished. The freedom of national governments to act individually is significantly restrained. Internationalisation has also put pressure on the public sector to improve its own performance. Any comparative inefficiency, for example in the provision of social and physical infrastructures, diminishes national competitiveness. In the meantime, the private sector has been forced to undergo painful change as companies have been exposed to competition and have sought to exploit the new opportunities. In this climate, pressure built quickly for public sector support for private sector efforts at structural adjustment. This meant reassessing the impact on business of government action, including regulation.

In many countries, the reform debate also provoked a fundamental questioning of the role of the public sector. The functions of the public sector reflect the community's expectations of government, constitutional responsibilities, external constraints and internal capacities and options. These all change over time. But growing appreciation of the implications of a large public sector for international competitiveness added impetus to the debate. People asked why the state was doing certain things and whether they could not be done more effectively in other ways.

The perception had grown, too, that public sector efficiency was inferior to that of the private sector and that the public sector should be more business-like. This view may misrepresent fundamental differences between the two sectors, but the overall impression of an under-performing public sector was supported by evidence emerging from privatisation and contracting out. Monopoly conditions, inadequate incentive structures and delivery of unpriced services were identified as principal reasons for efficiency problems.

Objectives of reducing budget deficits and public debt have also increased pressure for reform in public sector management. The financial balances of general government in OECD countries have shown substantial deficits for a number of years.[1] Their legacy has been a dramatic increase of the public debt in the OECD area (see Figure 2). A major reduction in structural budget deficits is now seen as essential, and probably the only way to redress current macroeconomic imbalances and make significant inroads into unemployment.[2] The task is not made any easier by resurgent expenditure pressures. Depressed economic performance increased expenditure on social security, for example, at a time when tax revenues were stagnating. Meanwhile, demographic factors such as ageing populations and changes in family structures are feeding into expenditure pressures, and servicing national debt has reduced the scope for discretionary spending.

These economic pressures for reform have been reinforced by other changes in the environment of the public sector. Organisations that do not learn to adapt themselves to ever-faster, multi-fronted change atrophy until external forces transform them. Governments no less than business have to adapt to an environment that is becoming more turbulent, complex and difficult to predict. Global transformations, caused by, among other things, developments in technology, communications and trade, demand new abilities. Flexibility and nimbleness have become key objectives. Inherited forms of governance appear outmoded and inflexible.

Concomitantly, the environment has been marked by a general downgrading of expectations and belief in the state as problem-solver; it is no longer seen to have all the answers in all situations. The effectiveness of government interventions has been increasingly questioned. Traditional remedies of additional expenditure or new regulations, even if available, seem inadequate, for example, to deal with problems such as violence, immigration, drug abuse and environmental degradation. Imaginative, innovative approaches are required. Confidence in the ability of the government apparatus to respond has been undermined.

Figure 2. **General government gross financial liabilities in the OECD area**
(As a percentage of nominal GDP)

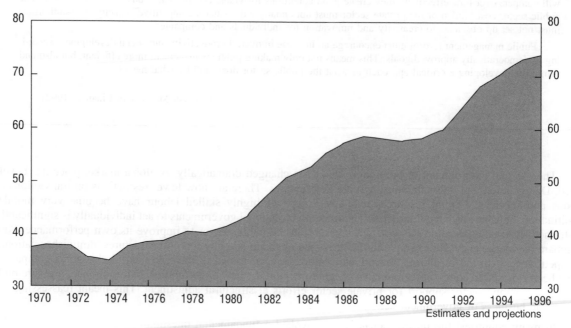

Estimates and projections

Source: OECD Economic Outlook No. 56, December 1994.

Citizens, whether individuals, businesses or other groups, have also become more demanding. They want options of "voice" and "exit". In other words, they want a greater say in what governments do and how they do it. They demand more responsive services and greater choice. They expect the same quality of service as they get from the private sector. They insist on better value for their taxes. They have become more articulate and better organised. They have become critical of administrations that appear over-bureaucratic and self-serving. Disaffection with government actions and questioning of authority are seen as symptoms of a perceived "democratic deficit" and wasteful and ineffective administration. Governance in the "information age" requires a new relationship between government and a better-educated and informed society, involving, among other things, greater transparency and participation.

The public sector itself has been a great source of pressure for change. For example, staff have mirrored external demands for more responsive service by demands for improved capacity to deliver quality services. More generally, if the public sector is to be successful in recruiting and retaining the high-calibre staff on which its performance depends, conditions of employment and the working environment must be competitive with those in other sectors. This goes beyond questions of remuneration to include other criteria such as opportunities for continued on-the-job development, challenging work, and appropriate incentives and rewards. Information technology has also been a key agent of change, providing both a tool to carry out change and a stimulus to further change. It has provided immense opportunities to do new things and to do things differently.

Are the public sectors in OECD countries in a state of crisis? Critics argue, in particular, that they are no longer affordable; they are inadequate, excessively involved in some cases and insufficiently in others; and they function on the basis of perverse incentives which send "wrong" signals to employees and clients. More damning, they are uncontrollable for many reasons, including bureaucratic rigidities, citizen demands, undue influence from powerful interest groups and lack of flexibility in adjusting to external shocks.

"Crisis" may be too strong a term to describe the situation that existed or exists in some countries. Nevertheless, it is certain that pressures on governments are considerable. Moreover, the demands in the years to come are at least equally impressive and challenging. Together, these pressures have resulted in a reappraisal of the rationale for government intervention and a re-examination of the management of the public sector, its programmes and regulatory activities.

22

NOTES

1. This is set to continue. For the OECD area as a whole, the deficit is estimated (in OECD, 1994*b*) to be 3.8 and 3.3 per cent of GDP in 1994 and 1995, respectively. For OECD-Europe the corresponding figures are 6.0 and 5.0 per cent of GDP.

2. As argued, for example, in OECD, 1993*a*.

Chapter 3

GOVERNANCE IN TRANSITION: THE MAIN LINES OF CHANGE

SUMMARY

OECD countries' reform strategies have many points in common. They are aimed at both improving the performance of the public sector and redefining its role in the economy. Key reform thrusts are: a greater focus on results and increased value for money, devolution of authority and enhanced flexibility, strengthened accountability and control, a client- and service-orientation, strengthened capacity for developing strategy and policy, introducing competition and other market elements, and changed relationships with other levels of government. Taken together, the reforms represent a paradigm shift. Yet there is no single model of reform, there are no off-the-shelf solutions. Differences among countries can be seen in emphasis and take-up of particular reforms. The reforms raise new issues, and potential negative impacts must be controlled. Implementation experiences are often too recent to allow firm conclusions about the conditions necessary for success. Monitoring and evaluation are therefore crucial.

Responses by OECD Member countries to the pressures for change show a remarkable degree of convergence overall. Clear patterns of reform emerge. Certainly, countries differ at the level of individual reforms. They place different emphasis on different aspects and implement reforms at varying speeds. The rate of take-up of reforms shows considerable variation among countries: not all countries are reforming in the areas described in this report. Likewise, there are several important divergences in reform objectives. Some countries, for example, have set a reduction in the size of the public sector as a specific objective, while others put more stress on improving its performance and strengthening its role.

Confusion of objectives, lack of accountability, inadequate adaptability to change, over-centralised control mechanisms, multi-layered management structures, excessive paperwork burdens, dispersion of responsibility, widespread internal protective mechanisms and, ultimately, an inability to exert appropriate control over government expenditure ... characterise large parts of the public sector.

(Dr. Roderick Deane, Chairman, New Zealand State
Services Commission, 1986-87, quoted in Martin, 1992)

The reforms are aimed principally at both improving the performance of the public sector and redefining its role in the economy. Key thrusts are elaborated below. Underlying the reform responses is the recognition that highly centralised command and control systems are unsuited to the new environment. In the early post-war period, countries generally tended to respond to pressures by trying to improve centralised systems, seeking to increase administrative efficiency, add new rules, adjust hierarchical structures, handle increasing amounts of information, use advanced computer systems, and so on. Complex hierarchical, rule-based systems are heavily dependent on top-down decision-making processes and showed signs of progressive sclerosis and inflexibility. They were increasingly distant from the citizens they were designed to serve. Now governments have been adopting less centralised ways of carrying out their functions and responding to pressures for change.

Initiatives to bring about a greater focus on performance aim, in particular, at focusing on outputs and results as well as inputs and processes. They involve establishing a framework for clarifying objectives, assigning clear responsibilities for achieving results, setting targets, providing appropriate signals and incentives, measuring and reporting performance, and taking necessary follow-up action. These kinds of initiatives are being applied at the level of both the individual and the organisation. Management development and training initiatives play a vital role, and a new impetus has been given to improving human resource management more generally.

The drive to provide greater value for money is a direct result of the pressure to do more with less. Ways are being sought to increase efficiency, reduce waste, and improve effectiveness. This has involved a critical reappraisal of government programmes and methods. Traditional public sector monopolies are challenged and elements of competition introduced. All options for service delivery are open for consideration: within the public sector, by the profit and not-for-profit private sector, and in various types of partnership.

There has been a major push to enhance flexibility, essentially by changing the nature of central steering and control. Reforms have aimed to empower organisations and managers, encouraging innovation and initiative. Various forms of devolution are introduced, aimed, among other things, at locating operational decisions closer to the point of service delivery. Detailed central controls are substituted by more aggregate controls, with greater flexibility at local level to achieve agreed objectives within more global budget allocations. Reforms in the area of human resources seek to provide greater flexibility in recruitment, termination, pay, and staffing policies generally, and to provide performance-related incentives. New institutional arrangements have been taken up in some countries as an option allowing greater autonomy in operational matters (*e.g.* Executive Agencies in the UK, deconcentration in France).[1] For commercial functions, this has included the establishment of more or less autonomous enterprises with commercial freedoms as well as full privatisation.

Strengthening accountability and control has been rendered all the more important in the context of greater devolution and flexibility. The counterpart of greater autonomy is accountability for actions. Reforms have focused, among other things, on translating broad objectives into operational targets, assigning clear responsibilities for achieving results, communicating agreed standards and enhancing reporting arrangements, both internally and externally. Information on performance is presented in more useful formats and made more generally available. Greater transparency has been a key objective.

The establishment of a client- and service-oriented public sector that is more outward-looking than inward-looking represents another major thrust of reform. Considerable efforts have been devoted to increasing responsiveness and service quality. A veritable cultural change is taking place in the way the public service views its clients and deals with them. Easier access, simplified procedures, more courteous service, greater transparency and provision of information are already common. Improving the choice available to clients is a key objective, being pursued, for example, through greater use of market-type mechanisms and the creation of markets. Organisations in many countries are committing themselves to public standards of service as a matter of client right. Consulting clients about their needs, requesting feedback on service provided, and other types of client participation represent another major thrust of reform. These efforts to improve service have been complemented by the development of avenues of redress. Organisations are investing massively in the use of information technology to offer improved service.

Reforms are also aimed at strengthening capacities for developing strategy and policy. The greater flexibility given to organisations and managers can free up the centre to concentrate more on strategy and policy, ''on steering rather than rowing''.[2] A major challenge has been to ensure adequate feedback from operations where the centre is less directly involved in implementation. Co-ordination mechanisms are being adjusted to the new environment of devolution and the involvement of other international and sub-national players. Efforts are being made to ensure the coherence of government action, all the more critical given the nature of challenges it faces.

Another major focus of reforms relates to the impact of government on overall economic efficiency. Driven by the need for international competitiveness, governments have been concerned to reduce the burden they necessarily place on the private sector in terms of tax imposition and compliance and administrative costs. Reforms have focused on the quality of service to business as a particular client, the management of the environment in which business must operate, and reduction of the compliance and administrative burdens. Regulatory management has received particular attention, beyond mere economic impact. Governments have strengthened regulatory disciplines and controls, forcing a closer look at costs and benefits and ways of achieving the same objectives with alternative instruments. More globally, the rationale for government action is being reappraised.

Finally, countries have been establishing different relationships with other levels of government. The relationship between central and lower levels of government is highly charged politically. Several countries have increased their reliance on decentralised service provision. The attractions of proximity to the client include better identification of needs and provision of more tailor-made, responsive services, as well as potential to improve local democracy. Reforms in most countries are also vitally concerned with adjusting to the opportunities, constraints and obligations of membership of international groupings and other forms of international co-operation.

Taken together, the reforms have been described as a paradigm shift. While it must be remembered that not all countries are moving on all reform fronts, the fundamental, comprehensive nature of the changes described represents a move to a new order. The culture of the public sector is being transformed. The role of government is being reassessed. New ways of ensuring service provision are being considered. New power-sharing relationships are being forged at several different levels. The move from centralised to decentralised, ''micro-oriented'' approaches is key.

But the potential drawback of reform cannot be ignored. The reforms are recent and their full impact is unknown. Many of the reforms are inspired by best practice in the private sector, but in the public sector they are, in many respects, journeys into unknown territory. Managing public services requires all the competences of private sector management plus the satisfaction of taxpayers' demands for equity, probity and accountability. The reforms raise many new issues that have the potential to derail at least some elements of the reforms. There is an acute need to monitor and evaluate reforms, adjusting them as necessary in the light of experience. In any event, future changes in the environment of government will require further modification of public sector structures, procedures, and capacities.

The reforms are the result of conscious choices involving trade-offs among different objectives. They raise several concerns that are discussed in more detail in the following chapters. Key concerns centre on the trade-offs between central controls (political, managerial, and financial) and devolved authority to managers and subcontractors. This covers a multitude of issues, including the likely impact on cherished public service values such as equity in the delivery of services and probity in the handling of public resources and the use of discretionary powers. It also raises various issues associated with agency theory, primarily related to the costs of contract formulation and enforcement and the recognition that agent and principal interests can never be exactly matched. The process of setting targets and measuring performance requires significant development. Some fear, on the one side, an erosion of autonomy and the imposition of unnecessarily detailed reporting requirements, and, on the other, a reduction in accountability and responsiveness to government wishes. A balance has to be worked out between satisfying legitimate needs of the centre and protecting local freedoms.

Particularly where devolution takes place or new institutional arrangements are set up, risks are also perceived regarding fragmentation of government, loss of policy coherence and consistency, and inadequate feedback from operations to policy-making. Other concerns include possible capture by clients and local interests, and loss of control over programme costs. Another key concern is that, despite precautions, government bodies will, in the long term, become dependent on particular subcontractors. Countries will also need to carefully monitor the immediate and long-term impact of various changes in human resource management on staff motivation and behaviour.

For the moment, it is too early to judge the merits and disadvantages of all the new initiatives. The diversity of public sector activities, as well as the rich array of instruments used, also renders it inappropriate to make sweeping recommendations or criticisms based on single experiments. What works in one case may not work in others. There are no ready-made solutions. It is of paramount importance in this context that countries monitor and evaluate reform experiences if they are to build on success and learn from failure.

In the current environment, public management reform is seen as a dynamic process and not a specific end-point. Countries are not seeking only to increase the static efficiency of the public sector, but also to create the capacity to react to external changes automatically, flexibly and at least cost. In other words, their goal is to develop a dynamically efficient system. They recognise, too, that it is not possible to identify best reform solutions at the outset. They accept a need for experimentation and adaptation, and competition among alternatives. The approach chosen is to create a framework rather than to specify end results.

Many difficulties arise in the application of these principles. Taking steps in the right order and at an appropriate speed are important considerations. Coherence has emerged as a necessary condition for success, without which the reform process is, at best, sub-optimal and, at worst, in jeopardy in its entirety. Reforms have to be both mutually-supporting and complete. For example, the creation of markets will not, by itself, allow the full benefits of reform to be felt: concomitant steps are needed to facilitate entry and exit of producers, ease contracting procedures, and ensure fair competition, not the least between public and private suppliers. The reforms are aimed essentially at longer-term change to systems and attitudes rather than being focused on spectacular one-shot reforms. Against this background, overcoming resistance to reforms and keeping reform on the political agenda are major concerns.

The following eight chapters examine the principal reforms initiated by Member countries to give effect to the broad reform strategies discussed. They set out objectives, report on experiences and impacts, identify advantages and disadvantages, and discuss new issues that are raised. Their focus is primarily on the public service rather than the wider public sector. Countries have placed different emphasis on different aspects of reform, taking account of national contexts, needs, constraints and opportunities. Some countries have taken a lead in respect of particular types of reform. Few have reached the stage of carrying out fundamental evaluations of results. It is inevitable, therefore, that a relatively small number of countries are cited to illustrate particular experiences or evaluation findings. This is not intended to imply that other countries have not introduced similar reforms.

For purposes of analysis, initiatives are grouped under the following headings, each treated in a separate chapter:

- devolving authority, providing flexibility;
- ensuring performance, control and accountability;
- developing competition and choice;
- providing responsive service;
- improving the management of human resources;
- exploiting information technology;
- improving the quality of regulation;
- strengthening steering functions at the centre.

NOTES

1. Based on the principle of subsidiarity, deconcentration redefines the role of each level of the central administration, organising services functionally so as to maximise their complementarity.
2. To use the terms of Osborne and Gaebler (United States), 1992.

Chapter 4

DEVOLVING AUTHORITY, PROVIDING FLEXIBILITY

SUMMARY

Devolving authority and providing flexibility are corner-stones of reforms aimed at improving performance. Reforms under this heading give managers and organisations greater freedom in operational decisions and remove unnecessary constraints in financial and human resource management. In exchange, managers are held more directly accountable for results. Control through detailed prescription is replaced by a framework of incentives and more global controls. Reforms include: greater end-of-year flexibility in managing resources; consolidation of budget headings, especially for running costs; medium-term resource planning; accrual accounting; net appropriations; and greater flexibility as regards staffing levels. Changes to organisational structures can underpin these reforms. Several countries have sought to separate policy-making and policy implementation functions, hiving off executive functions to agencies with greater flexibility in resource management to achieve agreed targets. Other countries have moved to rationalise the number of government departments and eliminate layers of management. Devolution has given rise to concerns about fragmentation and loss of coherence of government action. Key questions concern the satisfaction of central co-ordination and control needs without eroding local freedoms, and the extent to which authority can be passed down organisations.

Devolving managerial authority is a corner-stone of reforms to improve the performance of the public sector. In essence, reforms under this heading involve giving managers greater flexibility and incentives to achieve results, relaxing traditional central controls on the use of resources. New managerial freedoms are balanced by greater accountability involving specification of targets, performance measurement and reporting of results achieved. Central control is enhanced at a strategic rather than operational level. In simple terms, this kind of reform is about letting managers manage and making managers manage. The reforms apply equally to relations between central management bodies and line departments and agencies, within line departments, down the line and to local offices, and between parent departments and subordinate bodies.

The need for control over the use of public money and authority is not disputed and the extent and nature of controls is not just a management issue. Political choices are involved and basic relations are affected between executive and legislative branches. Existing controls were built up over time to prevent abuse, fraud or illegality in the spending of public moneys. This goal of propriety in public spending remains valid.

However, controls can and did get in the way of performance. Control systems have been criticised as having become, over the years, too detailed, rigid, stifling, impenetrable and, in many cases, counter-productive. Performance was seen to suffer because the systems in place put a higher premium on compliance with internal rules than on achieving objectives. Efforts to prevent abuse such as theft and fraud led to a different kind of abuse: waste, ineffective expenditure and unwillingness to shoulder responsibility.

Today's reforms aim to establish an appropriate balance between performance and control. Overall, their purpose is to institute a new framework of incentives, remove unnecessary constraints, and bring about a radical change in culture and performance. In some countries, where there is mistrust of the administration, perhaps because of associations with discredited governments or high perceived risk of corruption, detailed controls may still be viewed as appropriate. The move to greater, but bounded, managerial freedom and flexibility is an attempt to meet the challenge of improving efficiency and effectiveness without compromising propriety.

Financial resources

Detailed budget controls are typically among the first to be relaxed in the interests of improving performance. This may at first seem paradoxical when there is such pressure to reduce public expenditure. But it is now clear that better quality expenditure, better value for money, and reduced expenditure require a different kind of control. Reminiscent of some of the excesses of Communist command economies, traditional control systems constrained responsible, rational public servants to spend money in foolish ways.

In the past (and it is true today in many cases), funds unspent at the end of the year had to be surrendered in full to the centre, regardless of the reason for underspending. Often, allocations in subsequent years were also reduced to reflect this underspending. The logical response was the well-known phenomenon of ''December fever'', the end-of-year rush to spend, regardless of whether the expenditure was cost-effective. Overspending was, of course, a greater sin. Coming in on target became almost an end in itself.

Reforms have aimed to reduce the annual rush to spend by allowing departments greater end-of-year flexibility in managing budgets. In the main, this has entailed flexibility to carry over a proportion of unspent funds to the following year. A smaller number of countries also allow organisations to borrow from the following year's allocation in certain circumstances. End-of-year flexibility is widely seen as a success. It has not caused any loss of control. It has eliminated existing penalties on efficient behaviour and has contributed to changing ingrained behaviour. The success of the measure can be judged by the fact that some countries have moved to increase the percentage of budget that can be carried over from one year to the next (*e.g.* Australia 3 per cent originally, now 6 per cent).

Reforms also aim to give managers greater flexibility in the use of funds by eliminating over-detailed categorisation of budget allocations and making transfers among budget categories easier. An increasingly common approach is to consolidate all administrative expenditures, including salaries, into a single running costs appropriation subject to strict overall cash limits. Such operational budgets are much smaller than programme outlays, but it is arguably the potential to redeploy operational resources which most assists good management.

Consolidation, like end-of-year flexibility, has also proved instrumental in establishing a performance culture: over-restrictive rules inevitably reinforce a focus on inputs rather than results. A single budget line for administrative costs makes it possible to use different combinations of staff, consultants, information technology, and other resources to produce results in accordance with programme targets, local needs and changing priorities. Increased flexibility can also include the possibility of converting a portion of funds for running costs into minor capital, and *vice versa*. Traditional controls over administrative costs were usually accompanied by central controls over staff numbers and gradings. Some countries have also relaxed or even abolished their staffing controls, satisfied with control over total costs through cash limits. This can be seen as part of a general trend to devolve responsibilities for human resources management and industrial relations, discussed in Chapter 8.

The consolidation of administrative costs into a single budget line has, in some countries, been accompanied by an enforced efficiency dividend so that programme managers are required to achieve a minimum target in terms of improved productivity (Australia, Denmark, Ireland, Sweden). The annual budget allocation is reduced by up to 2-3 per cent in real terms. This is justified by budget offices on the basis that the increased flexibility allows greater efficiency and that the benefit should be shared between the Budget and spending departments. It also includes an element of forcing improvements. This productivity growth rate is significant compared with estimates of long-term public service productivity growth and may be unsustainable even in the medium-term. If unrelated to other attempts to improve productivity, such as use of new technology or flexible work practices, there is a danger of expenditure reductions being achieved at the expense of quality or level of output. The same efficiency objectives are pursued in the UK through the establishment of firm (cash) limits for running costs, which in recent years have not been adjusted upwards for changes in inflation but held constant in cash terms.

Consolidation of running costs has its counterpart in the area of expenditure. This shares the same objective of increased flexibility – to achieve more effective expenditure with less waste – but also aims at a more meaningful presentation of information to facilitate decision-making and control. The carry-over of unexpended programme appropriations from one year to the next and transfers within programmes have also been made easier, but the scope for these kinds of changes is more limited for programme expenditures than for administrative costs.

What has proved particularly beneficial, however, is the adoption of a medium-term planning framework. ''Forward appropriations'', based on projections of the financial consequences of existing policies and programmes, involve a measure of agreement regarding resources for up to three years ahead. These may be enshrined in formal resource agreements (Australia). The resulting greater stability and flexibility has improved expenditure planning and, importantly, has forced governments to focus on the out-year implications of policy changes. It has also further enhanced control by helping to ensure that savings in one period are not achieved simply by deferring expenditure. A move by some countries (Iceland, New Zealand) to full accrual accounting is also aimed at improving resource allocation and providing managers with better tools to achieve their missions.

Transfers between programme and administrative budget allocations remain subject to restrictions: the spending of programme funds on salaries, accommodation or other administrative overhead requires explicit authorisation from central authorities and budget framers. This is entirely consistent with the emphasis of reforms on efficiency and the objective of keeping administrative costs low. The ratio of running costs to programme expenditure can provide a useful indicator of operational efficiency.

The introduction of net appropriations is also aimed at providing positive incentives. These allow organisations to retain all or some revenue raised from user charges. Gross outlays can be increased to the extent of the additional revenue retained. Even in tight budgetary situations, some minimum retention is highly recommended as an incentive to generate revenue that would not otherwise be generated. Net appropriations are a tool for achieving better performance: the closer matching of revenues and costs highlights changes in efficiency; they create pressures to regularly review and justify fees; and, by linking the extent of operations to willingness of users to pay, they ensure greater responsiveness to customers' needs.

Net appropriations have raised concerns about a weakening of parliamentary control, where deliberate underestimation leads to excess revenue, which is then used to supplement expenditure. These concerns can be accommodated without serious loss of incentive either by placing limits on the amount of gross spending over and above that approved by the parliament, or by setting ceilings beyond which receipts must be credited to general revenue.

The same kind of reforms – increased flexibility, devolved decision-making, and performance-oriented approaches – also feature prominently in the area of human resources management (HRM). In a recent PUMA assessment of HRM reforms, 12 of the 19 respondent countries listed devolution-type initiatives among their three most important reforms. Nevertheless, it is evident that, with some notable exceptions, the extent and rate of devolution is limited. The general pattern is that responsibility for determining HRM policy still rests solely or primarily with central management bodies. Limited policy independence has been achieved as regards recruitment, selection and promotion.

Devolution has raised concerns about a potential loss of service-wide perspective as departments and agencies focus on their own affairs and become what have been described as "individual fiefdoms". The consequential threat to service unity and the overall coherence of government action is accentuated by a diminished capacity to generate service-wide information. Reforms in other domains, *e.g.* performance management and creation of agencies, may aggravate the problem.

The extent of devolution from central management bodies to line departments and agencies is only one issue. Even where this has been successful, it is not clear that devolution within organisations has taken place to the desired extent. The impression gained in the PUMA HRM study, for example, is of a strong tendency for personnel units to retain control. This impression is reinforced by informal contacts with countries, and might be especially true for smaller departments and agencies. Reviews of reforms in Australia and New Zealand have pointed out the special support needs of smaller organisations in this respect. There are, at any rate, grounds for speculating that organisations themselves will become more centralised than central management bodies as they adjust to taking direct responsibility. This tendency might be expected to ease as organisations gain experience and confidence in their managers.

This highlights a key question for reformers: what is the appropriate level to which decision-making powers should be devolved in an organisation? There is no easy answer. It depends very much on the nature of the powers devolved, the organisation's management capacities, the adequacy of support systems (*e.g.* the availability of guidance, standards, performance monitoring) and external environmental factors (*e.g.* imposed expenditure cuts, the behaviour of oversight bodies). In some organisations devolved activities have been recentralised. The final outcome, if there can be such a thing, is likely to emerge from an evolutionary, trial-and-error process and from learning from experience.

Organisational structures

Changes to organisational structures have been an important element of reforms aimed at facilitating devolution and improving performance. These changes frequently are the most visible signs of reform. They can be important catalysts for change in behaviour and values. In some cases, structural changes have involved hiving off executive, research or commercial functions to separate organisational units with varying degrees of autonomy. A number of countries have seen merit in the agency model, well established in Nordic countries, of small policy-making ministries with attached boards or agencies that enjoy greater managerial freedom in executing policy. Structural changes may also underpin a separation of funder and provider roles, opening up the way for key reforms in other areas, such as competition, standards, or the adoption of a regulatory approach. Other countries have favoured the creation of a smaller number of larger ministries and the grouping of related, complementary functions. Some countries have also sought to introduce organisational structures with fewer layers of management.

There is, of course, no single correct organisational model. Even within countries, there needs to be a variety of organisational models, testament to the diversity of government functions and accountability requirements.

In several countries, one of the main reasons for changing organisational structures is to separate policy-making from policy execution. The UK, for example, embraced the Executive Agency model for this reason. Some 350 000 civil servants, or about 60 per cent of the total, already work in Executive Agencies headed by a chief executive directly accountable to a minister, who sets performance targets. Canada has established similar agencies. Reforms in New Zealand have formalised the separation of ministerial responsibility for policy outcomes and civil service responsibility for production of outputs. Ministers effectively purchase outputs (services, including policy advice) from their departments. Formal performance agreements between Ministers and department heads set out objectives to be achieved and performance standards against which the chief executive will be judged. The chief executive is free to choose the mix of inputs required to produce the agreed outputs.

Other countries question the utility of separating policy-making and its implementation in this way. They are concerned that it may weaken feedback from operations into policy-making, compromise the collective interest, and dilute public accountability. These concerns continue to surface from time to time in countries pursuing a more formal separation of policy and operations, but the remedy is seen as lying in attacking the perceived inadequacies rather than change the overall system.

Thus, attempts are being made to strengthen consultative linkages between policy formulation and execution and to improve management information systems. The challenge here is to strike a balance that ensures adequate information feedback while avoiding the erosion of managerial freedoms. Flexibility is also clearly required for mid-period policy changes and renegotiation of programme targets where circumstances dictate.

Similarly, concerns about protecting collective interests are being tackled by including specific references to it in performance agreements, strengthening reporting and evaluation of it, and making other modifications to devolution mechanisms. In New Zealand, for example, performance agreements between ministers and chief executives now include objectives for collective interest obligations. These are, among other things, related to overall government policy, interdepartmental co-ordination of policy-making, and management standards in the areas of purchasing, accommodation, and information technology.

Chapter 5

ENSURING PERFORMANCE, CONTROL, AND ACCOUNTABILITY

SUMMARY

*More stringent performance requirements and enhanced control and accountability
are being introduced in a number of ways in many OECD countries. A contractual
approach is frequently being implemented in many countries at organisational and
individual levels: typically, performance agreement sets out financial allocations
and flexibilities, expected performance levels, and indicators by which performance
will be judged. Much effort is being devoted to refining objective- and target-setting
processes and developing measurement and reporting capacities. These initiatives
are complemented by periodic in-depth programme evaluation, now compulsory in
a few countries. Public accountability is being strengthened through improved
reporting and transparency, but there are concerns that the new arrangements may
cloud or diminish ministerial responsibility. There are also concerns that the
contract approach may itself become cumbersome and inflexible, and that imperfect performance measurement will cause attention to be focused on the wrong
things and create dysfunctional incentives.*

Giving managers greater flexibility and freedom to manage resources is a necessary but insufficient
condition for achieving improved performance. Autonomy alone is not enough. The counterpart of the devolution
of authority is more stringent performance requirements and enhanced accountability. The new management
reforms require managers to accept responsibility for achieving specified performance targets while managing
within resources. Accountability is strengthened through a more contractual approach, performance measurement
and reporting requirements.

If a manager is to be held accountable, certain conditions must be met. A definition of tasks and goals, as
well as measures of performance must be agreed upon and appropriate systems for monitoring, reporting and
analysing results must be in place. Accountability also implies that the manager of an organisation is responsible
for ensuring its long-term viability and its ability to adapt to changes in policy direction. Incentives, both rewards
and sanctions, are vital elements.

The translation of strategic governmental objectives into operational targets and actual performance is the
very essence of public management. There are many points in the process where divergences can occur. To begin
with, departments and agencies are, in most cases, faced with multiple, sometimes conflicting, objectives.
Managers may be given little indication of their relative priority. Reforms aimed at improving performance have
begun with a clarification of objectives, targets and responsibilities. This process is all the more critical in the
context of devolved management, but it is a feature of reform even where functions remain highly centralised.

Performance agreements

In a context of devolution of authority, some kind of performance agreement is usual. This can take many
forms, from explicit contracts through less formal negotiated agreements to more generally applicable principles.
It may also take the form of statements of service entitlement or "charters" that commit an agency to supplying a
particular level or quality of service to its clients. At the core of any agreement lies the objectives to be achieved,
the resources provided to attain them, accountability and control measures, and the freedoms and flexibilities that

managers will receive. The agreements do not, strictly speaking, have legal force because they fall within the hierarchical system of the state. Rather, they indicate the parties' intention to respect certain mutual undertakings.

The agreements cover different relationships and differ accordingly in scope and nature. Resource agreements between the central budget office and departments and agencies may provide financial allocations and flexibilities in return for an agreed level of performance. Sanctions or rewards in the form of budget alterations may be set out. Formal legislative appropriations may also be made on the basis of the agency producing an agreed level of outputs. Australia, Finland, New Zealand and Sweden, for example, have amended their budget systems to include references to outputs and outcomes.

Formal performance agreements also exist at the level of the individual, primarily between the chief executive of an agency and either the minister or central management body. In addition to performance targets in terms of outputs or outcomes, such agreements may cover processes to be observed, partly to prevent dysfunctional behaviour in the pursuit of such targets. The interests of the chief executive and the agency are assumed to be synonymous, as is their performance, but the agreements may also include specific personal commitments by the chief executive. The logic of the reforms is that these higher-level agreements permeate to lower levels of the organisation. They are now common in a number of governments and typically relate divisional objectives to corporate objectives through a corporate planning process.

Contracts in different Member countries generally share a common framework which defines a global, sometimes multi-year budget outlook. However, there are significant differences in the level of detail in contracts among countries and organisations. Some contracts define roles in great detail and cover the entire range of types of performance indicator (output, efficiency, effectiveness, quality). Precise objectives presuppose an in-depth diagnosis of the unit's programmes and processes. In other cases, contracts are more succinct, containing a few overall productivity objectives expressed in quantitative terms.

Several problems arise with implementation of the contract approach. Even where there is a strong desire to make line units autonomous, the relationship remains a hierarchical one, with the government and central bodies the final arbiters of objectives and regulations. If line units alone agree to the new constraints while their parent ministry or central bodies do not feel similarly bound, the initiative is likely to fail. The political authority must retain the power to unilaterally amend the terms of contract but only exercise it on rare occasions when strategic government requirements demand it. Problems have arisen in particular regarding mid-year resource cuts. Where changes prove unavoidable, early, frank dialogue helps relieve management problems caused by mid-term changes in plans.

Centres de Responsabilité, France

Since 1990, many state services at both central and devolved levels have been established as Responsibility Centres in France. A contract with their Ministry gives Directors greater management flexibility in operational matters in exchange for a commitment to put management control in place and achieve agreed objectives. It also stipulates a method for evaluating results. Contracts, negotiated case by case, are for three years. Some 207 centres existed as of January 1994.

A contractual approach may institute very cumbersome procedures. By seeking to formalise formerly implicit ground rules, contracts run the risk of going into excessive detail and fixing mechanisms that were previously open to continuous adjustment. Even with contracts, there is a well-documented tendency to define procedures rather than simply state objectives. Excessively detailed contracts may also take away with one hand what they give with the other, restraining autonomous management with niggling obligations.

Performance measurement

The contractual approach, and management reforms in general attach great importance to performance measurement. This has two main elements: the use of performance indicators to signal whether performance is on target, and programme evaluation involving an in-depth assessment of performance.

Performance indicators are quantitative measures of aspects of performance. They provide a *prima facie* indication of whether a programme's performance is adequate. They may relate to issues of efficiency, effectiveness, or service quality. An indication of poor performance is a signal for more detailed investigation. Indicators say nothing, for example, about the link between performance and budget. Most governments have put considerable emphasis on requiring agencies to develop performance indicators as part of performance agreements and/or in published budget documents and reports for parliament.

Based on experience to date, countries stress the importance of focusing on a selection of key indicators and keeping the process simple, ensuring that all important aspects of performance are covered but not trying to cover every aspect. In setting objectives and targets, there is a danger of focusing on the wrong thing: any performance that can be measured automatically becomes an objective. Countries also stress that indicators must be useful to both internal managers and external examiners. It is important to constantly review and refine indicators to ensure that they reflect what really matters. In this respect, there is most value in indicators related to outcomes and outputs, although early efforts have often focused on costs and processes. The process of refinement is therefore on-going. However, therein lies a potential difficulty, since it is equally important to develop a consistent series of indicators so that trends can be identified. There is also a perceived need in countries to get beyond debates over definition and into concrete action.

A critical issue is the link between individual and organisational targets and indicators of performance. Careful choice of indicators is necessary at both levels to avoid dysfunctional behaviour – *e.g.* maximising performance in areas that generate improved indicator ratings but that are sub-optimal in terms of overall programme objectives. Countries stress the importance of concordant human resource management frameworks that link individual performance to organisational objectives through, for example, performance appraisal, performance-related pay, and incentive structures generally.

Programme evaluation

Programme evaluation involves going beyond performance indicators to assess performance in depth and judge the effectiveness of government policy and programmes. It seeks to identify cause-effect relationships and reasons for a particular level of performance. Evaluation is seen primarily as the responsibility of individual agencies and managers, as an essential element of good management. If an organisation continuously evaluates itself, control ceases to be exceptional and loses any inquisitional character. Management and control become highly complementary.

In the context of financial management reforms, a number of countries have formalised requirements for programme evaluation. In Australia, for example, since 1987 all departments are required to evaluate each of their programmes every 3-5 years and to prepare annual evaluation plans. New policy proposals must incorporate arrangements for future evaluations. There is evidence that evaluations are increasing in rigour and influence. For example, two-thirds of the new policy proposals in the 1992-93 budget were a direct result of evaluations. Experience elsewhere, notably in Canada and in the United States, suggests that, however valuable they may be when policy changes are being considered, *ex post* evaluations are of more limited use in annual budget expenditure control. Difficulties arise for several reasons: the information analysed is complex, there are timing problems between evaluations and the budget cycle, and a focus on reducing expenditure limits the number and quality of evaluations.

Policy Evaluation: France

An interdepartmental system of policy evaluation was established in 1990. Evaluations are conducted by a group that is independent of policy makers. The quality of evaluations is assured by a Scientific Council composed of recognised, independent experts. Reports are made public. Ten policy areas have so far been subject to such evaluation.

Performance measurement is not an exact science. It has to be undertaken with recognition of its conceptual and practical limitations. In the general government sector it is used to get a better feel for performance in order to assist in decision-making, rather than to arrive at some precise bottom line. In particular, a performance measure does not speak for itself: it must be evaluated with reference to some base. Compiling a time series of indicators and making comparisons with other similar organisations are seen as useful ways to develop benchmarks. Appropriate benchmarking is a key aspect of performance evaluation.

At the same time, performance measurement is critical to control and accountability. Control, by definition, involves the measurement of variances between objectives and results, the interpretation of these variances, and some confirming or corrective action. It also involves attributing results to a person (individual responsibility), organisation (collective responsibility) or cause (making it possible to modify objectives). In this sense, the stakes are high: the performance of individuals, organisations and programmes is judged and key decisions are made about changes in the nature and content of programmes, and about sanctions and rewards. Performance measurement and control are corner-stones of the reforms aimed at devolving responsibility, but they require significant investment. There may be only limited time to perfect a working system and demonstrate its full value before ministers and department heads lose patience with the effort required in the developmental stages.

Accountability

In countries that have pushed devolved management furthest, there is a lively debate about the impact of the reforms on public accountability, *i.e.* the accountability of those who govern to elected bodies and thence to the public at large. Some are concerned that increased management autonomy and more frequent use of agency relationships clouds or diminishes ministerial responsibility and thus public accountability. In this view, increased public power is given to appointed officials at the expense of elected representatives. It has also been suggested that autonomy has been granted before proper accountability mechanisms, such as performance measurement, have been put in place.

Others argue that it is desirable to separate accountability for administration (operational management) from that for policy (strategic management) to enhance overall accountability and performance. The deliberate distancing of ministers from operational decisions on service delivery clarifies and enhances accountability to the public and allows their elected representatives to focus their attentions on strategic decisions regarding policy and overall results. Any potential democratic deficit can be made up by strengthening various other safeguards that focus on transparency (public reporting and audit) and on greater client influence.

As regards parliamentary examination, ministers are required to defend their policies and actions from time to time. What is changing is the extent to which ministers feel obliged or able to answer for the detailed operations of organisations to which they have devolved powers and from which they purchase specified services. This raises the question of whether top managers or agency heads should become accountable directly to parliament. While traditionally senior civil servants have been called upon to give evidence before parliamentary committees on the administration of their departments, the principle of ministerial accountability remained paramount. The management reforms giving greater autonomy to managers are thus calling into question this traditional concept, and new rules and procedures may be required. These may include new forms of accountability.

A key issue is the adaptation of oversight bodies such as parliamentary committees and audit bodies to the new management approach. In particular, it needs to be determined whether they are prepared to focus on larger strategic issues or have the capacity to do so. It is clear from country experiences that many parliamentarians have yet to make the adjustment. They remain focused on inputs or compliance issues rather than on outputs and outcomes. For a number of reasons, they are not always well placed to adapt to the new management systems and to avail of the increased volume and diversity of information that is reported. For example, they are frequently hampered by insufficient support systems and staff. Although not a new problem, it is brought into sharper relief by the management reforms. In some countries similar observations are made about parliamentary auditors, although in some cases this may reflect a limited audit mandate.

As more and more emphasis is placed on a results-oriented and client-sensitive culture and on devolution, and as the environment of public sector management becomes more diverse and complex, the importance of effective accountability becomes correspondingly greater. Thus, the provision of more, better quality information to parliament and the public has been a significant feature of reforms. It is an important counterbalance to managerial freedoms. In many countries, enhanced information is now provided at various stages in the management cycle. For example, published corporate plans and performance agreements provide information on strategic objectives; budget documents increasingly set out spending plans in a more meaningful programme format and often include performance targets; and annual reports give account of achievements against these targets. The independent audit of performance is an issue of growing importance in this context. Furthermore, policy evaluations are increasingly made public. Improvements in financial reporting, such as with the introduction of accrual accounting, also enhance the utility of information provided.

Chapter 6

DEVELOPING COMPETITION AND CHOICE

SUMMARY

Introducing greater competition in the public sector is doubly attractive, offering gains in economy and efficiency as well as in quality and choice. Countries differ significantly in their take-up of reforms under this heading, especially when more innovative approaches are involved. Reforms range from the creation of internal markets (e.g. with user charging, freedom of choice with regard to suppliers, autonomy of commercial entities, separation of funders and providers) to greater involvement of non-government suppliers (through contracting out, partnerships, privatisation, etc.). Promising reforms in sectoral areas include the creation and modification of property rights and use of vouchers. Benefits from market-type mechanisms are not automatic: they are not instant formulas for success and there remains much to learn about the conditions under which they best function.

The development of competitive environments has become a key part of management reform strategies. The basic rationale is to improve performance by exposing the sheltered public service to market disciplines. Common reforms include breaking up monopoly power and introducing market-type mechanisms. These encompass all arrangements that feature at least one significant characteristic of markets (competition, pricing, dispersed decision making, monetary incentives, etc.). The most common instruments include internal markets, user charges, contracting out, the creation or modification of property rights, vouchers, and intergovernmental contracts. Reforms have also entailed structural change such as the establishment of government entities operating on a fully commercial basis, full privatisation, and partnerships with the private for-profit and not-for-profit sectors.

Economists don't agree on much, but they do concur that monopolies provide poorer service at higher prices than competitive companies. Our public monopolies have brought us higher costs, endless delays, and reduced flexibility. Monopolies don't suffer the full costs of their inefficiency. With nowhere else to go, customers absorb them. A monopoly's managers don't even know when they are providing poor service or failing to take advantage of new, cost-cutting technologies, because they don't get signals from their customers.

(US Vice-President Gore, 1993)

Strengthening market elements is an attractive strategy because it offers the possibility, under certain conditions, of gains in economy and efficiency at the same time as higher-quality service and greater choice for both internal or external consumers. Market-related reforms have also been introduced in particular sectors in response to technological changes or the deficiencies of previous policies (*e.g.* property rights in fisheries or telecommunications).

Yet differences among countries' reform strategies are perhaps greatest when it comes to developing competition. Some countries have placed systematic introduction of market elements at the heart of their reforms. Other countries are still studying the extent to which they want to use them. Still others are implementing significant changes which involve a *de facto* expansion of market instruments but without reference to an explicit market model. In some cases, market-type mechanisms are being used within the context of an overall readjustment of the respective roles of the state and the private sector; in others, they are seen purely as techniques for improving efficiency and flexibility in an otherwise unchanged balance between the public and private sectors.

Internal markets, user charging

Elements of competition have been introduced in many ways and in different spheres. As regards inter-agency provision of services, most budget-funded agencies have traditionally received services such as property and printing from a central body at no cost to themselves. Consequently they have had no incentive to economise in terms of quantity or quality, while the service provider has been happy to lobby on behalf of its clients. Several countries have introduced user charging for these services and changed the rules of the game dramatically by this single reform. The supply of services is now determined by the amount that the consuming agencies are prepared to pay for.

A number of countries have gone further in attempting to create internal markets. Consuming agencies often had no choice but to take their services from the central supply bodies. This kind of requirement was aimed at achieving economies of scale and using combined purchasing power to negotiate favourable terms on bulk purchases. Considering these requirements incompatible with reforms aimed at giving greater management autonomy and unable, in any event, to guarantee better value for money, several countries have moved to allow the purchase of services from alternative suppliers. The public sector provider must compete directly against the private sector for public sector business. This is the case, for example, of information technology services in Scandinavian countries. Countries have been slower to allow the public sector to compete for private sector business. This might be envisaged in certain circumstances, *e.g.* a transition to full privatisation, to use temporary spare capacity, or to exploit a particular product or service not yet developed in the private sector. The reluctance has been partly due to concern about fair competitive conditions.

The main benefits of these internal markets are significant productivity increases and substantial changes in the amount and composition of services purchased. To some extent they also offer an alternative or complement to performance measurements. Subjecting operations to market discipline provides crude but robust bottom-line indicators of performance.

The creation of internal markets is also being pursued as an instrument of sectoral policy, albeit on a more restricted scale. An example in some countries is the health sector, where arrangements have been made to implement managed markets allowing choice and competition. The equivalents in the market economy are internal transfer prices within large groups, when those are allowed to reflect full costs, as in the auction system utilised by General Motors for choosing the factory in which a particular model will be produced.

Internal Market in the UK Health Service

An internal market has been created within the health service by transforming local health authorities and general practitioner groups into purchasers of hospital services on behalf of their patients. Competition has been established among hospitals as a decentralised mechanism for reallocating resources and a market-type link has been created between the loads and effectiveness of a hospital and its access to public funds. Since the notion of profit does not apply, reliance is placed on incentives linked to the size and growth of the establishment, its prestige and the performance of its managers and professional staff. Hospitals are also given a large degree of autonomy as regards the techniques and approach they adopt for the management of all their resources. Prices charged to customers reflect all costs (including capital charges) and act as the markers for reallocating business among different suppliers of hospital services. The purchaser/provider split has been most successful where there is real competition, in areas with several hospitals competing to provide services and many general practitioner fundholders shopping for them.

The rational allocation of funds among establishments is achievable in other ways, for example through the use of reliable shadow prices which approximate market prices. In France, sophisticated indicators of costs already exist or are being developed within a framework of managerial autonomy for hospitals and global budgets. The adoption of private sector management practices (*e.g.* organisation along cost and profit-centre lines) and the establishment of a professional management cadre are also receiving wide interest.

In terms of contributing to expenditure control, it is not clear how these market-type instruments affect total resources used in the sector. Nevertheless, preliminary evidence suggests that they do have considerable potential for allocating available resources more efficiently among establishments, generating productivity gains and improving capacity utilisation. The extent of this potential, however, remains largely unmeasurable for the present, but encouraging results already achieved can be interpreted as good omens for the future.

The imposition of user charges on external customers is a similar attempt to strengthen market signals, as well as recover some or all of the costs incurred in production. Charging has helped to ration demand and reallocate resources to higher priorities. Just as for internal markets, the introduction of charging linked with the breaking of monopoly supply can considerably strengthen market discipline. It institutes stronger incentives to control and reduce costs, increase quality and generally be responsive to consumers' needs. Even if demand is inelastic and the client has no alternative supplier (as is the case with passports, for example), the same kinds of pressures are felt, albeit not to the same degree. To put it in perspective, however, user charging remains largely insignificant as a percentage of expenditure.

Contracting out

Increased competition is perhaps most frequently accomplished through contracting out after competitive tendering. In many countries, contracting out has been normal practice for many years for simple activities involving little risk (maintenance, catering, etc.). A common view has been that "activities of a commercial kind are generally best performed in the private sector, where they are open to greater influence from consumers and to the disciplines of competition" (Commonwealth of Australia, 1981). What is new is the extent to which countries are now prepared to contract out more complex and more central activities (such as information technology functions and prison services). A number of governments have made it obligatory to consider external supply options for many services, expressing an implicit or explicit preference for that option. Government policy in the UK, for example, as set out in the White Paper *Competing for Quality* (CM 1730), envisages that the widest possible range of activities should be subjected to competition. Firm targets for market testing have been set for ministries and agencies and officials are appointed with clear overall responsibility for each organisation's market testing programme.

The benefits of contracting out in terms of efficiency savings can be significant, although measurement difficulties are acknowledged.[1] The UK, for example, has obtained typical savings of 25 per cent from its market testing (*Complex Contracting Out for Information Technology,* Occasional Paper on Public Management, Market-Type Mechanisms Series No. 5, 1992, p. 18). Even where services are retained in-house, US experience with contracting out under its Circular A-76 is that savings of 20-30 per cent can be achieved. Clarity of service specification and performance monitoring are also benefits.

Anticipated cost savings are not the only reason for contracting out. In some cases, organisations have no choice but to contract out to meet needs which exceed the capability of in-house staff or to provide the necessary flexibility to meet temporary or one-off requirements. Another reason is the desire to accelerate capital investment programmes through partnership arrangements with the private sector (the "partnership" arrangement itself being subject to competition). This is of increasing interest in several countries. In each case, major issues concerning the nature, extent and sharing of risks and rewards need to be resolved.

Experience with contracting out relatively simple activities suggests several essential conditions for achieving real benefits are actually realised, notably: the existence of a competitive market among suppliers; open, verifiable procurement procedures; and solid skills in contract management. These pre-conditions may set practical limits to contracting out more complex activities in some countries, at least in the shorter term. And, as is the case for all market-type mechanisms, it is evident that potential improvements in performance can be dissipated if implementation issues are not given sufficient attention.

A major and controversial consideration in contracting out is the costing methods used by internal and external bidders. Arriving at an informed decision requires the fullest possible comparison of comparable elements. The public sector bid needs, for example, to be based on full costs, including overhead and cost of capital. The evaluation of private sector bids needs to take account of costs of staff displaced and contract management. Short-term gains must be balanced against long-term performance.

Market Testing in the UK

The advantages of market testing are:

– competition helps ensure value for money;
– focusing on performance outputs will produce clearer standards and improved quality of service;
– an explicit customer/supplier relationship;
– external and in-house bidders will be given the opportunity to be more innovative in the field; and
– monitoring of contracts and service level agreements will focus on the outputs, objectives and targets required in improving the efficiency and effectiveness of targets.

In identifying an activity as a possible candidate for market testing, managers should consider it in detail and:

– Confirm whether it needs to be performed. If not, it should ease.
– Confirm whether it is a suitable candidate for privatisation, and, if so, act accordingly.
– Where the government wishes to retain responsibility for the service, consider whether competition for its provision should be introduced. The possibility of a Next Steps Agency should also be considered at this stage.
– In considering how to introduce competition, a key decision will be whether for policy or management reasons the work should be done by the private sector (in which case strategic contracting out without an in-house bid would be the appropriate way forward), or whether to have an in-house bid (market testing).

Few activities cannot (or should not) be subject to market testing, and therefore managers will be required to justify their decision not to market test activities. From past experience, those activities which offer the greatest scope for contracting out include:

– those that are resource intensive (running costs or capital investment);
– relatively discrete areas;
– specialist and other support services;
– those with fluctuating workloads;
– those subject to a quickly changing market and where it is costly to recruit, train and retain staff; and
– those with a rapidly changing technology requiring expensive investment.

In the case of new services, where there is no in-house operation, there should be a general presumption in favour of contracting out subject to management or policy requirements and relative value for money.

(Office of Public Service and Science, HMSO, 1993*a*)

Critics of contracting out argue that transition costs are high and frequently underestimated. They further argue that the involvement of a third party in the production and delivery of a service results in a weakening of accountability and control. A key concern is the danger of dependence on a particular supplier. Certain steps can be taken to mitigate the danger (such as stipulating specific hand-over procedures in the contract) and several organisations have already successfully changed supplier. On the other hand the ability to take the service back into the public sector is likely to be undermined. Some also argue that, contrary to claims, contracting out inevitably reduces flexibility to adapt to changing needs and opportunities. This may be true if the specification is over-prescriptive; putting the emphasis on the quality and quantity of resources needed, and not on how to provide them, facilitates greater innovation and creativity.

There is a general consensus that contracting out is not always appropriate, but no hard and fast rule emerges from country experience. Organisations are generally reluctant to contract out sensitive or strategic functions and, in any contracting out situation, ensure that critical decisions remain the sole responsibility of in-house staff. The final choice as to whether and what to contract out is a matter for ministers and delegated officials after assessment of the appropriateness in each case. Nevertheless, it is clear that, to achieve its full potential, contracting out needs powerful support from the centre.

Markets in property rights

Despite their novelty in most contexts, markets in property rights are seen as a highly promising device, especially in the management of common goods (such as fisheries, the environment, radio frequencies) and state-controlled assets (such as airports and forests). Markets in fishing rights illustrate this potential (see Chapter 15). The total allowable catch is calculated and divided into quotas, which are then distributed to fishing operators. Each quota is itself divisible, and all or part of it can be traded on the market. A number of countries adopted this kind of mechanism as an alternative to regulating access and fishing effort (Australia, Canada, Iceland).

The success of property right systems lies in the fact that they eliminate the perverse incentives of regulation of vessel size, equipment, length of season, etc. Individual tradeable quotas allow operators to behave like rational firms. An indication of their success is that there is no intention anywhere of returning to the previous regime.

Property right markets in pollution control (principally tradeable emission rights) appear to offer similar advantages. Although the experience with them is much less extensive than in fisheries, they seem more effective than command regulations in encouraging adaptation, minimising transitional disruption and costs to firms and the economy, and ensuring fairness. However, they require rather complex institution-building and the creation of a legal framework.

The main virtue of property rights is their ability to bring about structural adjustment. In the past, additional regulations or expenditure programmes were often needed because the industry had "adapted" to the existing regime or the regulations had been overtaken by technology or innovative operators. With property rights, this vicious circle is broken. Collective and individual objectives can be pursued simultaneously, resulting in increased efficency.

Vouchers

Vouchers have been around for some time under different guises, *e.g.* tax expenditures for child care and housing allowances integrated within welfare payments. But there is new interest in their expanded use as a way of empowering consumers. A voucher's distinguishing characteristic is that it restricts consumers in their choice of goods and services, while leaving them free to choose the suppliers. Ensuing enhanced competition among suppliers is expected to lower prices and/or enhance quality and diversity of services. For this to happen, markets must be competitive or have the potential to become so with, for example, few barriers to entry. On the demand side, voucher holders must have adequate information to exercise their choice.

Other potential advantages of the voucher include its ability to limit the government's expenditure commitment, provided, of course, that the number of recipients is predictable and controllable. Administrative costs are also lower. Vouchers allow recipients to search more efficiently for the services they want. They are also likely to generate positive income effects, all the more so if they are means-tested. Thus, two basic features of vouchers should be: a ceiling on the amount paid to the individual (as opposed to a government commitment to shoulder all costs associated with the provision of a service) and non-transferability from the specified goods and services or from the voucher recipient. Vouchers also offer advantages in terms of facilitating change: a key argument in their favour is that they will break up the producers' monopoly of supply. Once in place, they enhance the capacity of service provision to adapt to future change.

Any qualitative advantage depends on whether quality is defined as a matching of consumers' preferences to market offerings or in more precise terms (verification of adherence to curricula in education, inspected physical attributes of lodgings, standards of care in nursing homes, etc.). If the latter, then the superiority of vouchers over traditional delivery mechanisms depends on the capacity and costs of controlling standards.

Vouchers are said to have two major distributive drawbacks. First, vouchers may be appropriated by others (for instance when the benefit of housing vouchers is cancelled out by higher rents). Second, they may create greater social inequality because people do not have equal access to information (*e.g.* about the relative quality of different schools). Also, they may impair social cohesion by, for example, accentuating existing divisions based on money, religion, race, etc., by replacing a uniform system with institutions reflecting those divisions. For the moment, the operational measurement of such effects does not seem possible. In any event, the distributive drawbacks may be no less significant for non-voucher methods, merely less transparent.

Corporatisation and privatisation

Reforms aimed at improving the competitive environment of government activity have also involved increased resort to corporatisation and privatisation. Public enterprises, which are financed mainly by sales of their products and services, can range from firms that are little different from their private sector counterparts to public utilities in which there is frequently considered to be substantial public interest. The broad direction of reform in respect of these enterprises is fairly clear. The aim is to develop a market environment that requires management to mimic the behaviour of the competitive firm. This requires, first, that they be given as much independence as possible and be placed at arm's length from departments, ministers and the parliament. They also need clear directions regarding strategic objectives and responsibilities, for which ministers remain politically responsible. Achieving objectives and meeting responsibilities is then left to the management of the enterprise. The process of corporatisation requires separating regulatory functions from service delivery functions.

Several countries have extended their use of the public enterprise model, with positive experiences in many respects. To give just one example, New Zealand, since 1987, has "corporatised" numerous government departments producing goods and services (*e.g.* electricity generation, forestry and mining) into "State-Owned Enterprises" that operate in a more businesslike way while remaining under government ownership. As fully commercial enterprises, they have achieved substantial productivity gains and higher service quality and returned dividends to the government. Government functions are now largely grouped in accordance with a new rationale: trading activities are in the commercial mainstream, policy advice activities are close to the government, and service delivery activities are being aligned more closely with their consumers, under the supervision of management boards. In several cases, corporatisation was accompanied or followed by regulatory reform and privatisation.

The principles governing the operation of State-Owned Enterprises (SOEs) in New Zealand were set out as follows (New Zealand Minister of Finance, as quoted in Mascarenhas, 1991):

- responsibility for non-commercial functions to be separated from major trading SOEs;
- managers of SOEs to be given a principal objective of running them as successful business enterprises;
- managers to be responsible for decisions on the use of inputs and on pricing and marketing of their output within the performance objectives agreed with ministers so that they can be held accountable to ministers and Parliament for results;
- the advantages (and disadvantages) thus far enjoyed by SOEs, including unnecessary barriers to competition, to be removed so that commercial criteria could then provide a fair assessment of managerial performance;
- individual SOEs to be reconstituted on a case-by-case basis in a form appropriate for their commercial purposes under the guidance of boards comprising, generally, members appointed from the private sector.

Later, these principles were further elaborated to require financing of expenditure from market sources and not from government loans, and payment of tax and dividends.

The public enterprise model is not without its difficulties. In practice, public enterprises serve as an important instrument of government policy, and their freedom of action is frequently restricted in areas such as wage policy, price setting and borrowing. In addition, they are often required to pursue social objectives that restrict their pursuit of normal commercial objectives. Reforms have moved in the direction of making the additional cost of meeting public interest requirements more transparent and compensating enterprises for it.

Countries are also still seeking to establish an appropriate balance between managerial flexibility under market conditions and political direction and public control. Initial operational freedoms have proved vulnerable to erosion by what some see as creeping political interference and others see as legitimate direction by the major shareholder. Others regret the loss of transparency that is required to protect commercial interests. New, more strategic controls and enhanced accountability are needed to counterbalance the freedoms granted to managers. Various approaches are being employed. They include target rates of return and price-fixing mechanisms (with or without built-in productivity adjustments), and strategic planning requirements that incorporate financial plans and qualitative objectives. Public enterprises are also often criticised for being subsidised by governments (they rarely face the threat of take-over or bankruptcy) and having an unfair advantage over domestic or international competitors.

Some commentators see full privatisation as the eventual solution and view corporatisation merely as an intermediate step towards this end. A number of countries have favoured privatisation in the interests of ensuring operational independence, reducing the risks of capture by special interest groups, and raising much-needed funds. But the problems of regulatory control remain unresolved where the privatised enterprises have natural monopolies and/or where there is believed to be a large element of "public interest".

Other countries have followed programmes of privatisation and regulatory reform against a background of widespread dissatisfaction with the performance of state-owned enterprises and concern about the drain on public resources that they engendered. For example, a study of nationalised industries in the UK during the 1970s identified shortcomings such as productivity declines (*e.g.* 7 per cent in coal, 12 per cent in postal services) and increases in unit costs (32 per cent in steel, 37 per cent in postal services). Even in faster-growing industries dominated by state-owned firms, where technological progress allowed real cost levels to be reduced, performance was well below international averages. The study attributed this overall poor performance to four underlying causes: over-staffing, poor product mix, poor plant mix, and poorly designed capital investment programmes (United Kingdom, HMSO, 1991). Numerous OECD studies show that other countries have had similar experiences. Recent studies of Greece and Italy, for example, show evidence of dual development patterns in which a relatively dynamic private sector competes with a large public enterprise sector showing long-term losses and poor market focus.

Competition is the essential spur to improved performance. The clearest lesson to be learned from OECD reform experience is that all enterprises, whether public or private, are found to be more efficient when product markets are competitive or contestable.[2] When market forces are allowed to operate in such settings, large efficiency and consumer welfare gains are forthcoming. In sectors characterised by total or significant market failure, a complex picture of ownership and regulation emerges. For example, in sectors retaining natural monopoly elements, such as water and electric utilities, the results of empirical studies of different ownership forms are very mixed: some give the advantage to public ownership, others to private ownership, and still others find no significant difference. In those cases where there are clear grounds for government intervention, the key question goes beyond the issue of ownership. Rather, it is how to find an organisational and regulatory mix that will induce the managers of the enterprise in question to serve the public interest in the most efficient manner.

The problem closely resembles its counterpart in the private sector, that of corporate governance: what are the best institutional arrangements for motivating and monitoring corporate performance? In the public sector, the reform process has given rise to experimentation with alternative organisational and regulatory arrangements, accompanied by intergovernmental imitation of successful regulatory innovations (*e.g.* price-capping, incentive regulation). This may mean that governments will eventually converge on a regulatory "best practice" for each of the regulated industries.

NOTES

1. *Cf. The United States Experience with Contracting Out Under Circular A-76,* Occasional Paper on Public Management, Market-Type Mechanisms Series No. 2, p. 17: "The lack of a general programme audit, differences in accounting procedures, general lack of a pre-study base-line for comparison, and controversy over what costs should be counted resulted in the widespread conclusion that the true savings cannot be calculated. ... savings estimates have varied from a net loss to 35 per cent."

2. Evaluation based on analysis provided in OECD, 1992*b*, reflecting the situation at end 1990.

Chapter 7

PROVIDING RESPONSIVE SERVICE

SUMMARY

Providing more responsive service to citizens is a principal reform objective in all countries. Much progress has been achieved in strengthening a customer-service orientation in public institutions. Initiatives to improve accessibility and transparency include greater provision of information on available services and remedies, greater convenience in opening hours and physical access, and better-integrated service focused more specifically on client needs. There is a growing commitment to more active citizen participation through consumer choice and consultation about needs and perceptions of service. Setting clear standards of quality provides a basis for fixing expectations, judging performance and, increasingly, rewarding or penalising performance. Action is also centred on alleviating the administrative burden imposed on business, reducing demands and speeding up administrative action. Key concerns are the perceived risk of capture by dominant client interests and balancing the needs of clients and other stakeholders, especially the general taxpayer.

Public management reform will be seen as a failure if it does not respond to the legitimate expectations of citizens. In the past, many have criticised government as being more concerned with meeting its own needs rather than those of its citizens. But now, better informed and more articulate consumers, be they business representatives, interest groups, communities or private individuals, demand more say in what governments do and how they do it. They expect value for money in the services they receive, including standards of service delivery as high as those of the private sector. They expect to be treated as customers, with responsiveness and consideration. This is just as true of the tax or employment office as of the supermarket. Improved responsiveness is a key objective of reforms. In the end, making government more client-oriented is a central element of making it more performance-oriented. This goes far beyond superficial adjustments to the interface between the citizen and the administration. It lies much deeper in the structures and processes of democratic government and administrative organisation and is also heavily dependent on high quality, capable staff.

The public service is required to deliver a wide variety of services to the community. Radical improvements are needed in the delivery of these services. Quality and speed of service are crucial; courtesy and efficiency must go hand in hand. Good government ensures that people are made aware of the services and entitlements to which they have a right. Particular emphasis will now be given to providing citizens with such information in simple language and in an accessible form. The recognition of the customer must be paramount.

(Government of Ireland, 1985, p. 57)

Improved service to citizens is an important objective of many of the public management reforms described in other sections of this report. Thus, market-type mechanisms such as vouchers have been introduced partly to increase consumer choice. User charges, especially where demand is elastic and alternative supply options exist, are aimed not only at recovering some or all production costs, but also at obtaining feedback on client demand. Likewise, in some countries, reforms of social security financing seek to strengthen connections between payments and benefits. Providing a better quality of service to consumers is a major objective of the overall trend towards improved performance. Moreover, policies to promote equal employment opportunities help to ensure that the public service workforce is representative of a diverse community. Countries have also introduced a variety of specific initiatives to improve responsiveness to clients' demands.

A starting point is recognition that there is no generic client. Different clients or client groups will have different experiences with the public administration and different attitudes towards it. Their reasons for contacting it and their ability to deal with it will be far from identical. Any one client will also hold different views depending on the circumstances of a particular interaction and over time. Furthermore, different categories of client will have different rights and obligations in dealing with the administration.

Improving accessibility and participation

Efforts to improve transparency have featured prominently in country programmes. Information on how services are organised and on what possibilities exist for the redress of grievances is now made more readily available. For example, organisation charts are displayed in public offices; posters, explanatory leaflets, simple guides, and videos are made available; information about complaint and redress procedures is provided. Public servants are required to identify themselves through the use of name badges, giving their name in phone inquiries and in typing names in written correspondence. The anonymous bureaucrat is largely a relic of the past. Several countries have also introduced new appeal institutions or have strengthened existing ones. Ombudsmen, administrative review bodies, data protection agencies, freedom-of-information acts all form part of the machinery designed to restore balance in the relationship between the administration and the client. Important reforms in their own right, they also reinforce cultural change and encourage individual public servants to assume greater personal responsibility.

Accessibility to services has been improved by the relocation of offices nearer client population clusters, the use of alternative delivery mechanisms (*e.g.* mobile services, new functions in post offices), the use of information technology (*e.g.* automated information services in shopping malls or rural community centres, payment of benefits via "smart card" or the direct crediting of bank accounts), and more convenient opening hours. The special needs of disabled or elderly citizens are addressed by programmes in many organisations, which also aim

---

Improving Responsiveness

There is general agreement amongst OECD countries that the administration should be responsive to its clients, the public. There is less consensus on how that should be achieved. Some common elements have been identified as essential for responsive service delivery:

Transparency – clients should know how the administration works, what the constraints on actions of public servants are, who is responsible for what and what remedies are available if things go wrong.

Client participation – clients resent being treated as passive recipients of whatever the administration dishes out to them. In many cases their involvement is necessary if the administration is going to perform many of its tasks, as, for example, with tax collection.

Satisfying client requirements – as far as possible, clients should be offered services which correspond to their particular situation. "One-size-fits-all" services are no longer appropriate nor are they necessary as the new flexibility in the public sector allows services to be matched to requirements.

Accessibility – clients should have easy physical access to administration at convenient hours and be offered information in plain language.

(*Administration as Service, the Public as Client*, OECD, 1987)

---

to take account of the needs of minorities. The physical attributes of reception offices have been improved as financing permits (*e.g.* to allow privacy, facilitate orderly queuing, and provide a modern environment). Particular effort has been made in several countries to make administrative communications simpler and more comprehensible, using plain language, and eliminating jargon and codes.

Engaging the active participation of clients is another key objective. Much administrative output requires, or at least can be made more efficient by active client involvement in the production process. Clients' participation helps ensure that the administration takes account of their needs, and fosters a sense of joint responsibility for outcomes. In order to give clients the service they need, government organisations must first find out what they want. Reform efforts have accordingly sought to establish or strengthen consultative mechanisms. Many organisations now make greater use of client surveys, public hearings, and meetings with interest groups, and have generally made it clear that they would welcome input from the public. Information technology has opened up new opportunities (*e.g.* disseminating information in electronic format via bulletin boards, computer networks, magnetic and optical disks, and neighbourhood electronic kiosks).

Improved client services has been a significant part of the government's reform program. The Government and Ministers will decide on what kind and level of services should be provided, on the basis of assessments of the needs and interests of client groups. ... it is the responsibility of the Public Service and its staff to see that the services desired by the government are delivered effectively, efficiently and in a timely fashion, with proper courtesy and sensitivity and with full regard to the legal rights and entitlements of clients. For the Public Service, this is the nub of client focus and service quality.

(Australian Management Advisory Board
and Management Improvement Advisory Committee, 1993*d*, p. 16)

Setting service standards

Service standards are by now a centre-piece of reforms in most countries. A number of countries have given them particular prominence in high-profile documents such as the *Public Service User's Charter* in Belgium, the *Public Service Charter* in France, the *Public Service Quality Charter* in Portugal and the UK *Citizen's Charter*. With clear and specific service standards, clients and staff know exactly what is expected, in some cases for the first time. In this sense, service standards set a limit on the demands that can be satisfied. Standards also provide vital benchmarks against which performance can be judged and complement internal performance targets. In the longer term, standards should reflect the needs of service users. And, although the level at which standards are set is so far the result of a negotiation in which clients are represented only indirectly, this does not greatly diminish their value. The need for standards to be politically plausible guarantees a certain level of ambition, and measuring performance against standards over time creates its own dynamic to ensure continued relevance and realism. The commitment to public standards has also made political choices over levels of quality more explicit: sooner or later, higher standards come up against funding limitations.

The Public Service Users' Charter, Belgium

Adopted in December 1992, the *Charte de l'Utilisateur des Services Publics Fédéraux Belges,* sets out general principles governing the public services (transparency, flexibility, accessibility, and legal protection) and lists various measures already in operation and to be taken to put these principles into practice.

To be meaningful, standards need to be linked in some way to compensation for clients. But who is to fund the compensation? It is not much of an advance if the general taxpayer ends up compensating users of a specific service or if compensation for particular users is funded by higher charges for all users. Performance in relation to standards also needs to be linked to incentives for the organisation and its staff. Compensation can be a useful substitute for the profit motive if it is used to identify shortcomings and reward good management.

Clients' needs are not defined solely in terms of outputs but also cover such factors as speed of service and cost to the client of obtaining service. Reform initiatives have included the establishment of ''one-stop-shops'' (where the citizen can receive multiple or integrated services from a single point of contact) and co-location of government offices (where costs of moving between government services are minimised). Several agencies (notably taxation offices) have reorganised along client-group lines rather than by function or type of service (tax). In other words, they have tried to organise in a way that suits the client rather than the administration. These kinds of initiatives have been slow to get off the ground for technical and organisational reasons. They were often initially limited to service referral or to co-ordination of services within a single organisation. Breaking down interorganisational boundaries has proved even more difficult. Much scope remains for using information technology to reorganise government, now that the physical location of information is no longer a constraint.

Reducing administrative burden

Reducing administrative burden is another vital aspect of improving service to clients, and particularly to the business community. Initiatives aimed at cutting unnecessary red tape have included:

- the simplification of requirements and standardisation of forms (*e.g.* customs clearance, licence application);
- the multiple use of information provided by clients, consistent with privacy protection (*e.g.* use of single identifier, sharing of information within government, pre-printing of entries on forms);
- the use of information technology (*e.g.* electronic exchange of data, access to information bases); and
- a generally increasing awareness of the costs imposed (*e.g.* in statistical inquiries).

Initiatives to speed up administrative action have also included the rationalisation of decision-making procedures and a commitment to specific standards concerning reply deadlines and accuracy. These are underpinned in many instances by quality improvement programmes and techniques, such as Total Quality Management, that stress a commitment to quality at all levels of staff and at all stages of business in an organisation.

Avoiding client capture

The idea of focusing on citizens as customers, although attracting many adherents, is more complex than it first appears. First of all, it is important to remember that the achievement of service quality objectives is but one aspect of performance management, and the recipient of a particular service is only one of many stakeholders. The interests of the general taxpayer, in particular, have also to be given due consideration. The pursuit of higher quality and responsiveness must be weighed against its opportunity cost. Some improvements can be achieved at low cost, but there is always a trade-off between cost and quality. Other stakeholders include partners in provision and overseers of performance. Furthermore, as lower levels of government and private sector (for-profit and not-for-profit) organisations become more prominent in service delivery, their needs as intermediate customers must also be considered.

A balance has to be achieved between client responsiveness and client capture. The public service is not seen to be directly accountable to its clients. Accountability to the public, as discussed earlier, is indirect through the government and the Parliament. Nevertheless, increased emphasis on performance, measured predominantly or exclusively by client assessments, may strengthen the influence of particular client groups. This may be more likely in cases where policy-making and policy execution have been separated and where there is significant delegation of authority to local offices. Front-line staff may begin to identify more with clients than with policy-makers who are geographically and hierarchically distant. Small, single-issue agencies may also be vulnerable to over-representing their clients' needs.

The Customers of Government

"Customer"	Perspective
Citizens as service recipients	Responsiveness
Partners in service provision	Effectiveness
Overseers of performance	Accountability
Citizens as taxpayers	Efficiency

(United States – DiIulio *et al.*, 1993)

The risk is all the greater given that interest groups are increasingly well organised in lobbying on their own behalf. The phenomenon of interest groups is not new, but current management reforms have the potential to give them more rather than less influence. A strategy for harnessing their energy without jeopardising the general public interest is still being sought. In the absence of such a strategy, uniformity and equity may evaporate, resulting in those who shout loudest being served first and best and the poorly represented being neglected.

Chapter 8

IMPROVING THE MANAGEMENT OF HUMAN RESOURCES

SUMMARY

Reforms in human resources management (HRM) are driven by a variety of factors. The most influential factors are broader public sector reforms towards more efficient, effective, and customer-oriented services, and ongoing fiscal pressures to contain public expenditure. While there are important differences in countries' goals and strategies for HRM reforms, most organizations are adopting a more strategic approach to HRM, integrating it with broader "corporate" objectives. Decentralisation and devolution of HRM practices appear as the principal reform trends, although there is a general tendency to retain central constraints on pay and in other areas where it is considered important to maintain unity and collective perspective in the public service (e.g. collective bargaining, equal employment opportunity policies). Countries with a high level of devolution/decentralisation are reporting clear benefits; however, in all countries implementing such reforms, the balance between control and flexibility is still evolving.

Other significant developments include: the use of devolved budget frameworks within central resource limits; a focus on accountability and performance through performance contracts for top management and widespread use of performance-related pay schemes for managers and/or line staff; and a renewed emphasis on training and development in response to rising knowledge and skills requirements and the need for a flexible and adaptable workforce.

HRM reform trends and strategies

New approaches to managing people have gained ground in most OECD public services over the past decade. The main impetus for change has come from a recognition that improvements in efficiency and effectiveness are closely bound up with pay and employment practices, working methods, the performance and attitudes of staff, and other aspects of HRM. Increasingly, therefore, public employees are regarded as an essential resource requiring careful and active management. This view is leading to an acceptance that managers need to be given more authority to manage their staff, that HRM should be adapted more closely to the particular circumstances of different organisations, and that more attention should be given to developing coherent HRM strategies, planning HRM needs, and developing and motivating staff.

HRM reforms have also been driven by a variety of other factors. Labour market pressures, demographic factors, considerations of equity and social justice, and the need to contain public expenditure, all affect HRM policies. As the average age of populations increases, the public sector, like the private sector, is having to adapt its employment practices to ensure that it can recruit and retain a skilled workforce. All OECD governments subscribe to the principle of providing equal employment opportunities in the public service. Budget constraints create a continuing pressure to cut costs, of which staffing costs are a major component.

While the extent and content of HRM reforms vary among countries, there are important points of convergence. Common features include:

- the devolution of responsibility from central bodies to line departments and agencies and to line managers;
- a greater focus on and new approaches to the management of senior public servants;

- an increased emphasis on training and development and on performance management;
- the development of more flexible policies and practices in areas such as pay and conditions of employment, classification and grading, staffing and working arrangements.

There are also important differences among countries in terms of the degree of change in HRM that is being sought. At one end of the spectrum are countries such as Australia, New Zealand, Sweden, and the United Kingdom, where fundamental reforms are being pursued. At the other end are countries such as Germany and Japan, where changes have been few. In Japan the main emphasis has been on reducing public service employment and working-time. For Germany the main concern has recently been incorporating the new Eastern *Länder* into the public service system. Other countries are ranged at various points along this spectrum, with Canada, Denmark, Finland, and the Netherlands towards the more change-oriented end. Consequently, while the nature of public service employment is being radically transformed in some countries, in many others the reforms are leaving the basic structures and principles relatively unchanged, at least for the present.

The influence of new public management ideas can be discerned in many countries. These ideas have, to date, been most influential in the English-speaking and Nordic countries. They have tended to lead to more integrated programmes of HRM reform and to HRM changes embedded in wider public management reform strategies. The varying attachment to new management ideas is most apparent in the amount of devolution and managerial flexibility that countries are willing to implement and in the adoption of private sector management techniques, such as performance management. For many countries, higher priority is being given to bringing unwieldy bureaucratic structures and procedures under control and developing more transparent and rational systems for managing people. In some important respects, therefore, increasing efficiency and effectiveness is seen as requiring more, not less, standardisation. Nevertheless, the objective of moving to a more efficient, results-oriented administration is, generally also a reform theme.

Devolution of responsibility for HRM

For the most part, devolution has concerned the operational aspects of HRM, with the responsibility for determining policy retained by central management bodies. What this means in practice depends on how detailed the policy framework is. In most countries, the management of people within the public service has traditionally been highly regulated. The introduction of more flexible policies and the simplification of rules and procedures are an important corollary of devolution, providing managers with increased room for man8vre. Notions as to what the appropriate balance is between managerial flexibility and regulation vary from one public service to another.

The Devolution of HRM in New Zealand and Sweden

The most extensive devolution of HRM has occurred in New Zealand and Sweden. In New Zealand, the 1988 State Sector Act transferred the role of employer to chief executives of government departments, making them responsible for most aspects of HRM policy and practice. They are required to respect certain procedures for the appointment of staff, discipline and dismissal, occupational health and safety and minimum leave entitlements. The 1988 Act also obliges them to be "good employers", requiring them, for example, to appoint staff impartially and to provide opportunities for staff development. The State Services Commission (SSC), which formerly held all HRM authorities, retains an operational role only in relation to the employment of chief executives, pay determination and contracts for the Senior Executive Service. Since 1992, authority for negotiating pay and other conditions of employment has also been delegated to chief executives, with the SSC setting broad policy parameters, participating in negotiations and approving departmental agreements.

In Sweden, the devolution of HRM is considered a lynch-pin of the programme for public sector reform. Agencies and boards now control most aspects of their HRM policies and operations, with very little intervention by central bodies. The Ministry of Finance fixes salaries for agency directors general and advises on their recruitment. Since 1990, agencies are free to determine their own pay structures and to set pay individually for their employees. Individual agencies negotiate pay increases subject only to a ceiling on the total pay bill and to centrally-negotiated minimum wage increases.

In many countries, the emphasis is shifting from detailed controls to providing looser guidelines and defining basic standards that must be observed. At the same time, efforts are being made to develop a more strategic role for central management bodies. This is well illustrated in Australia, where a central human resource management framework has been developed that defines general principles under which agencies determine appropriate action in a devolved management environment. Implementation of the framework is promoted at the central level by the Public Service Commission with the following mission:

> In an environment where departments and agencies have greater flexibility and greater responsibilities to manage their resources to meet corporate goals, this framework provides a conceptual and communications tool to help managers manage their people more effectively...[B]y clearly showing the links between the various aspects of people management, [it] provides a sound basis for ongoing strategic human resource management.
>
> (Australian Public Service Commission, 1992*b*, p. 1)

In practice, the framework is designed to function as a continuous point of reference for the ongoing and cyclical process of corporate planning, communication of HRM policies, and evaluation.

Some features of the devolution of HRM are common to many countries. Devolved budgetary frameworks with single running-cost appropriations have provided an essential basis for relaxing central controls over key aspects of HRM such as staff numbers, classification and grading, and pay. Most countries have preferred to maintain central control over pay. Only in Australia, New Zealand, Sweden and the United Kingdom has pay determination been devolved to any significant extent and, even in these countries, an overall limit is applied to pay expenditure. This is bolstered by some involvement of central management bodies in setting pay-negotiation parameters, as in the United Kingdom, or in negotiating basic pay increases within a service-wide pay and grading structure, as in Australia.

In all countries there is continued involvement by central bodies in the appointment, pay, and classification of top public service positions, and in managing the performance of top officials. Often this also applies to senior management positions below the top level. The devolution of HRM is subject to laws or collective agreements that set basic standards and procedures. Usually, central management bodies maintain an oversight responsibility in areas such as equal employment opportunities, health and safety, and ''good employer'' requirements. Central management agencies also have a significant role in identifying and disseminating promising practices across the public service. Departments and agencies express most concern about controls affecting recruitment, termination of employment, classification and pay, and feel that procedures could be simplified and made less time-consuming, especially procedures for terminating employment. Where there has been significant devolution, the size of central management bodies has diminished appreciably (*e.g.* by half in Australia and New Zealand).

Where extensive freedoms from central control have been granted, there has, in turn, been a significant shift of authority for HRM to line managers (Australia, Denmark, the Netherlands, New Zealand, Sweden and the United Kingdom). Current practice in these countries is in striking contrast to that prior to the reforms. Even in other countries, increased managerial flexibility has resulted from reduced central involvement in areas such as classification, the control of staff numbers and recruitment. The spread of performance appraisal and flexible pay arrangements administered by line managers has also contributed to giving them a more active role in managing their staff.

The devolution of HRM to departments and agencies implies a much closer integration of HRM with organisational goals and strategies than has been typical of public service organisations in the past. A case study was carried out for this report, involving the following countries: Australia, Canada, Denmark, France, the Netherlands, New Zealand, Spain, Sweden, the United Kingdom, (see Chapter 16 below). In all of these countries, the organisations examined acknowledged the importance of integrating HRM with corporate strategy. However, most organisations felt they still had some way to go in achieving a satisfactory level of integration. In several of the case study countries, corporate planning processes were only beginning to be developed, and even where such processes were already in place, HRM planning and strategy were often not yet well integrated. There were weaknesses in most of the organisations studied in terms of translating HRM objectives into specific targets and strategies, which are then followed through in business planning and performance planning systems throughout the organisation; and in terms of the linkages between individual goal-setting and performance review and organisational performance planning targets. In contrast, training and developing measures were often quite well integrated with organisational planning processes. For large departments and agencies in particular, devolution raises the issue of insufficient co-ordination and organisational focus in HRM unless there is effective strategic integration. This issue emerged, for example, in some organisations in New Zealand and Sweden where there had been extensive devolution to line units.

Performance management systems are a key instrument for linking the management of people to organisational goals and strategies. Yet, this too is often a weak point. In practice, it takes a considerable length of time to establish performance management systems, and achieving the desired linkage among individual, unit and corporate target-setting is far from easy. Nevertheless, most countries recognize that such linkages are crucial, and consequently are investing time and effort into strengthening them. As a result, the attention of both management and staff is being brought to focus much more clearly on the importance of achieving specified outputs and service standards.

On the other hand, the new HRM flexibilities have enabled organisations to tailor structural and managerial reforms to their particular needs. Distinctive organisational cultures have begun to emerge. Key aspects of the reforms in most cases have been flatter structures, a reorganisation of the way work is carried out, simplified and more flexible job descriptions, and major efforts to train staff. In general, less has been done to alter pay and grading systems. New rigorous performance and accountability frameworks have created an incentive to use HRM flexibilities more actively in an effort to improve organisational performance.

Restructuring has, at the same time, put considerable pressure on both line managers and HRM specialists and has, in some respects, diverted attention from HRM. As reorganisations have generally involved staff reductions, much energy has had to be channelled into managing redeployment and redundancy; this has meant that managers have focused less on other aspects of HRM, and that staff have tended to be unreceptive to HRM initiatives. A more comprehensive, strategic approach to HRM is likely to take hold only when organisational changes have settled down.

Managers are often slow to take full advantage of the new flexibilities available to them. There appear to be a number of reasons for this. Managers see HRM as more complex and time-consuming than financial management and tend to push problems back to the centre of the organisation. In many cases, line managers are given HRM responsibilities before they have an opportunity to develop the necessary skills. It is sometimes felt that HRM expertise has been lost at the corporate centre without being replaced at the line management level. Line managers also complain of a lack of clear and easy-to-apply guidelines. They are also reluctant to accept HRM responsibilities if the delegation is only partial; they feel that they cannot successfully tackle some aspects while others are outside their control. Holding managers accountable for their performance of HRM functions is seen as one way to influence their handling of these functions.

Most countries are anxious to ensure that increased devolution does not result in the loss of a service-wide perspective or a dilution of basic public service principles and values. There are also concerns about the capacity of central bodies to monitor compliance with service-wide requirements. Reaching a balance in practice between devolution and due attention to service-wide goals and values is difficult, and in all countries the balance between control and devolution continues to evolve.

Devolution has provided clear benefits. Countries that have implemented significant devolution of HRM are generally very positive about its value. Central management bodies report that it has:

– enabled the implementation of organisational change and a greater diversity of practice among departments;
– enabled departments to recruit and retain staff more easily and to manage their people efficiently;
– increased the responsibility and accountability of managers and enabled them to manage their resources more actively;
– contributed to a sharper focus on efficiency and effectiveness, with positive impacts on service delivery and responsiveness;
– improved the link between policy and execution.

Positive assessments of the impact of devolution are generally borne out by the experience of line departments and agencies. Available evidence suggests that neither management nor unions wish to return to the previous situation of centralised control. Concerns are focused on the appropriate degree of devolution rather than the principle (in general, line departments and agencies want more freedom), on the ability of line managers to carry out their new responsibilities and on the adequacy of training and support.

Accountability and performance

HRM policies and practices have an important role to play both in the accountability mechanisms needed in a devolved management environment and in the development of a focus on results and performance in the public service. Performance management systems and accountability arrangements for senior managers are key factors.

Several countries have adopted a more contractual approach to HRM management, typically involving fixed-term employment contracts for top managers, annual agreements covering personal and organisational performance targets, annual performance appraisal, and appropriate rewards and penalties. Performance-related pay constitutes the main system reward. Penalties normally take the form of provisions for termination or non-renewal of contracts. Greater flexibility in recruitment is also a feature, aimed at recruitment from a wider pool, especially the private sector.

In New Zealand, for example, chief executives are appointed for 5-year terms and subject to detailed annual performance agreements. A 1991 review found that this model was proving reasonably robust and effective, despite initial difficulties with the specification, measurement and reporting of performance. The system also extends to senior managers. In 1994, the Australian public service instituted a system of statutory employment contracts for heads of departments. Contracts are for a fixed term not to exceed five years, they include a loading factor of 20 per cent above the basic rate of pay to compensate for loss of tenure, and the appointee has no right of return to the public service after the term of the contract (although contracts are renewable and there is special compensation for early termination). The possibility of introducing fixed term contracts for senior managers is under review. In the United Kingdom, chief executives of Executive Agencies (but not heads of departments) are recruited on fixed-term contracts on the basis of open competition, and a substantial portion of their pay is linked to key agency performance targets. Canada and Sweden have also strengthened performance management systems for department and agency heads.

More generally, techniques such as performance appraisal have spread in recent years. Up to two-thirds of public services in OECD countries have introduced at least some elements of performance management, although many systems are still in their infancy. Formal systems of performance appraisal and review linked to performance agreements are most developed in English-speaking countries, at least with respect to managers. Performance management systems for non-managerial staff are less well developed. The extent to which these systems link individual objective-setting and performance review to organisational goals and service standards varies greatly.

There is not a strong tradition of performance management in the Nordic countries, where less formalised approaches are felt to be better suited to the public service culture. Several of these countries have introduced performance discussions between managers and staff, usually on a voluntary basis. The focus is often on the development of individual skills and abilities rather than performance against set objectives. In France, the service-wide system of performance grading is becoming increasingly based on objective-setting and clear performance criteria. Elsewhere, the development of performance management has been very limited.

Although not an essential component of performance management, there has been increasing interest in performance-related pay in a number of public services. In Denmark, the Netherlands and New Zealand, for example, performance pay applies in principle to all levels in the public service; in practice, the spread of schemes across agencies has been uneven, and there is a tendency to concentrate the available funds on rewarding the more senior levels. In Australia, Canada, Ireland and the United States, schemes are confined to senior managers.

A previous study by PUMA suggests that many performance pay schemes are not functioning effectively (OECD, 1993a). Common problems include the appraisal of performance for pay purposes, poor management of performance appraisal ratings and the distribution of performance pay awards, the excessive standardisation of schemes and control by central management bodies, and insufficient funding. As a result, staff involved in such schemes are often unclear or cynical about the relationship between performance and pay, and feel that awards are not sufficiently large to be worth the effort. In addition, managers often feel that the schemes do not provide them with sufficient flexibility and discretion.

The study found little evidence that departments and agencies were using performance pay to implement their corporate strategies or to shape the culture of their organisations. This could be due to several factors: the inability of systems to adapt to specific agency requirements, the involvement of unions in pay allocation decisions, the lack of highly developed corporate planning systems, a perceived incompatibility with a teamwork culture, etc. This may be changing, however. The introduction of workplace bargaining in 1992 in Australia and the devolution of pay determination to large agencies in the United Kingdom provide greater flexibility to adapt to organisational requirements. In the United States, agencies are encouraged to develop their own schemes since the demise of the service-wide scheme for middle managers and supervisors. Individual and group bonus schemes exist in some agencies in Spain and Sweden, with rewards linked to the achievement of work unit goals derived from corporate goals.

Developing the skills and abilities of managers and staff has received increased attention and is widely targeted for continuing emphasis. Commonly cited reasons include the need: to invest managers with the necessary skills to handle newly delegated responsibilities; to keep pace with the increasing amount of knowledge and skills required by public service jobs; to develop a client focus and improve standards of service delivery; to adapt to new technology and new working methods; to address skill shortages. More generally, training and development programmes are seen as playing an important role in inculcating new values and bringing about desired cultural change.

It is clear that training is an important element in managerial and financial devolution. Devolution will have disappointing, if not disastrous, results if managers are not provided with adequate training and support to take on new tasks that had formerly been handled through central offices or agencies. As noted earlier, even where countries are moving forward quickly with devolution, many managers still do not look upon HRM as an important part of their work. Lack of attention to HRM may be less a function of resistance or reluctance than of transition adjustments for the current generation of managers who were neither schooled in integrating HRM functions into their management role, nor saw these functions carried out by their own mentors and managers. Consequently, it is not surprising that virtually all OECD countries have initiated new training and development measures in recent years.

In response to a growing recognition of the need for agency-specific training given both devolution and changes in the work being carried out by many departments or agencies, there is a renewed emphasis on encouraging (or requiring) departments or agencies to develop their own training programmes. Integrating staff training and development into agencies' strategic and resource planning is also thought to be an important part of developing a corporate culture. Several countries have also reported establishing service-wide training frameworks that maintain a focus on core values, while providing maximum flexibility to departments and agencies in tailoring programmes to meet targeted staffing needs (Australia, Canada, Denmark, New Zealand, the United States). On the other hand, the development of leadership and management skills, especially at the senior management levels (a matter of high priority for many public services), is an area where central management bodies should retain responsibility or, at least, remain involved. A centralized training agenda for senior management is a useful tool for imparting and maintaining a service-wide perspective on HRM principles and the co-ordination and communication of HRM reforms across the public service. In several countries (Australia, New Zealand, the United Kingdom) programmes are based on a set of core skills that senior managers are expected to acquire.

More flexible, cost-effective pay and employment practices

Reforming public service pay and employment practices is central to the aims of increasing managerial flexibility and obtaining better value for money. There have been efforts in many countries to gain tighter control over pay costs by changing the methods of determining general pay increases (*e.g.* elimination of indexing, reduction of the role of market comparisons, removal of pay linkages among different groups of public servants) and in the rules for individual pay progression (*e.g.* giving less weight to length of service as a criterion for pay progression).

Some countries have introduced more explicit linkages between pay increases and increased productivity, through productivity bargaining, as in the Australian public service, or requiring agencies to fund their own pay increases out of efficiency gains, as in recent pay rounds in New Zealand and the United Kingdom. Efforts to gain flexibility are reflected in provisions for: greater variation in individual pay based on performance, skills or recruitment and retention considerations; allowing flexibility for departments and agencies to reclassify positions; and variation according to labour market conditions for particular groups of employees or in different localities.

A crucial issue is whether the increased managerial flexibility that undoubtedly results from giving departments and agencies more freedom to decide their own pay arrangements can be combined successfully with the control of pay costs. To date, all of the countries that have devolved pay-fixing have addressed the cost issue by maintaining some measure of centralised control over the total pay budget, and several have also limited the level of pay settlements.

Reforms of industrial relations systems have been undertaken in several countries (*e.g.* Italy, Netherlands, New Zealand, Spain) with the aim of bringing them into line with private sector practices and "normalising" the conditions of employment of public servants. The New Zealand reforms, covering both the public and private sectors, removed the right of arbitration, abolished the special legal status of registered trade unions, introduced freedom of choice in industrial representation, and made the form and nature of bargaining a matter for negotiation between individual employers and employees.

More flexible and less complex job classification systems have been an important element of reforms in a number of public services. In Australia, a move to fewer, more broadly defined classifications, combined with a policy of multi-skilling, has helped to break down job demarcations, to facilitate new working practices and to provide greater flexibility to redeploy staff. Canada, France, New Zealand and the United States have also undertaken reforms in this area.

There has been a range of changes in employment practices in OECD countries. Most common have been the introduction of more flexible working time arrangements, measures to increase mobility, and provision for easier redeployment. Recruitment arrangements have been simplified and made more flexible, and open recruitment has been introduced in a number of countries that previously operated closed career systems. Flexible terms of employment, including contract employment, casual employment and part-time employment, have spread. Several countries have simplified provisions for terminating employment contracts and laying off surplus staff, and there are moves in this direction in other countries.

In addition to undertaking HRM reforms, most countries have implemented cost-cutting measures involving reductions in the number of public service employees (via controls on recruitment, redundancy, or both) and pay restraint measures.

Conclusions

In all countries that have devolved HRM, the balance between control and flexibility is still being struck. There are areas where central bodies are clearly unwilling to relinquish control completely; this applies especially to public sector pay, where devolved bargaining is usually combined with mechanisms for ensuring adherence to budgetary limits. There are also concerns about the balance between allowing departments and agencies the freedom to develop their own HRM practices, maintaining some degree of unity and a collective perspective across the public service. Very few countries (Sweden and possibly the United Kingdom) appear willing to take the route of total fragmentation of the public service. Most appear committed to retaining a basic common core of conditions that apply across the public service, although this may prove increasingly difficult as the effects of devolution take hold. Attempts to reinforce a collective perspective are reflected in centralised arrangements for the appointment and management of senior civil servants and in efforts in a number of countries to develop a capacity in central bodies for strategic planning of service-wide HRM policies.

Although the use of performance management techniques, especially performance review and appraisal, is spreading in the public service in many countries, such systems seem, with a few exceptions, to be underdeveloped. Links between individual goal-setting and performance review and organisational performance planning and targets are especially weak. However, managerial devolution is leading to a greater focus on this issue and, more generally, to efforts to forge a closer link between HRM and organisational goals and strategies. This is particularly evident in the increased attention being paid to staff training and development and to integrating training and development measures with organisational planning processes.

There has been little systematic evaluation of HRM reforms. Australia and New Zealand have undertaken an assessment in the context of overall reviews of public service reforms; several other countries have conducted reviews of specific reforms. PUMA's assessment provides some further insight into impacts. However, many of the reforms are too recent for a full and balanced assessment and, because the effects of some HRM reforms can take a considerable time to work through the system, the impacts may not become apparent for a number of years.

The reviews in Australia and New Zealand concluded that the overall public management reforms had been well directed and had brought significant benefits that had outweighed their costs. The devolution of HRM and associated reforms in New Zealand were considered to have permitted more efficient recruitment, retention and management of people and to have improved HRM overall in the public service. In this context, the accountability and responsibility of chief executives for HRM were seen as critical. In Australia, the working environment for staff had been improved by devolution, better job design, more participative approaches to work and fairer HRM policies and practices. HRM reforms were seen by staff as crucial to increasing the quality of service.

The case studies undertaken by PUMA in these two countries support this positive view of reforms. Although departments and agencies were not satisfied with all aspects of the reforms, none wished to return to the pre-reform situation, and all felt that the changes had given them much more "ownership" of their HRM policies, thereby enabling them to improve their efficiency. Managers were generally positive about the reforms; staff and unions, while generally supportive of the overall thrust of the reforms, had more mixed reactions. Factors such as organisational restructuring, redundancies, pay restraint and, in some cases, a perception that line managers were not handling HRM issues competently had had a detrimental effect on staff morale and were, in the view of management impeding the necessary cultural change. However, these problems were gradually being overcome and a service-wide survey of staff attitudes in Australia showed levels of job satisfaction and interest that compared favourably with other organisations.

Reviews by central management bodies in Denmark, Ireland and Sweden have also been generally positive about the effects of reforms. In the United Kingdom, the fact that Executive Agencies have met or exceeded a large proportion of their performance targets is considered to be evidence of the succeful delegation of HRM responsibilities.

Country experience has highlighted the existence of:

– where limited devolution has occurred, a demand from departments and agencies for further freedoms and a perception that effective management is hindered by the limited powers available to them;
– a need for further devolution from the centres of line departments to agencies and regional offices;
– concerns that line managers are not making full use of the HRM flexibilities they have been given;
– concerns about line management competence and a perceived need for more training, support and communication;
– a need for measures to hold line managers more accountable for their responsibilities;
– a need for effective monitoring of Equal Employment Opportunities (EEO) and other basic principles and standards, and a perception that this is not occurring in some countries;
– concerns that devolution of HRM may impede staff mobility and erode the unity of the public service.

PUMA's assessment indicates that most OECD countries foresee growing emphasis on reforming HRM in the coming years. The most commonly identified priority is further emphasis on training and development, especially the development of management skills and abilities. Other priorities for the future include:

– the development of strategic human resource management in departments and agencies;
– the need to improve the management and monitoring of devolution of HRM and to address issues of co-ordination and central steering;
– securing increased mobility within the public service;
– greater flexibility and tailoring of human resource management to the needs of departments and agencies;
– more flexible pay and grading structures;
– workforce reduction and policies for exit from the public service.

These priorities indicate that the current thrust of reforms will be maintained and indeed intensified in the coming years.

Chapter 9

OPTIMISING INFORMATION TECHNOLOGY

SUMMARY

OECD countries are investing heavily in information technology (IT) as a key support to reforms in public sector management. Many of the reforms would not be possible without IT. It is an important catalyst for change and offers significant benefits, especially in improving productivity and quality of service. At the same time, IT provides no magic formula for achieving modernisation objectives. For many, the potential of IT has never been fully realised. Its track record is marked by both success and disappointment. Making the most of IT will require linking it more closely to organisational change and corporate objectives, ensuring cost-effective delivery of IT, and keeping pace with changes in the technology itself.

IT in government: from efficiency to effectiveness

The original function of IT in public administration was primarily to increase productivity. Most IT projects had to be justified by staff reductions and increased workloads. Internal administrative and financial systems predominated. The emphasis has shifted in recent years, in tandem with technological developments and reform objectives. Efficiency and economy remain critical objectives, but now equal emphasis is put on the use of IT to increase effectiveness and improve quality of service. The whole thrust of IT is changing in order to achieve maximum gain. Applying new technology to existing ways of doing business is no longer enough. It must be used to change processes and structures, within a wider strategic framework.

Traditional productivity gains remain important, but countries are also focusing increasingly on efficiency across organisational boundaries and with respect to actors in the external environment (clients, both individuals and businesses). The real efficiency benefits of IT are seen in improving government-wide interaction and in reducing administrative burden on clients. A recent evaluation of government IT in France, for example, noted that "the greatest productivity gains result from changes to organisational structures and procedures, too often neglected. This is true for applications within ministries but even more so for applications that affect several ministries" (Commissariat général du Plan, 1992, p. 7). The report was critical that measurement, where it occurs, is based more on the return to the organisation's own budget than on resultant savings on a much broader front.

Five factors emerged as particularly important in facilitating the achievement of maximum organisational benefits from IT systems:

- a business-driven, strategic planning framework;
- a performance-related approach to IT investment appraisal;
- active user participation;
- clear responsibility for the management of IT budgets;
- strong project management.

(Ireland – Clince *et al.*, 1992)

Countries are seeking to use IT to achieve efficiency gains in a variety of ways. The use of preprinted forms that require minimum input by clients and, therefore reduce mistakes that are difficult to identify later and costly to rectify, is already commonplace. This provides benefits to both the public sector and its clients. Shared benefits are also a feature of single points of information collection and distribution (*e.g.* one-stop-shops for small businesses; the collection of social security information on behalf of several government departments and agencies). More recently, countries are investing in the development of electronic data exchange and generally conducting business electronically (including, for example, the use of electronic bulletin boards in the area of procurement). There is also interest in using IT to improve the management and access to regulation.

IT's contribution to improved effectiveness can be seen at several levels. The introduction of IT in recent years has typically involved a strategic planning process in which organisational objectives are clarified and prioritised. This has been a useful contribution in its own right to organisational effectiveness. IT has also facilitated access by policy-makers to timely and comprehensive information, through better communication systems and the generation of policy-relevant information from operations. This has become all the more crucial in an environment of devolution and separation of policy-making and executive functions.

There are many examples of innovative use of IT to improve service delivery and responsiveness, and countries are keen to go further in this direction. IT has been central to several initiatives to improve access to information and services outside normal office hours, in locations which best suit the client and in multiple forms (*e.g.* different languages, touch-screen interrogation). Thus, information and services are beginning to be provided to individual citizens, for example via kiosks situated in shopping malls, community centres or other public places. Some developments bring together a wide range of information from many central and local government departments (*e.g.* INFOCID – the Portuguese inter-departmental system for information for the citizen). Others provide both information and services such as job seeking and vehicle licence renewal, with the facility for payment by credit card (*e.g.* INFO CALIFORNIA – the California State system that provides a multiple-service window to all state departments). There are also initiatives that combine public and private sector information, such as the French MINITEL system and the Project VEREDA in Spain.

Two major issues that have arisen are: *a)* authenticating identification when services are specific to the individual; and *b)* ensuring equity of access from both urban and rural areas. A step towards addressing this second issue is taken by experiments in using IT to provide services to remote rural areas. Examples are the "LAMDA" project in the Highlands and Islands of Scotland, partially funded by the EU, and "tele-cottages" in Nordic countries. In addition to improving service delivery, these initiatives offer considerable potential for reducing the running costs of public administration by reducing the need for paper forms and transferring clerical tasks to the individual citizen. In this way, they are similar to the introduction of "self-service" automated teller machines (ATMs) by banks.

Electronic delivery may lead not only to improvements in current services, but to new ways of thinking about and organizing government programs and delivery mechanisms.

(US Office of Technology Assessment, 1993)

IT has also underpinned efforts to provide an integrated service based on the "whole person" concept rather that on administrative function (*e.g.* all tax or social security matters relevant to a particular client are dealt with by a single office rather than separated according to individual tax or benefit type and dealt with by different offices). This kind of system has many advantages for administration and client alike. For the administration, it improves efficiency (*e.g.* by eliminating duplication), control (against fraud and evasion) and effectiveness (*e.g.* by increasing tax in-flow or better targeting of service). For clients, it reduces intrusion and compliance costs. But it requires major changes in work practices, communications, organisational structures and computer systems. Although many countries are committed to the approach, progress in implementation has generally been slow. This is due not to technological limitations, but rather to organisational barriers between departments or agencies and local levels of government and the attitudes of civil servants.

Countries are also developing more interactive and easy-to-use systems that enable point-of-contact officials to provide relevant information and service to clients. Many front-line offices now have immediate access to main databases storing information on clients and providing opportunities to establish their entitlements and ultimately to customise the service to their needs within defined limits of discretion. On-line access to information holdings, more intense use of information already collected and greater integration or connection among systems are reducing form-filling and permitting speedier, more reliable responses. IT holds out promise as regards greater client involvement in the identification of needs, the design of systems, and feedback on operations, but this aspect is perhaps the least well understood or exploited.

Realising the benefits of IT

Listing these and other applications could give the impression that everything is rosy in the IT garden. There have indeed been successful applications of IT, but many are isolated incidences or are at early stages of development. Technical and organisational factors have often hampered the full exploitation of IT. Some organisations have gone further than others in using IT to support general reform objectives, but they illustrate what might be possible rather than the general state of play. There have been also many failures and disappointments in the IT field. There has been much concern that IT investments have not provided best value for money or delivered all the promised benefits.

Evaluations of IT strategies and investments in several countries have shown that, although important benefits have been achieved, they have not been as great as they could have been. The evaluation of government IT in France, referred to earlier, criticised the overall lack of profitability of investments. It attributed this to four main factors: missed opportunities to make fundamental change; a lack of clear, quantified objectives and measurement of benefits; a narrow focus on benefits within existing organisational boundaries; and poor cost control. An evaluation in Denmark revealed a similar situation. A lack of integration between IT use and organisational change and a lack of appreciation of IT as a strategic element were identified as the main obstacles to deriving more benefit from IT (Ministry of Finance, 1992). In Ireland, an evaluation noted that "the overall picture, then, is one of substantial and diverse benefits which prove the value of IT tempered with instances of under-achievement of benefits" (Clince *et al.,* 1992).

In fact, IT is quite capable of having negative as well as positive effects. In PUMA work, based mainly on public service case studies, IT was frequently described by countries as a "double-edged sword", capable of cutting both ways, for good and bad (*Information Technology in Government – Management Challenges,* PUMA Occasional Paper, 1992). IT projects usually have multiple objectives, including greater control and the reduction of fraud, better working conditions for staff, and improved quality of service. It is undoubtedly possible to make progress towards achieving several objectives simultaneously, but usually not with equal emphasis. The dominant focus has tended to be on productivity, and technological and financial considerations have preoccupied project managers. This is a natural tendency when financial constraints and implementation deadlines are tight. Objectives regarding quality of service risk being diluted along the way, and improvements to the working environment, relegated to second place.

The uneven use of IT can also increase external inefficiency and administrative burden. Thus, governments can add to the costs of firms by not keeping up with their IT investments or by imposing different technical and information standards. They may handicap smaller firms by effectively increasing entry costs if they impose particular IT solutions. Policy-makers may be tempted to use IT's information-handling capacity to introduce more and more complexity into schemes and regulations, making comprehension and compliance more difficult. A balance needs to be struck between tailoring administrative acts to the needs of individual clients (but adding overall complexity) and maintaining uniformity and relative simplicity and transparency.

The same phenomenon has been observed as regards IT's impact on organisational structure and culture. Countries acknowledge that, in order to maximise the return on IT, they must use it to bring about structural change in organisations. IT offers options of organisational design that were not previously available. The location of information is no longer a design criterion. This allows a greater geographical spread of offices, bringing service closer to the client. Information holding and processing can take place in low-cost areas without adversely affecting service in high-street offices. It enables different parts of different organisations to interact in new ways, based on common functions and objectives. IT also facilitates the establishment of task-oriented groups of finite duration, communicating across long distances. In short, it can allow greater organisational flexibility.

But countries are also concerned that, paradoxically, IT may act as a brake on desired structural change. IT "repairs" may perpetuate out-dated models of organisation, when more radical change is in fact required. Fixing old procedures and routines, even in new systems, will limit flexibility. One organisation's ageing systems may also limit the development of a partner organisation because of the need to make progress in tandem. A key challenge to management is to ensure that IT solutions do not impose new barriers to organisational change. Technological choices must allow for new organisational forms and relationships.

IT can have an important impact on organisational culture. On the positive side, it can help underpin values such as client responsiveness and quality of service. Its effective use can help provide an attractive working environment and motivate staff. It can provide new options for flexible working arrangements such as working from home or from other locations outside the office. It can enrich jobs, allowing machines to take over repetitive tasks. Better motivated staff are more likely to accept change and also to look for opportunities for further change. But IT can also bring about uncertainty and de-skilling. It can eliminate the interesting parts of some jobs and it may simply replace old procedures with new, more complicated ones. It can reinforce bureaucratic culture through, for example, the value it places on detail, accuracy, and adherence to procedures.

Although working from home ("teleworking") may generate benefits, it may also have some shortcomings. The benefits are substantial savings on office accommodation costs for departments, travel costs and stress for the individual, and a general improvement in productivity, particularly for those involved in policy formulation and other "knowledge based" activities. The problems are both human and regulatory. As organisations become increasingly flatter, middle managers find their positions further threatened if their staff are not in an office where they can see and control them directly. Current experience suggests that those who telework are isolated by the organisation and their potential is often underexploited. Current conditions of service in several public administrations discourage staff from working at home and in some cases penalise staff.

Implementing IT

The way in which IT is introduced and implemented is therefore critical. Countries have accumulated a wealth of experience in this respect. Large-scale projects have brought into sharp relief many of the problems of introducing IT. Despite some noteworthy successes, IT projects have an overall reputation for being over-budget, behind schedule and disappointing in terms of achieving their objectives.

Inadequate project management is the most frequent cause of failure. Success depends heavily on having a strong project leader and project management team from the outset. The personal characteristics of project managers are more important than where they come from in the organisation. The project manager needs clear authority from top managers and ready access to them for purposes of reporting progress and at key decision points. The continuity of project leadership and team membership is also important, but can be difficult to achieve in a large project, which is necessarily of long duration. In addition, many of the control issues raised by contracting out are also particularly relevant to IT projects.

Breaking down large projects into more easily managed parts, using modular or incrementalist approaches, is seen in some countries as a way to overcome problems concerning changing organisational needs and technology, project management and control of partners, and also as a way to ensure early benefits and a more rapid return on investment. However, projects may become fragmented under this approach. Down-sizing thus needs to be part of a strategic planning framework if it is to be effective, and co-ordination mechanisms, such as those involved in programme management, must be put in place.

A sustained, visible commitment from top managers is critical to success, just as for any major change. They are vitally involved. They must set the strategic direction and ensure appropriate structures and capacity for implementation. Only they can bring about the conditions for the organisational change necessary to capitalise fully on the IT investment. Only they can ensure that interdepartmental co-operation takes place. In the end, only they can ensure that the impact of IT is positive.

IT cannot be left to technologists. There is a need for new skills and a multidisciplinary team to introduce and manage IT, including skills from the behavioural sciences and in organisation design. To achieve maximum benefit from IT systems, users need to "own" them, and this ownership requires their active participation. Users at all levels of an organisation, especially at the operator level, need to be involved from the design and development stages to the end of the process. This is now generally accepted practice, aimed at bridging the gap that existed in the past between users and technologists. IT benefits flow not from the technology but from its effective use.

Most countries have been emphasising the need for a results-oriented approach to IT, integrating IT with organisational priorities. As they see it, a strategic focus is necessary. Common technical and information standards are crucial to achieving cost-effective, flexible systems in the long term. Investing in open, instead of proprietary, systems offers the benefit of a uniform environment enabling systems of different types and sizes to work together. Governments have a key role in identifying and demanding the standards and products that they need.

Increased reliance on IT has raised concerns about security and privacy. Organisations are increasingly dependent on IT systems for most aspects of their operations. The dangers of infiltration, sabotage, accidents, etc., are of greater consequence. Various initiatives have been taken to provide adequate protection, including legislative changes at the national level and issuance of guidelines within administrations. The responsibility for the security of systems is seen to lie primarily with individual organisations. As a minimum, all have taken steps to ensure back-up facilities and the storage of data.

As regards privacy and protection of data, new information technologies may be undermining the goals of first-generation laws in this area. Desk-top computers make it difficult to monitor the use of personal information because individual users can use them to create their own systems of records and as remote terminals to access centralised systems of records. The power and flexibility of networked IT allows a vast increase in the exchange and manipulation of information, and in the number of people having access to it. Taken together, these factors have necessitated a fresh look at the benefits and risks of information-sharing and the relevance and effectiveness of existing procedures, guidelines and legal powers.

It is also felt that a changed role for the central IT function is necessary for realising the benefits of IT. The emerging need for a central co-ordination function across the public administration to ensure that economies of scale and scope are not lost has contributed to the creation of, for example, the CCTA, the Government Centre for Information systems in the UK and the Secretariat for Administrative Modernisation (SMA) in Portugal. The general trend is towards greater devolution of responsibility for IT, both within organisations and between central bodies and line agencies, mainly in response to demands from users. If line managers are held accountable for resource use and programme outputs, they expect quality service from IT units and want to be able to go elsewhere for services if the standard is unsatisfactory or costs are too high. The devolution of IT has gone furthest in countries that have introduced extended managerial devolution as part of their wider public management reforms. Concerns about the devolution of IT relate essentially to aspects of the balance between local autonomy and service-wide considerations.

The introduction of greater competition through market-testing and contracting out is also an increasing trend, pursued more vigorously in some countries than in others. This, too, has major implications for the organisation and role of the central IT function, at the level of central management bodies and line departments alike. The centre retains a key advantage in providing advice and guidance that is independent and commercially impartial. It holds an important function in providing direct services for procurement, consultancy and telecommunications. It has a significant role in supporting customers, especially smaller units, in the new business environment, bolstering contract negotiation and management skills and generally helping customers to be competent and comfortable in dealing with contractors.

The centre also has a role in promoting best practice, keeping in touch with technological research and innovation, and providing and managing common infrastructure. It will retain a responsibility for developing and co-ordinating IT policy as it affects the administration as a whole. Central IT bodies also need to strengthen links with other central bodies responsible for public management reform, so that IT can be integrated fully with the reform process.

Concluding remarks

Much more needs to be done in order to increase the return on IT investment and to capitalise on IT's immense potential. Countries recognise the potential but, given past experiences, are now more cautious and realistic. Thus, Denmark notes that ''The 90s *might* be the decade in which information technology (IT) makes a serious contribution to new, better and cheaper solutions in the public sector'' (Ministry of Finance, 1992*b*). It sees that, thanks to past investments, the public sector now has a good base for moving forward.

The evaluation of government IT in France saw IT as constituting ''an indispensable instrument in responding to future challenges'' and recommended that IT should occupy a more central place in modernisation efforts and as a tool of reform (Commissariat Général du Plan, 1992, p. 7). IT is a catalyst for providing improved public services, better decision making, efficient resource management and streamlined work practices. For this to happen, action is required on a number of fronts, notably:

- enhanced management, planning and control of the IT function;
- using technology to redesign and improve administrative processes;
- providing better access to quality information;
- harnessing the potential of new technologies;
- developing and applying standards;
- attracting and retaining high-calibre IT professionals;
- increasing research into the economic, social, legal and political implications of new IT opportunities; and
- assessing experiences.

Chapter 10

IMPROVING THE QUALITY OF REGULATION

SUMMARY

Improving the management of the regulatory system is a high priority for many reasons. Regulation is and will remain an essential policy instrument of government. Yet traditional regulatory approaches have often been disappointing in achieving policy objectives and have proved costly and inflexible. Unrelenting growth in regulation has imposed heavy burdens and prompted calls for relief. Regulation has not kept up with developments in microeconomics, technological innovations, globalisation and decentralisation. The effectiveness of government intervention is seen to be at risk while the external demand and internal pressures for regulation continue unabated. Reforms are directed, therefore, both at reducing the quantity and cost of regulation and at improving its quality. New management frameworks to discipline and control regulation rely on strategies such as the use of regulatory checklists, regulatory analysis, the establishment of explicit quality standards, and greater resort to alternatives to traditional regulation. These latter include approaches such as information disclosure, economic incentives, voluntary agreements, self-regulation, and compliance innovation. A host of political, economic, social, and institutional interests have hampered progress but, nevertheless, several country successes suggest that there are solid grounds for optimism.

Regulation in its many forms has, in the post-war years, become one of the most widely-used policy instruments of modern governance. Its use has become so pervasive that many scholars suggest that OECD countries today are best described as "regulatory states". By many standards, the development of intricate and far-reaching national regulatory systems must be judged a successful governing response to social and economic demands. Regulation has played a vital role in serving and balancing the diverse interests and values of complex societies and economies.

Regulatory reform initiatives in many OECD countries over the past several years have substantially improved the capacities of governments to respond to the governing pressures outlined in Chapter 2. These initiatives therefore constitute a significant step forward in public sector management. Regulators are paying more attention to regulatory costs, and are seeking practical methods by which negative impacts can be assessed and disciplined. Programmes of administrative simplification and de-bureaucratisation are beginning to lighten the burden of meeting regulatory requirements. Regulatory quality is receiving more attention, and regulatory decision-making at national and international levels is increasingly transparent and empirically-based.

What were good regulatory practices in 1986 may not be good enough now.

(Treasury Board of Canada, 1992, p. 4)

Most importantly from a longer-term perspective, several governments have established permanent institutions with the tools and expertise to guide the reform process. In the 1990s the reform of rules is evolving into the management of the regulatory system. The creation of regulatory management bodies in the central management structures of government can be compared to the creation of central budgeting offices earlier in this century.

Current regulatory trends

What is the regulatory situation facing governments of OECD countries today, following a decade or more of reform? Two opposing trends are clear. On one side, through privatisation and economic deregulation, governments are withdrawing from the direct regulation of economic decisions, albeit unevenly among countries and sectors. Economic deregulation can be seen as one of the most important experiments in economic policy of the past several decades. There are a number of reasons for economic deregulation: a better understanding of industrial organisational structures and market failures, a growing awareness of the extent and nature of regulatory failure, technological changes, growing budgetary demands from failing public enterprises, and liberalised regional and global trading systems.* Governments are now concentrating more on regulating the conditions of competition.

Against this, two other types of regulation have been on the increase. Regulation intended to provide social protection and benefits – such as better environmental quality, improved working conditions, reduced risks of accident or illness, and consumer protection – increased rapidly in the 1980s and, if anything, further growth is likely, since public demand for these kinds of regulation appears to be intensifying. And administrative requirements affecting the private sector, sometimes called "process" regulation and needed to carry out government programmes such as tax collection, have proved to be an increasing burden.

Objectives of regulatory management and reform

Regulatory reform in OECD countries serves a variety of objectives that encompass, in one country or another, most of the major issues on political agendas. Yet the core problems of regulation identified in OECD countries can be grouped into three areas: quantity and cost, quality, and legitimacy. Since quantity is the dominant concern, it is given the most in-depth treatment here; the others are mentioned more briefly.

Quantity and cost

Evidence is mounting that governments are approaching the practical limits of the regulatory state. The volume and complexity of new regulations from all levels of government reached unprecedented heights in the 1980s, threatening to overwhelm the capacity of government administrations and private sectors alike. Have the governments of OECD countries reached the point where continued regulatory growth will undermine the regulatory system? It is impossible to say, but warning bells are beginning to ring, some sounded by governments themselves. For the United States, for example, the comprehensive Code of Federal Regulations swelled from 20 000 pages in 1960 to over 120 000 pages by 1990; in Australia, lower-level regulation doubled from 1982 to 1990.

Similar messages are heard in other countries: In Sweden, the government noted in 1985 that simpler and fewer rules were necessary for the regulatory system to operate as intended; Portugal stated in 1990 that reform was needed to stem an "excessive production of rules"; in 1988 the Japanese Government identified the reduction of regulation and government instructions as a top priority of administrative reform.

The cost of regulation is rising as or more quickly than its quantity. Administrative costs to governments are a continuing problem as budget constraints become tighter. In 1992, Canada found "the cost of implementing regulation to be high... [and] the money is simply not there anymore" (Treasury Board of Canada, 1992, p. 4). Far greater, however, are compliance costs borne directly by citizens and businesses. From an economic perspective, the cost of regulation can be seen as a form of indirect taxation, and regulation as a mechanism for government spending. Yet no OECD country has a system in place to account for the cost of regulation and to control it. In fact, regulation is the last major area of government spending that is not centrally managed.

---

* The reasons for economic deregulation are discussed more fully in OECD, 1992*b*.

The lack of accounting makes it difficult to assess the true cost of regulation. Data, covering the system as a whole, are available from only one country: in the United States, aggregate costs of federal regulation were estimated at $500 billion per year in 1992, or about 10 per cent of GDP and one-fourth of on-budget spending, and were projected to grow steadily in the future. Since the administrative costs of federal US regulation amounted to about $9 billion in 1992, every dollar spent by the government on administering regulation represented a corresponding cost of $55 to citizens and businesses.

Costs of this magnitude are clearly significant for economic growth, and many studies have suggested that some regulations reduce productivity, job creation, and innovation, and hence the speed of structural adjustment. Small businesses are likely to be disproportionately affected. In addition, the direct and indirect effects of regulation on international competitiveness have recently become an object of concern.

Obviously, the current rate of regulatory growth cannot continue. Could UK company law, 500 pages in 1980, over 3 500 pages in 1991, exceed 20 000 pages in another decade? How could companies, already complaining, cope with such an increase? How could governments? And yet, how can regulatory growth not continue? Public demand for regulation is not abating; on the contrary: as the director of regulatory reform in Canada has noted, "there seems to be no natural limit to the potential demand for regulatory intervention". Environmental quality, consumer protection, working conditions, safety and health – regulations are rapidly increasing in all these areas in response to emerging values, interests, and scientific understanding of risks and externalities.

The creation of regulatory institutions has generated its own dynamic in which regulation begets regulation. Regulators tend to regulate. "Social intervention becomes a race between the ingenuity of the regulatee and the loophole-closing of the regulator, with a continuing expansion in the volume of regulations as the outcome," the

---

Alternatives and Complements to Traditional Styles of Regulation

Information disclosure: the provision of information to consumers and workers has been used to reduce health and safety risks (cancer warnings), change eating habits (food labels), protect the environment (eco-labels), and promote energy conservation (energy efficiency labels).

Economic incentives, such as taxes, charges, subsidies, and refund schemes, change behaviour by changing the relative benefits and costs of private actions. They leave the way open for citizens and businesses to react in the ways they themselves see as the most beneficial. They provide incentives to innovate in the longer-term by allowing regulatees to profit from doing better.

Tradeable property rights: government-issued permits that can be bought and sold in the market can provide significant incentives for innovation and competition. Possible types of permit include "rights" to discharge a quantity of pollution, tradeable fuel efficiency credits for automobile manufacturers, fishing rights, and air transport landing rights.

Liability combined with insurance based on previous behaviour can provide an economic incentive, administered by the court system.

Voluntary agreements between governments and businesses or other interest groups are essentially non-mandatory contracts in which incentives for action arise from mutual interest rather than from sanctions.

Self-regulation, an arrangement in which an organised group regulates the behaviour of its members, can take many forms ranging from informal or implicit agreements among group members to formal bodies which may have legal and sanctioning powers.

Persuasive approaches: the use of information, communication, encouragement, peer pressure, and education strategies to convince the public of the need for change.

Performance-based regulation sets out the desired objectives, along with criteria (performance measures) for determining whether the objective has been achieved. This approach, by focusing on results (outputs) rather than on the means for achieving them (inputs), allows regulated entities greater freedom of action to find the lowest-cost means of complying.

Compliance innovation is aimed at improving the effectiveness of enforcement while reducing its cost. One approach is to rely on third-party certification of compliance with rules. Another is to establish incentives for third parties, such as employees, consumers, or communities, to monitor compliance.

Market forces and deregulation: not all problems are amenable to government solutions. A cost-effective option may be deregulation to allow market forces to work efficiently.

director of regulatory review in the United States has observed (Schultze, 1977, pp. 56-57). And as the Prime Minister of France noted in 1988, "Certain civil servants seem to consider that no situation exists that cannot be made subject to a regulation" (Conseil d'État, 1992, p. 24).

Most importantly, political systems encourage regulatory growth. Politically, regulation is extraordinarily convenient. In many ways, regulation plays to the weakness of democratic systems. The underlying dynamic of regulation is that it serves visible and vocal groups, and imposes costs on diffuse and unsuspecting groups (such as consumers). There is no easier way for governments to spend money than to regulate. And if governments are finding it difficult to control fiscal costs, which are highly visible, how much more difficult will it be to control the invisible costs of regulation?

Nothing less than the rule of law might be at stake. The present rate of growth would lead inevitably to over-regulated societies in which complete compliance with the law is impossible, and citizens and governments pick and choose which rules to obey and enforce. The French Conseil d'Etat has warned as well that citizens might be divided into classes: "the few who can afford expert advice on how to exploit to the full the subtleties of the law, and everyone else, hopelessly lost in the legislative maze, with no recourse to law" (Conseil d'État, 1992, p. 21).

The dilemma of regulatory growth has no single answer. The only obvious response is development of a new management framework to discipline and control regulation. Such controls have succeeded in curbing the rate of regulatory growth in some OECD countries. Many countries are also resorting to alternative and complementary policy instruments that can be more effective, less costly, and more flexible (see box). But the reform initiatives of the past several years have faced not only a daunting inventory of existing problems, but also established laws, processes, and institutions that are well suited to creating more problems, and are highly resistant to change.

Quality

Given the formidable political interests that protect existing regulations and support new ones, governments have naturally tended to emphasize "quality" rather than "quantity" reforms. Everyone can agree on the need for "good" regulation. "We may not end with far fewer regulations," stated the UK Government in 1986, "but they will be better regulations" (Secretary of State for Employment, 1986, p. 2). In Canada, the motto has been "regulating smarter".

Several OECD governments have set explicit quality standards for regulations, and others have implicitly pursued a wide range of standards: user standards such as stability, predictability, clarity, simplicity, and accessibility; design standards such as flexibility and compatibility with other rules and international standards; legal standards regarding structure, drafting, and technique; and analytical standards, such as cost-benefit and cost-effectiveness tests. Regulatory analysis, in particular, has been a widely used technique for focusing attention on the impact of regulation and on possible alternatives.

Some countries have made significant gains towards improved regulatory quality. The United States has applied since 1981 a rigorous cost-benefit test, and believes that the costs of new regulations have been reduced by billions of dollars as a result. The Single Market Programme of the European Community is expected to produce large gains in economic growth by eliminating regulatory inconsistencies that block trade and competition. Several countries have swept away outdated laws and reordered legal systems to improve clarity and accessibility. Turkey completed a codification programme that eliminated 1 600 laws and consolidated 12 000 others into 700.

Other countries, such as Germany, have noted that simply asking the right questions, through the use of "checklists" or lists of principles, can help sensitise regulators to a broader set of issues. The checklist approach can be useful in many ways. It provides a mechanism for communicating the values and policies of a government and thus fosters responsiveness to political priorities. It improves efficiency in regulatory development by providing consistent information and a predictable decision-making process. It helps improve the quality of regulation by specifying the use of consultative procedures and requiring the inclusion of cost estimates. It assists the improvement of regulatory programme design by raising the question of enforceability. A longer-term benefit derives from its value as an educational tool and mechanism for cultural change. Finally, it facilitates managerial oversight of the regulatory system.

Experience to date suggests that good regulatory practices and techniques may significantly reduce burdens and improve effectiveness. Yet it is unclear whether, on the whole, today's regulations are of better quality than their counterparts of ten years ago. Regulators' compliance with quality standards has been problematic, since it has proved difficult to establish incentives within bureaucracies for regulators to change their behaviour. Few countries have established any system for measuring regulatory improvement.

Legitimacy

As more decisions affecting people are made through regulation, regulatory processes and requirements have become key determinants of the scope and form of government authority. In some countries, there is a sense that control and decision making within centralised regulatory bureaucracies are reaching their limits, given the democratic values of these societies. Some of the reforms intended to strengthen legitimacy – public participation and consultation, information disclosure – affect regulatory processes. Others, such as devolution to lower levels of government, affect the distribution of regulatory authority. Still others, such as parliamentary oversight and reporting to ministers, are intended to establish direct links to politically-accountable officials. "There is widespread concern, well merited in our view, that Parliament has lost control of the regulatory process," a parliamentary committee in Canada warned in early 1993 (House of Commons, 1993, p. 7).

Issues of legitimacy are likely to intensify through the 1990s, because of the increasing use of international bodies and agreements to regulate issues formerly left to national governments. Regulatory co-operation is no longer a policy choice for governments. There is relentless pressure for mutual action as economic, environmental, and social issues become increasingly intertwined. This "regulatory diversification" amounts to a complex web of vertical and horizontal linkages extending from the lowest to the highest level of government (see Figure 3).

Figure 3. A multi-layered Regulatory system

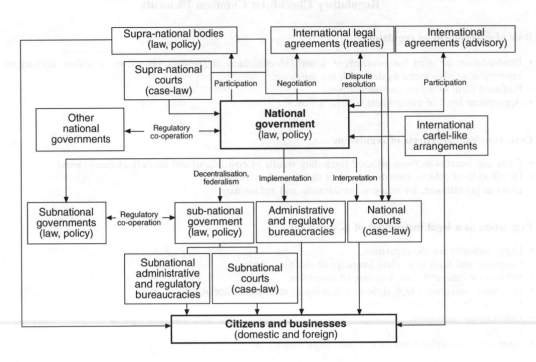

Source: OECD.

Lessons learned

Progress has proved to be more difficult and slower than anticipated. In light of the array of political, economic, social, and institutional interests opposing change, the regulatory reform programmes have often seemed quixotic in their quests to change long-standing trends and regulatory cultures. At the same time, regulatory management and reform have not been made any easier by regulatory interdependence. Governments no longer act in isolation: internationalisation and decentralisation have had profound impacts on how they use their regulatory powers.

Nevertheless, the past decade of regulatory reform does suggest grounds for optimism. Management and reform strategies have yielded important successes. The elimination or revision of regulations that were outdated, unworkable, duplicative or anti-competitive have produced immediate economic and political gains. A few countries have succeeded in slowing the rate of growth of new regulations. Improving regulatory processes has been slower, but may yield more long-term benefits.

Even more significantly, reform strategies are becoming increasingly effective as understanding develops about the nature and dynamic of the regulatory state, as reform strategies are better designed, and as regulatory management becomes more established as a central management function. The trend toward addressing "system" issues rather than individual rules illustrates the increasingly sophisticated and ambitious nature of these regulatory reform programmes.

Chapter 11

STRENGTHENING STEERING FUNCTIONS AT THE CENTRE

SUMMARY

The fast-changing policy environment requires the development of a strategic capacity at the centre of government and puts a premium on coherence of government action. Meanwhile, the public sector management reforms require a different relationship between the centre and operating departments and agencies, one based more on consultation and co-operation than on command and control. Managerial devolution and flexibility present an opportunity for central bodies to focus more on cross-cutting issues, major questions, and long-term perspectives. The challenge is to adjust co-ordination and monitoring mechanisms to satisfy the centre's legitimate requirements for policy information without undermining departments' and agencies' operational freedom. Central bodies also have a key role in embedding management reforms. In this respect, they must often combine the roles of consultant and controller.

Reforms aimed at devolution and increased flexibility have transferred varying degrees of operational control from central management bodies, and from central units in line departments and agencies, to line managers. At the same time, they have sought to maintain effective central control at a more strategic level through changes in incentive and accountability frameworks. While providing line departments with greater operational freedom, the reforms have presented the centre with opportunities to focus more on strategic policy issues.

Devolution is not abdication by the centre. There is a continued need for central control and co-ordination. To the extent that devolved activities play a policy role, and as long as they engage public funds, the government remains responsible for them. The need to ensure value for money encourages the elimination of duplication and the early detection and resolution of policy conflicts.

Ensuring coherence of government action

The need to strengthen the coherence of government action has never been greater – or more challenging. The range and complexity of issues facing governments increasingly require a clear and consistent response across the government. The centre of government plays a key role in providing the leadership required to achieve that objective. It must provide policy direction and actively seek to anticipate and defuse conflicts.

The very nature of devolution and other management reforms makes co-ordination more hazardous. For example, the greater focus on individual targets for more autonomous units risks undermining the collective interest. Co-ordination mechanisms need to be adapted to harmonize action in a more decentralised environment.

It is recognised that there are intrinsic limits to coherence. Political factors, such as party platforms, coalition arrangements, and electoral imperatives, bring into play an array of forces that rarely converge toward coherent sets of policies. Complete coherence in all fields is an elusive goal. Moreover, it may not be the only standard of good decision-making. Given unavoidable policy conflicts, good decision-making is not as simple as avoiding contradiction. A test of the quality of a decision-making system is whether inconsistent decisions are made wittingly or unwittingly; that is, whether a conflicting decision results from a well-informed political choice, or from a failure of the advisory system to inform decision-makers of possible inconsistencies. Information, supported by analysis, is essential for ensuring coherence.

Countries are reviewing the structures, processes, and methods of work they employ to maximise coherence. A basic objective is to ensure the provision of important information from a wide range of sources; well-analysed, clearly defined issues; and realistic options for decision. For some, the contestability of policy advice is a key objective. A common practice in many countries is to insist that the centre constitute a single point of passage for all proposals submitted to the council of ministers, and that certain procedures be followed: for example, listing other ministries consulted and reporting their views.

There has been much interest in clarifying and strengthening links between the policy-making and budgetary processes. As well as being an instrument of economic and financial management, the budget is an expression of the government's policy priorities. There is an increased risk, in times of large budget deficits, that the budgetary process will dominate the policy agenda. This reduces the government's range of options. Countries are continuously searching for better linkages to reconcile policy and budgetary goals, and to ensure that they are mutually reinforcing. One promising development concerns the changing role of budget ministries. They are moving away from their traditional role as naysayers, and are developing expertise in identifying cost-cutting and efficiency measures. They are thus in a better position to advise ministries on how to cut administrative costs without reducing programmes.

An important aspect of the centre's role is to ensure the implementation of policy decisions. This is a difficult task, because, once a decision has been taken at the centre, individual ministers are generally responsible for implementation. Devolution reinforces this tendency. In the new devolved environment, the centre must increasingly rely on good communication networks throughout the government in order to follow up on implementation. The principal factors of improved policy implementation are *i)* the careful, co-ordinated preparation of decisions, and *ii)* their clear documentation, for example, in written records of decision that identify implementation time-frames, resource implications, and ministerial responsibilities (especially when a decision has ramifications in several policy sectors).

Developing a strategic perspective

Freed of many of the detailed tasks involved in input control, the centre can devote more resources to strategic policy issues and evaluation. Reforms can also help strengthen the centre's capacity to provide a long-term perspective and satisfy the need for government to be pro-active as well as reactive. Strategic policy development does not imply "state planning". It reflects a recognition that solving the problems confronting government requires coherent policies within a strategic framework. Although the responsibility for sectoral strategies rests primarily with line departments, the need has increased for a strategic overview at the centre.

Adapting to a devolved environment

Critical to the success of the devolution and flexibility reforms is the way in which central management bodies – and line ministries and agencies – adapt to their changing roles. The same is true for relationships between central offices in line departments and their programme delivery areas, whether at headquarters or local offices. Devolution requires a shift by central management bodies toward setting the overall framework rather than micromanaging. Line departments and agencies must assume responsibility for difficult decisions without the cover of central diktats. They must also agree to provide information that the centre needs to fulfil its monitoring role.

The relationship between centre and line changes from one founded on command and control to one based on consultation and co-operation. This calls for more informal procedures and communications between them, as well as changes in attitudes and behaviour on both sides. For many, the change is not easy. It is almost inevitable that some individual officers remain wedded to a traditional outlook, reluctant, for example, to relinquish their perceived authority over programme managers through the budget system. Australia's evaluation of its reforms found evidence of this, but also reported a common view among heads of departments and agencies that, overall, the Department of Finance had successfully changed its culture. (The evaluation also found that current consultative arrangements were not sufficiently effective.)

An early test for central bodies comes in devising and operating monitoring arrangements appropriate to the new environment. Devolution does not absolve the centre from knowing how policies for which it is responsible, *e.g.* equal employment opportunity, are working in practice, but it will typically deprive it of information it is used to having. A number of countries have remarked that the shift away from centralised control has resulted in a decline in the quantity and quality of information received by central bodies. This has hampered their ability to monitor effectively. Monitoring systems are needed that satisfy the centre's legitimate requirements for policy information without transgressing the new operational autonomy of line units.

The actual production of information for central management bodies may not be the problem, since the centre should not, for the most part, require information that the line management would not itself wish to have. In other words, there may be no new burden of information collection. Even the centre's need for more strategic, long-term information should coincide to a large extent with needs of line departments and agencies, which are also concerned with these issues. The sharing of the information is more likely to be the cause of tensions if line departments and agencies feel that their autonomy is threatened. Much depends, therefore, on the way in which the information is to be used, and the degree of mutual trust built up. The centre can develop incentives for information provision by making available both the information it has collected and information it generates itself.

The centre also plays a key role in embedding the management reforms in departments. It provides an overall view of reform objectives, and of how individual reform initiatives fit together in an integrated package. It has a responsibility to identify future needs, and to help find ways to adapt to those needs. A major part of its role is providing consultancy-type support to line departments and agencies. This has proved especially important for smaller organisations having limited skills in some of the newly devolved areas. The centre can provide an overall sense of direction on the reforms, through guidelines or less formal advice. It is in a position to foster the exchange of information on experiences and promising practices. The centre can also use its particular responsibilities for the development of senior-level managers to encourage a more collegial attitude toward interministerial co-operation. The centre's dual role of consultant and controller involves an inevitable tension of purpose; in a continuing process of devolution, this question of balance is important.

Chapter 12

IMPLEMENTING REFORM

SUMMARY

Current reforms aim to bring about lasting change, transforming behaviour and values. This kind of reform takes time. Implementing reforms is more than changing structures and rules. Implementation issues need to be addressed right at the reform design stage. The capacity to manage reform is also critical. Incremental change may be inadequate, while the complete redesign of governance may be too ambitious. A reform strategy of selective radicalism could be optimal, i.e. the pursuit of a number of key reforms that are radical enough to make a real difference and generate political interest, yet remain realistic and manageable. The pace and sequencing of reforms may vary within this overall strategy. The early identification of potential sources of support and resistance is also crucial. Building external constituencies for reform can help sustain top-level support for reform and overcome inevitable resistance to change. Sources of support include the media, labour, business, and citizen groups. Resistance can be diluted through a variety of approaches, including ongoing dialogue, the demonstration of early benefits, and a commitment to staff training and development. The responsibility for implementing reform rests primarily with operating departments and agencies, with appropriate direction and support from the centre.

The capacity to manage the reform process may be the most important factor in the search for new forms of governance. It is difficult to generalise from Member countries' experiences of managing change. The complexity of change, the diversity of organisations, and differences in national circumstances and traditions mean that there is no generic model of change management. Nevertheless, some general principles suggest themselves.

Implementing reforms does not just involve changing structures, rules, and procedures. This is really only a beginning. Countries hope to achieve lasting change, transforming attitudes, not just incentives. This implies a need to examine how changes influence people and their relationships with each other and their work. It underlines the importance of appropriate training and support.

Implementation issues should also be addressed as part of reform design, considered explicitly from the outset. Change strategies have to be developed that identify ways to build support, generate a cumulative effect and deal with resistance to change. The change strategies themselves must be dynamic and flexible, adapting as the tasks of reform change. An overriding concern is that the reforms may themselves create new rigidities. Experience shows the value of diversity and flexibility to adapt to emerging challenges. A centrally imposed, monolithic structure is inconsistent with these objectives.

> The change process is one where there are few model solutions. Change involves uncertainty and calls for ongoing experimentation. It is best founded on harnessing the energies and insights of staff in a situation where staff are informed about, and identify with, the broad direction of the organisation and have access to information about good examples as a basis for local comparison and inspiration.
>
> (Australian Management Advisory Board, 1992, p. 520)

Strategies of reform

How comprehensive can or should the overall reform effort be? Alternatives are a comprehensive package of reforms, across a broad front (the "Big Bang" approach), or a more targeted, gradual approach. The grand design approach has the advantage of communicating a vision of a desired end-point, presenting the reforms as an integrated package and ensuring a consistent message. Staff and other stakeholders need to see how various reforms fit together. Commitment to the reforms will be less than wholehearted without this understanding. A consistent message is needed to avoid confusion and possible failure caused by different parts of the system sending different signals (*e.g.* as regards risk management). The actions of external review bodies such as auditors can be particularly influential in this regard.

The grand design approach also offers opportunities for trade-offs among different interests, and is helpful in generating and maintaining political and top-level interest. On the other hand, it may overwhelm management and staff in both the centre and line departments, and raise expectations unrealistically. It may involve significant costs, not least in terms of management time. It must be borne in mind that, for most organisations, management reforms will coincide with major policy and programme reforms, adding substantially to the complexity and burden of change.

A more gradual approach provides greater flexibility to adapt along the way and a longer time-scale within which to build management capacities. It also spreads costs, and many successful reforms have been introduced over a longer period of time, building on and supporting each other. A disadvantage of this approach is that it may dissipate interest and energy. Special effort must be made to maintain the coherence of reforms. Unless introduced within an overall framework, piecemeal reforms risk having only limited or conflicting impacts. Where responsibilities for different aspects of reform are spread among different central management bodies, effective co-ordination and communication mechanisms are vital.

Selective radicalism may be the optimum strategy. Incrementalism is not enough, because "more of the same, but a little better" cannot provide an adequate response to the fundamental changes and pressures in the environment. The complete redesign of governance is too enormous and overwhelming a task. Selective radicalism, in the sense of a limited number of reforms that are radical enough to make a real difference, can combine the benefits of the "Big Bang" and more gradual approaches, while reducing associated risks.

Within this framework and for particular types of reform, there are choices to be made about implementation. One option is piecemeal, voluntary change. In this case, there are no *ex ante* selection criteria, and organisations or units are chosen on the basis of their readiness and capacity to make the particular change in question. Pilot projects are a variation on this theme. This option allows reformers to draw conclusions from early experiments before extending the reforms. Pilot experiments have strong demonstrative effect, generating demand from other units as well as providing lessons from experience.

Another favoured option is allowing units to pursue reform objectives at their own pace, while making the intention to reform clear at the outset. This central approach has tended to predominate in many countries. It permits a pacing of reform more in tune with the requirements and capacities of individual units. Finally, reforms can be compulsory or at least promoted vigorously and pushed through as quickly as possible. This allows a critical threshold in reform to be crossed earlier, and alleviates problems such as managerial imbalances (*e.g.* central units retaining interventionist modes of conduct unsuited to the new requirements). It also makes it easier to transform the culture of the entire administration. It is the approach most likely to be adopted where legislative changes or lengthy union negotiations are required, *e.g.* in altering terms and conditions of employment of public servants (France, Germany).

It is difficult to draw firm conclusions from country experiences as regards the sequence of reforms. It is not clear, for example, whether the development of management systems is a prerequisite for giving line departments and agencies more autonomy, or whether financial management reforms need to be firmly in place before responsibility for human resources management can be devolved to line management. These and other questions – such as whether priority should be given to improving services or accountability to users and taxpayers, or whether a change in the legal status of staff and units is necessary – illustrate that these are not absolute choices but matters of political emphasis and, sometimes, common sense. There is no simple answer.

Responsibility for reform

How are countries organised to carry out reforms? Primary responsibility for overall reform rests in two key central locations: "centre of government" offices, such as the Prime Ministry, Federal Chancellery, Ministry of the Presidency; and "central management" bodies, such as the Ministries of Finance, Public Administration, and the Interior. In some countries, new institutions have been set up to initiate, co-ordinate, and monitor reform (*e.g.* the Secretariat for Administrative Modernisation in Portugal, the Management Advisory Board and Management Improvement Advisory Committee in Australia). In others, new functions have been allocated to existing institutions. Several countries share responsibilities among a number of institutions. Others have reinforced change mechanisms by replicating them in line departments and agencies, with some central presence to facilitate the process.

Each option has its own merits and disadvantages. For example, entirely new institutional arrangements highlight the reform agenda and provide initial impetus. On the other hand, they carry risks: reforms may be marginalised or undermined by conflicts with powerful control units in existing central management bodies. Shared responsibilities, for their part, may facilitate specialisation and assimilation but require a special effort to ensure that reforms are presented as a comprehensive, integral package.

The role of the centre is only a part of the picture. Other organisations can also play a vital role. Line departments and agencies have not passively waited to be prodded into action by central bodies or elected government leaders. Many have been a source of innovation and individual initiative within the limits of central rules and procedures. They also generate pressure for centre-driven reforms, and contribute to reform design. In many instances, reforms succeed precisely because line departments and agencies respond to demands articulated by managers. And, while overall reform initiatives may be guided or driven by central bodies, primary responsibility for implementation lies at the local level.

Reform is not a matter of the centre deciding policy, formulating implementation procedures, providing resources, and then leaving execution to spending ministries or lower level management. Without a shared, participative approach, the ability of central authorities to influence the behaviour of local implementers is limited, particularly when the goal is long-term, deep-rooted change, and when reform is a process rather than an end-point. In this sense, implementation is an integral part of the policy process, not a separate phase. It can be seen as a series of interactions among several actors with their own interests, objectives and strategies. The response of target groups and of officials implementing policy can rarely be guided effectively through formal structures and powers alone. Officials executing a policy enjoy a certain amount of discretion. They are continually engaged in interaction, negotiating, forming and reforming coalitions, and making use of various tactics to influence decisions.

The capacity of individual organisations to implement reforms is clearly critical to success. Country experiences have highlighted three particular aspects of this. First, smaller departments and agencies require a greater level of continuing support than larger units. For example, they typically do not have the same level of initial expertise or appropriate management systems for all functions being devolved; they are also vulnerable to turnover of key staff. In addition, they need on-going support to access and absorb information on best management practice, emerging technology, developments elsewhere, and so on. Second, as they adapt to new roles, central management bodies need to develop skills in several areas, including analytical and consultancy skills. Third, training and development efforts need to be adapted to the new environment and intensified to develop management and leadership skills and more generally enforce the reform message. This is a critical contribution to building the commitment of staff to the reforms, which is essential to their success.

Country experience suggests two other factors that are critical to successful implementation: *i)* gaining and keeping support and *ii)* dealing with resistance. They are closely related.

Implementing administrative reform in Belgium

Administrative reform has been receiving special attention in Belgium since 1986. By bringing together the relevant actors, tools, structures, demands, and values, the reform process aims to break vicious circles and turn them into "virtuous spirals". The main goal, namely the transformation of habits and attitudes, is achieved through "soft" measures (training, consultation, the encouragement of new ideas, informal or non-compulsory programmes) as well as more binding ones (regulations, government decisions). The "soft" measures encourage compliance with the more binding measures, which, in turn, tend to give rise to even more "soft" ones.

The reforms are taking place in a context of closer communication between ministries and their departments. Their shared concern is better management, with the guiding theme of improving relations with the public and achieving legitimacy in the public eye.

Paths for communication are provided by the College of Secretaries-General, meetings among civil service heads, the network of modernisation units, the information officers' group, and other management expert groups (such as the one for vetting official forms).

The directorate for training, the consultancies (on management and organisation, computerisation, readability), and the federal information service act as support bodies.

Among the instruments for aiding improved management are master plans for training, performance rating models, factsheets, job analysis, catalogues of public relations practices, strategic planning aids, and staff journals.

Examples of the more binding reforms, designed to enforce changes in behaviour and attitude, are the Users' Charter, programme-specific budgets, new statutory principles for the civil service, career reform, and staff performance appraisal reform.

The College of Secretaries-General, founded in 1989, is made up of the most senior officials in each Ministry. It advises the Cabinet on public administration matters and oversees the broad implementation of major interministerial reforms.

Building support for reform

Public management reform is a long haul, not a quick fix. It requires sustained, visible political support. Keeping reform high on the political agenda is a major challenge. Political enthusiasm for management reform is common enough among newly elected governments, but it has often been short-lived: political attention shifts to other subjects. To compound the problem, there is usually a mismatch between the time-scale of reform and the political cycle. Implementation, especially where devolution is concerned, is a gradual process. It usually takes longer than the average term of political office. Maintaining support for reforms through a change of government presents particular challenges. Yet a sequence of unfinished or abandoned reforms may lead to cynicism, making subsequent reform efforts even more difficult.

Building constituencies outside the public service that favour public sector reform can be crucial in generating political interest as well as overcoming barriers to change. Pressure from the media, labour, business and citizen groups has influenced reforms in many countries. This has been achieved without any one interest dominating and becoming itself a barrier to change. Briefings, symposia, ongoing dialogue, and the diffusion of information on experiences elsewhere are ways of building interest in reform. Reformers also stress the need to be opportunistic in the sense of spotting windows of opportunity and making the most of them. Particular circumstances in specific countries may combine in a way favourable to reform and should be utilised.

> ...a private sector firm's transition from traditional management practices to total quality management may take as long as 6 years, a government agency's as long as 10.
>
> (Comptroller General of the United States Bowsher, 1993, p. 9)

With internationalisation, the importance of a well-performing and cost-effective public sector becomes even more apparent. The current environment, with such pressures as discussed in Chapter 2, is giving new impetus to reform. Public management reform has moved up the political agenda in most countries, creating a kind of peer pressure for others. For example, if one country seeks national competitive advantage through structural adjustment and improved performance in its public sector, other countries cannot afford not to do likewise. And high-profile reform in some countries (*e.g.* "Public Service 2000" in Canada; "The Public Sector in the Year 2000" in Denmark; Programme for the renewal of the public service in France; "Renewing the Administration – Challenge and Commitment" in Portugal; Citizen's Charters in the UK; the National Performance Review in the US; radical change in New Zealand) can generate renewed political interest elsewhere. Similarly, increased international co-operation in so many fields requires equivalent governance capacities and approaches. The economic situation in most countries has also put a premium on expenditure control and doing more with less (although it may make some reform options, such as layoffs, politically unpalatable in the short term).

As with all projects of change, demonstrating early benefits is also important. It may not be possible to deliver all benefits immediately, but there will be some that can be realised earlier than others. Clear responsibilities need to be agreed for achieving intermediate reform targets by specified dates. The discipline of strong project management also needs to be applied to reform management.

The review and evaluation of reforms are essential to generating and maintaining broad-based support. This remains a relatively weak part of country reform processes. If anything, countries have concentrated on assessing different aspects of the reforms rather than the impact of reforms overall. So far, few have so far conducted formal, independent evaluations of how public management reforms across the board have contributed to improved performance. Notable exceptions include Australia and New Zealand (Australian Management Advisory Board, 1992; New Zealand State Services Commission, 1991). Both the centre and line departments and agencies need to develop capacity for monitoring and evaluation. New tools of analysis must also be developed. International comparison and exchange are potentially powerful methods of analysis.

Overcoming resistance

Strategies for reform must take into account the existence of resistance to change. It is necessary to come to terms with it rather than try to ignore it or deny its legitimacy. Reform needs to go hand in hand with an understanding of the organisational dynamics of the change process. Many reform initiatives have met with difficulty because the sources of resistance were not properly understood. Resistance is inevitable unless the changes harmonize with the organisation's culture, informal rules and routines, concepts, and conventions. Public management reforms are aimed precisely at changing beliefs and attitudes so as to permanently change behaviour. Change, in any event, involves power shifts, and there are always winners and losers. Resistance is therefore to be expected.

Resistance manifests itself in a variety of ways, both overt and subtle. These include industrial action by staff; the withholding of necessary agreements by parliament; sabotage by managers (*e.g.* through misinformation, or the perverse use of management incentives); vociferous lobbying by affected interest groups; deliberate delay; and feigned acquiescence. It is possible to identify several different sources of resistance, at different levels in an organisation and in its external environment: the conscientious objectors, *i.e.* those who disagree with the reform concepts and direction, perhaps because they see them as invalid or unworkable; those with vested interests in the status quo, *e.g.* lobby groups, parliament, civil servants, trade unions, professional groups; the cynics, who see the reforms as no more than a passing fad, something which can be sat out; the "old dogs" who cannot or are unwilling to learn new tricks; those who feel threatened because of uncertainty over the content of reform and its implications (*e.g.* job security) or are confused by different signals (*e.g.* about risk-taking); those who are wearied by what they see as never-ending change. An environment of pay restraint and cut-backs in numbers may also increase internal resistance to reforms.

In order to overcome resistance, reformers must first identify, both in advance and throughout the reform process, those who are likely to view reform negatively, and then take appropriate action to prevent or overcome any resistance that may result. Many of the actions aimed at generating and maintaining political support also, by definition, help overcome resistance (*e.g.* creating lobby groups for reform; improved communications; demonstrating benefits, telling about success, acknowledging disappointments; the involvement of the media). Similarly, the elements of good reform strategy discussed earlier can avoid or diffuse resistance. For example, open dialogue may eliminate resistance based on uncertainty or misunderstanding; an early commitment to training and development will reduce resistance based on fear of lacking proper skills or being poorly prepared for the new environment; widespread top management support can help convince people that the reforms are not just a passing fad; highlighting the attractions of the new working environment, such as more opportunity for innovation and personal advancement, helps present the reforms in a more positive light.

More entrenched resistance may require additional approaches. The assumption here is that communication, consultation, and negotiation are not enough to persuade those who deny the need for and merits of reforms. Of course, much depends on the particular country, including its traditions, and relative political strengths, as well as opportunity and judgement. As with implementing reforms generally, using a combination of approaches seems preferable to relying on just one particular approach. The basic idea is to build support for reforms while outflanking sources of resistance. This might include replacing senior staff unsympathetic to reform, buying out other sources of resistance (*e.g.* early retirement programmes), enacting legislation, strengthening reporting, and changing incentives and choices for lobby groups.

Chapter 13

GOVERNANCE IN TRANSITION: WHAT NEXT IN REFORM?

SUMMARY

Pressures for reform will continue, if not intensify. Current reforms need to be pursued vigorously in most fields. For example, the pace of devolution is uneven as yet; performance management frameworks need to be enhanced and performance measures refined; a culture of quality and responsiveness to clients needs to be embedded at all levels; the co-ordination and steering functions of the centre need to be developed further; the potential of market-type mechanisms is still largely untapped. Monitoring and evaluation of reforms is essential to ensure that key assumptions on which they are based are valid in practice, that the inherent tension and trade-offs among different reform objectives work out as planned, and that the reforms adapt to changing needs. The assessment of reforms must not be postponed because measurement techniques are not yet wholly satisfactory. For the future, the role of the state will evolve further, with, among other things, greater reliance on other partners for service delivery and the development of the government's strategic and policy-making capacities.

No one expects the driving forces behind current reforms to diminish in the future. If anything, the pressures for reform will intensify. The scope of the world-wide changes in progress is not yet known. Major new challenges are inevitable. The stakes continue to be high: continued reform is required precisely because of its essential contribution to economic development, the quality of democracy, and social cohesion.

Doing more with less will continue to be a feature of the public management environment. Expenditure pressures show no signs of abating. Health costs, to give just one example, are likely to rise given ageing populations, technological advances, and citizen demands. Unemployment levels are expected to remain high in many countries. What is more, there is a constant demand for new and improved services across a range of sectors. Financing these by increased taxation or borrowing is no longer an acceptable or sustainable option. The limits of taxation and borrowing are already judged to have been reached in several countries. Innovative solutions are needed to provide public services within tight resource constraints.

The stakes in all of this are very high because it is public sector efficiency that will make the crucial difference to national prosperity in the modern world economy... Those countries that see the writing on the wall and act now to reform the state apparatuses will have the lead. Thus, our understanding of the forces at work and of the changes that are necessary in the public service is a fundamental element in the future prosperity of our country.

(Canada – Massé, 1993, pp. 61-62)

If we are to keep the capacity to govern, it is essential that we be able to adapt, radically if necessary, and to continue to adapt. Three overall needs stand out. First, reforms must be pursued with vigour, and refined and refashioned as circumstances change. The public sector must therefore be composed of adaptable organisations that are open to learning. Second, reforms must be monitored and evaluated to ensure that the desired results actually materialise. Finally, the reform process has also given rise to renewed discussion about the appropriate role of government, stressing its role as enabler as well as provider. The evolving role of the state must be guided and managed.

Reforms need to be pursued with vigour

Many countries have made considerable progress in reforming their public sectors. Efforts have been made to improve the quality of service and responsiveness to clients. New tasks have been undertaken with little additional resources. Managers have been given greater flexibility in using resources to achieve objectives. Many wasteful practices have been eliminated. Steps have been taken to strengthen expenditure control. Commercial functions have been privatised or corporatised in many cases. Several countries have introduced competitive elements in hitherto sheltered parts of the public sector. Perhaps the most important progress is in bringing about a wider acceptance of the need for change and for awareness of the impact of government actions on its clients.

Even those countries that have been pursuing reform longest acknowledge that there is still much to be done. The evaluations mentioned above in Australia and New Zealand, for example, support the general direction of the reforms but identify factors critical to success and areas needing further work (Management Advisory Board, 1992; State Services Commission, 1991). The Australian report, noting that "a return to the previous arrangements, even if possible, would not be desirable. The new framework has strong support and is seen, overall, to have increased the cost-effectiveness of the APS (Australian Public Service) including outcomes for clients", goes on to point out that the reforms need to be firmly embedded, extended across the public service, and incorporated into its culture. In any case, the business of reform can never be finished; it is an ongoing process.

Several specific areas requiring further action have been identified by countries. The process of devolution of authority from central management bodies to line departments and agencies is not yet complete. The pace of devolution is uneven. Some countries are moving cautiously, fearful that relaxing central control of expenditure will undermine fiscal consolidation efforts. But the process has also been slowed by some line managers' reluctance to use their new freedom and by the entrenched behaviour of some managers in central management bodies. Devolution entails strengthening capacities at local level, with smaller departments and agencies having particular needs in the initial transition period. The pace of devolution within organisations is even more uneven, but the full benefits of greater flexibility will not be realised unless the empowerment of managers filters downwards and outwards.

Successful devolution requires a strengthening of the overall framework of performance management. This entails clarifying objectives, establishing performance targets and measuring actual performance against specified levels. These three processes are lynchpins of reform. Managers with devolved powers must know what they have to achieve and what they are answerable for. They must have control over resources, including information, to ensure that they are meeting performance requirements. Those with oversight responsibilities (higher levels or external bodies) must have information for strategic control. Countries acknowledge teething problems in developing and refining performance measures and indicators that focus on what is important rather than on what is easily measured. More work is required on refining performance measurement techniques, both in the development and analysis of performance indicators and in in-depth programme evaluation, recognising at the same time the limitations of any such performance measurement. Internal management information systems and external reporting mechanisms are currently criticised for imposing cumbersome and costly reporting burdens and eroding local autonomy.

Devolution requires greater clarification of objectives for different levels of management. But objectives can rarely be specified so unambiguously and flexibly that there is never a need for interpretation or adaptation to changing requirements. If they could be so clear and controllable, there would be a strong case for contracting out. An element of obfuscation and conflict among objectives in a political environment is inevitable, and perhaps even desirable. Nevertheless, the success of public management reform depends on converting broad government objectives into operational targets. Countries are still refining this process. Much also remains to be done to develop appropriate incentive systems and to ensure that the goals of the organisation and those of individuals are complementary. Human resource management policies and practices need to be further developed to ensure that they are consistent with the new environment and adequate for its requirements.

As regards quality of service and responsiveness to citizens, more work is needed to reinforce cultural change so that concern with quality becomes second nature at all organisational levels; develop service standards, grievance and redress mechanisms; and make techniques such as total quality management part of ongoing management.

Much remains to be done, too, to establish effective consultation with clients about their needs and their views of the service they receive. As one approach, organisations in many countries have been developing sample surveys. One-stop-shops, the co-location of offices and the use of information technology to provide improved services are far from fully developed, despite the rhetoric to the contrary. Efforts to estimate and reduce the totality of costs of administrative and regulatory demands on enterprises is only beginning in many countries. Work on the alternatives to regulation and mechanisms to improve regulatory management is still at the embryonic stage.

There is unfinished business, too, as regards improving the steering functions of the centre. Co-ordination mechanisms need to be further developed to take adequate account of local autonomy and of the increasing need to manage policies through relationships with other levels of government and complex partnership arrangements. Some central management bodies have still to adapt fully to their new "hands-off" relationship with line ministries, *i.e.* advising on broad principles rather than stipulating detailed procedures, and monitoring policies for which they retain overall responsibility in a non-intrusive fashion. They need to develop their capacity to provide support, particularly to smaller departments and agencies, and disseminate information on promising practice. Countries are also still developing planning mechanisms that take full advantage of new opportunities for the centre to take a strategic perspective when it is less involved in detailed control.

Many of the efforts to develop competitive environments within the public sector are recent. Analysis to date shows that, under certain conditions, market-type mechanisms have significant potential to improve cost-effectiveness and quality of service. They are nevertheless relatively untried in many countries and policy areas. There appears to be much scope for their introduction on a wider scale, subject to adaptation and refinement as required.

Evaluation of the reforms is crucial

Many of the reforms are still in their infancy and are just beginning to take effect. Much of the reform is pioneering, and there are no universal models. Reforms that work well in one country or in one set of circumstances may backfire in another. The dynamics of reform necessarily involve a considerable amount of learning-by-doing. The reform process also entails making choices and striking delicate balances among competing objectives and values. Implementation shapes the final outcomes. Close monitoring is required in order to control emerging balances and make trade-offs explicit.

But it is not enough to focus merely on particular groups of reforms (*e.g.* the management of human resources, financial resources or regulation). The reforms are interlinked in complex ways and must be coherent to be fully effective. The chances of success are reduced if signals are mixed and incentives inconsistent. Just as importantly, the full effects of the reforms are difficult to assess and their longer-term impact is necessarily unknown. Many of the changes are radical and are based on certain key assumptions. Proponents and opponents alike recognise trade-offs and tensions among the reforms, and acknowledge risks. The jury is out, so to speak, on many important issues.

Measuring the impact of reforms poses difficult problems of methodology. The reforms are aimed at improving the performance of the public sector and its contribution to overall economic performance. How can that be proved conclusively for reforms overall or for individual reforms? It is difficult to establish clear cause-and-effect relationships between reforms and overall economic performance. It is also difficult to measure aggregate public sector performance. The Australian evaluation, for example, took the view that "There is no definitive way to measure the APS-wide savings from these reforms, those comprising the [Financial Management Improvement Program] or even some of the major elements. To have produced even indicative figures... would have entailed more resources well beyond those reasonable to apply to such an effort and to little purpose" (Management Advisory Board, 1992). Much work remains to be done to improve evaluation methods, including the development of quantitative and objective measures and indicators, if hard evidence is to be provided of improvements in performance. Initially, a focus on individual organisations may be the most fruitful approach to evaluation, but overall government-wide performance must also be considered. The construction of internationally comparative performance indicators also holds potential.

Change in government employment is sometimes proposed as a partial indicator of the impact of reforms. Figures for general government employment (OECD average) show consistent growth over the last thirty years with only six countries recording a decline in recent years (see Table 2), testifying to the difficulties of achieving reductions. There are, however, several drawbacks in use of employment figures as a measure of reform success. For example, not all countries have set reducing employment as an explicit reform objective. Furthermore, a depressed economic climate poses particular problems for reducing public sector employment. Also, employment figures say nothing about changes in productivity or quality and, in many cases, additional tasks have been assumed without increases in staff. Likewise, the transfer of functions and staff among levels of government and types of organisation may not be adequately reflected in the figures selected.

The reforms are also based on certain assumptions. It goes almost without saying that the conditions that are assumed need to be verified in practice. For example, reforms aimed at an institutional separation of policy-making and policy execution are based on the premise that satisfactory arrangements can be put in place for the necessary feedback from operations to policy-making. A key assumption of devolution generally and of a more formal, contract-based relationship is that overall government objectives can be translated successfully into operational targets and standards. Countries need to attack quickly any inadequacies in these areas if the basis for the overall system is not to be undermined.

Other issues and inherent tensions also require close monitoring and evaluation. Devolution has raised concerns about possible loss of necessary central control. As long as overall controls are strengthened at the same time, there is little evidence to support this concern. Many, on the other hand, see a danger that organisations or units will become "individual fiefdoms" that are overly concerned with pursuing narrow objectives to the detriment of overall national or service-wide objectives. Early experience in New Zealand, for example, revealed a need to strengthen collective interest clauses in chief executives' contracts. There are related concerns about undermining the unity of the public service and what this means for co-operation and co-ordination, mobility, common values, or commitment to overall government policies (equal employment opportunities in human resource management, for example).

Table 2. **Government Service Employment:* Average Annual Growth Rates**

(per cent)

	1963-1973	1974-1978	1979-1983	1984-1989	1990-1992
Australia	3.6	8.3	1.7	1.9	0.6
Austria	2.5	3.4	2.2	2.6	0.2
Belgium	2.2	3.8	1.7	0.7	–
Canada	5.1	3.6	2.0	1.9	2.0
Denmark	6.8	4.4	3.8	0.6	0.2
Finland	4.7	5.0	3.6	2.1	–0.5
France	2.3	1.9	1.7	1.0	0.5
Germany	3.4	2.2	1.5	0.9	1.0
Greece	2.5	3.3	2.3	2.7	0.4
Iceland	6.5	5.2	5.1	2.3	0.2
Ireland	2.9	4.4	2.7	–0.4	0.7
Italy	2.9	2.8	1.4	1.4	0.2
Japan	1.7	1.8	1.0	0.1	0.6
Luxembourg	3.2	2.4	2.5	–	–
Netherlands	2.2	2.4	1.2	0.1	–0.8
New Zealand	2.8	3.7	–0.2	–0.8	–5.0
Norway	4.1	5.1	4.6	2.8	2.8
Portugal	6.6	5.1	6.9	3.5	2.1
Spain	3.0	5.5	3.0	2.4	4.1
Sweden	6.0	5.0	2.6	0.8	–0.1
Switzerland	3.9	2.7	1.8	0.9	–0.1
Turkey	2.7	4.9	1.5	0.9	2.1
United Kingdom	2.6	1.5	0.0	–0.1	–1.0
United States	4.1	2.7	0.3	1.9	1.4
EC**	3.7	2.4	1.4	0.9	0.5
Nordic Countries	5.6	4.9	3.4	1.3	0.5
OECD Europe**	3.7	2.7	1.6	1.0	0.5
OECD**	3.4	2.8	1.1	1.3	0.9

* National and sub-national levels, *i.e.* the general government sector.
** Excluding Belgium and Luxembourg.
Source: Assessing Structural Reform: Lessons for the Future, OECD, Paris, 1994.

Accountability is another important concern. The architects of reform see accountability protected and strengthened under their reforms. To begin with, true accountability requires autonomy and flexibility. The nature of accountability changes: extensive rules are replaced by guidelines; policy and operational objectives are clarified; reporting is greatly enhanced, including to parliament and the public; *ex ante* control is replaced by *ex post* review. Accountability is also strengthened through contracts with service providers and improved responsiveness to clients. Nevertheless, a number of potential dangers are recognised. The rules of the game need to be developed further, for example regarding the responsibilities of public servants towards parliament and external examiners, codes of conduct, and the protection of public servants as well as clients.

Countries are also anxious to instil new values such as responsiveness and cost-effectiveness without undermining the traditional values of probity, equity, and political neutrality. The new arrangements need to be monitored to ensure that there is no undue deviation from these norms. For example, several countries and organisations have drawn up new guidelines or readdressed old ones on ethical behaviour. Desired common values are also reflected in overall mission statements such as that of Australia (see box).

The effects of increased flexibility also need to be kept under review. In the area of human resource management, for example, changes in terms of employment, such as more flexible hiring and firing, or contract employment rather than tenured, are designed as an incentive to better performance. But the new system may lead to insecurity and effects on productivity no different from those pertaining under a system of tenured positions. A diminution of security of public sector employment may also result in recruitment difficulties at some levels and a need to offer individual remuneration packages more in line with the private sector. It is vital to monitor the

---

Australia: Key Public Service Values

Responsiveness to governments

- serving loyally and impartially ministers and the government;
- providing frank, honest and comprehensive advice.

A close focus on results

- pursuing efficiency and effectiveness at all levels;
- delivering services to clients conscientiously and courteously.

Merit as the basis for staffing

- ensuring equality of opportunity;
- providing fair and reasonable rewards as an incentive to high performance.

The highest standards of probity, integrity and conduct

- acting in accordance with the letter and spirit of the law;
- dealing equitably, honestly and responsively with the public;
- avoiding real or apparent conflicts of interest.

A strong commitment to accountability

- contributing fully to the accountability of the agency to the government, of the government to the parliament and of the parliament to the people;
- fully supporting the administrative and legal measures established to enhance accountability;
- recognising that those delegating responsibility for performance do not lose responsibility and may be called to account.

Continuous improvement through teams and individuals

- striving for creativity and innovation;
- making individual and team performance count.

impact of overall reforms on morale and motivation. PUMA work also points up the need to assess initiatives such as performance-related pay which have not yet worked as planned.

Other aspects which require close monitoring are the longer-term impacts of market-type mechanisms (*e.g.* do the conditions necessary for their successful use actually exist and if not, can they be developed sufficiently?), the evolution of client-administration relationships (*e.g.* how real is the risk of client capture) and indications of politicisation (the Australian evaluation found no evidence to suggest that this was a problem). More importantly, what are the wider effects, on social cohesion for example, of reforms aimed at expenditure reduction and cost-effectiveness?

The list of issues discussed above is not by any means exhaustive. The discussion in Chapters 4-11 is more comprehensive. The critical point is that monitoring and evaluation are essential if reforms are to be carried through successfully and if short-term gains are to be protected and perpetuated in the longer-term. The issues highlighted throw relief on reform as an on-going process, where the answers will come through only slowly.

The evolving role of the State

What governments do is a matter of political choice, a matter for democratic decision by the people through their elected government. The choice differs from country to country and over time. The performance of both government and the free market will have much to do with determining what mix is chosen at any one time. Two extreme cases illustrate possibilities and limitations.

At one extreme, the cost of public services is such that "the levels of taxation and borrowing necessary to finance them are killing the rest of the economy. High interest rates, inflation, loss of competitiveness, a growing black economy, increasing unemployment and a failure of confidence ultimately force a government to pull back in response to both domestic pressure from the electorate and international pressure (often focused on the rate of exchange)''. At the other extreme are low levels of taxation and public expenditure, with state intervention limited to a narrow range of core services. In this scenario, the benefits of low taxation and expenditure must be set against "such considerations as decaying infrastructure, poor quality public services which hit the disadvantaged in society more, inner city neglect, increasing pollution, greater political and social divisions and rising crime'' (Ireland – Murphy, 1993).

In both these extreme cases, the hoped for benefits are lost. In one case the high level of public services exacerbates the very problems it was aimed at resolving but the answer cannot be to spend more. In the other the benefits are not spread widely enough quickly enough, conspicuous consumption by the few contrasts with decaying public services for the many, and the overall quality of life is diminished. In some countries at least, there is recognition that the first limiting case is becoming a reality. But the other limiting case is also unacceptable and unworkable in free market democracies. In practice there are pendulum swings between these extremes. The debate about where the pendulum might rest provides the backdrop for public management reform. Such reform is aimed primarily at improving the performance of the public sector for any given level of public sector intervention, but it also inevitably raises the broader issue of the appropriate role of the public sector.

How the public sector plays its role in promoting economic and social development and structural adjustment is changing and will evolve further as its environment changes and reforms are carried through. Well-performing public sectors in the future will look and act quite differently than today. Government will be less of a producer and more of an enabler. It will be more about providing a flexible framework within which economic activity can take place. It will have a more disciplined approach to regulation, conscious of the burdens it imposes and informed about the expected impacts. It will evaluate policy effectiveness on an on-going basis. It will seek to be more strategic and nimble to meet the economic and social challenges of the future, developing its planning and leadership functions. It will adopt a more participative, partnership approach to governance, alive to the expectations of a better educated and better informed citizenry and conscious of the need to explain and persuade. In service delivery, it will increasingly be overseeing provision of services produced by others rather than delivering services it itself produces. The boundaries of the public sector are already becoming more blurred as new relationships are being forged (and forced) with other levels of government, the private for-profit and not-for-profit sectors, community groups, client groups and individuals.

The public service is likely to be leaner as a result. Down-sizing may become a reality as reforms are pursued further and pressures to reduce public expenditure bite deeper. The new structures, incentives and rules of the game are likely to lead to reduced numbers. Functions which can be carried out more cost-effectively outside the public sector are likely to continue to be privatised and contracted out. Economic realities and political imperatives may force government to withdraw from some areas (*i.e.* eliminate or substantially reduce certain categories of spending) and redefine welfare systems (*e.g.* by making welfare programmes more selective).

Governance in transition: the new agenda

The major goal of reform is to improve cost-effectiveness in the provision of goods and services decided by the government of the day and within the framework of public accountability. The strengths of both the public and private sectors must be harnessed to this end. Reform must also address other aspects of the performance of the public sector, including its wider role in the economy and in society generally. Pushing current reforms further, monitoring and evaluating progress, and managing the evolving role of the state must remain broad priorities. Reform must also assume continuing global and societal change and the need to adjust capacities to govern in consequence.

The analysis in this report points to many areas where further reform effort is needed. Although the focus will differ as between countries and organisations, the reform agenda will need to include action under the following headings:

Government as policy-maker

 – facilitating coherent and effective policies by improving the decision-making and rule-setting processes of government, especially as regards the flow of policy-relevant information and policy evaluation.

Government's performance

 – further developing strategies, structures ,and systems to let and make managers manage; removing unnecessary constraints and providing appropriate incentives;
 – providing effective ways to measure and monitor performance, strengthen accountability for performance, and engrain a focus on quality performance;
 – developing and maintaining a motivated, skilled, and flexible public sector work-force committed to a set of common public service values.

Government's strategic capacity

 – enhancing the capacity of the public sector to respond flexibly and automatically to future changes in its external environment;
 – improving government's capacity to operate strategically, to ensure adaptation to emerging opportunities and threats, to guide the overall evolution of the public sector, and to harmonize the efforts of central management bodies;
 – adopting a strategic approach to human resource management and industrial relations, and ensuring the sound discharge of the state's functions as employer.

Government as enabler

 – setting a framework for the public, private, or mixed supply of goods and services; enhancing consumer choice and quality of service; introducing competition wherever practicable; and generally promoting an efficient and effective use of resources;
 – identifying ways to improve interaction between the public and private sectors.

Government as reformer

 – strategically managing the overall reform process; monitoring and evaluating experiences in implementing reforms so that public sector organisations can learn from one another, exchange information and compare performance.

Part B

SPECIFIC REFORM INITIATIVES

Chapter 14

BUDGETING AND PERFORMANCE MANAGEMENT

Context of the reforms: doing more with less

Reforms to the budgetary process including a greater focus on performance issues have been a major element of most countries' public management reform strategies. They are founded on a desire to limit budget outlays using two interrelated strategies: *i)* enhancing aggregate controls by fixing targets for medium-term budget outcomes and monitoring performance, and *ii)* improving public sector performance in terms of economy, efficiency, effectiveness, and service quality. These strategies are aimed at generating budget savings, as well as providing resources to meet expanding demands in some areas.

The procedures followed in budgetary formulation and execution have been a natural starting point for countries considering public sector management reform. The budget is the principal mechanism through which governments give effect to their economic and social priorities. The effectiveness of expenditure policy and resource allocation decisions is affected by the practices and tools employed in budget formulation and implementation. Budgets, as instruments of economic and social policy, are of course affected by and intended to affect economic conditions. Similarly, budgeting practices are influenced by and designed to influence the decision-making environment. The nature of the rules, procedures, and incentives inherent in budgeting systems conditions the manner in which public sector activities are viewed and managed.

The principal objective of budget reforms is to encourage a greater focus on performance and results, as opposed to adherence to administrative processes and rules. In order to achieve this, governments generally are attempting to change the management culture of their organisations. This is not to say that governments and managers have not in the past been concerned with performance, but rather that there has not been a sufficient systematic focus on performance. Nor is it to say that rules designed to ensure probity and adherence to legal requirements are removed. Rather, it recognises that in most cases there is scope for changing the nature of such rules and for devolving more authority to managers.

Moves to focus on performance are, in fact, not new. For example, many governments have modified their budgetary processes during the last two decades by instituting new arrangements such as programme budgeting, planning-programming-budgeting-systems (PPBS), and zero-based budgeting. Others sought to focus on performance through the introduction of management-by-objective (MBO) processes. Overall, these efforts are regarded as having had mixed success. What is different in the current reforms is a comprehensive approach seeking to embrace all aspects of management, and a recognition that an overall cultural change is required in public sector management. It is not simply a matter of changing bureaucratic procedures. Managers' mentalities need to be changed and appropriate signals and incentives provided.

Changing management culture is a long-term process. Governments cannot expect instant results. There are sometimes unrealistic expectations, not least on the part of legislators, about how much the reforms can achieve and how quickly.

The pressure for this greater focus on performance varies among countries. In many instances, strong budget pressures are driving the reforms; in other cases, there is a perception that government programmes and public expenditure generally are ineffective or provide poor value for money. There are also demands for more services which must be provided within the limits of existing resources. Whatever the reason, public sector managers are being required to do more with less.

In addition, in several instances, there has been pressure to improve the accountability of governments and their organisations. The reforms aim to do this by extending the accountability of governments and managers to performance, rather than limiting it to compliance with processes and rules. Enhanced performance and enhanced accountability are inextricably linked in the reforms. In particular, a significant expansion in both the quality and quantity of information on government programmes and operations has contributed to both sets of objectives.

The change in culture being pursued is well illustrated by an Australian government survey carried out in 1983, before the introduction of the Financial Management Improvement Program. The survey revealed that the vast majority of middle managers perceived financial management as ensuring that resource allocations were neither overspent nor underspent, with no explicit or systematic consideration given to what was actually achieved with the resources. The new culture requires managers to accept responsibility for both managing within budget resources and achieving performance targets. Thus, every manager has definite budget and performance targets. For many, this represents a major change from previous management practices, where no explicit performance targets were set and where budgets were perceived as the responsibility of financial units, not of line managers.

The reforms are sometimes described as the adoption of private sector approaches in the public sector (New Zealand, United Kingdom). One key reform, for example, has been the introduction of markets or commercial arrangements in certain areas of the public sector. Some governments have emphasized the adoption of best private sector practices as the essence of the reforms, while others have preferred to portray the reforms as based on a generic approach to performance management.

Differing descriptions notwithstanding, there has emerged a common recognition of the need to balance policy objectives against financial capacity, and a sharpened awareness of the need to promote improved performance (in economy, efficiency, effectiveness, and service quality) in the management of public activities. Traditional budgetary and financial management systems – characterised by compliance and detailed central control over inputs – have been perceived as inadequate to meet these needs.

The concepts of performance, accountability, and control encapsulate the management reforms. They have three complementary elements:

- *strengthening aggregate expenditure control:* increased emphasis is being placed on a framework of high-level multi-year budgetary targets;
- *letting managers manage* through the devolution of decision-making authority lower down the organisational structure and a reduction in prescriptive rules, giving managers the necessary flexibility and authority to produce required results;
- *making managers manage,* requiring them to pursue performance goals through the strengthening of accountability requirements that focus on results, and the establishment of new performance measurement, contracting, and reporting arrangements.

Strengthening aggregate expenditure control

In order to prevent the public sector from claiming an ever-increasing share of national resources, many governments have established and published goals for total spending. Subsequent reallocations and detailed decisions about programme changes, cost increases, etc., must be accommodated within these limits. Such fiscal constraints or norms are intended to make politicians, interest groups, bureaucrats, and other claimants for funds aware that there are limits to the ability of governments to meet their demands. They are viewed as an important element of an educational process to shift expectations from expansion to expenditure restraint. Global budgetary targets and multi-year expenditure and financial planning, are among the most common and significant reforms that countries have introduced to enhance aggregate spending control.

Global budgetary norms must be expressed in simple terms, though they are likely to be based on complex considerations such as fiscal and monetary options, the size and role of government, the built-in momentum of revenue and expenditure, and sectoral policies and pressures. Targets that cannot be readily grasped by politicians, civil servants, and the general public stand little chance of influencing decisions. They must be summed up in a few key numbers. Virtually all OECD countries now articulate some form of high-level budgetary goal expressed in terms of specific quantitative targets rather than general qualitative statements of intent. This precision provides a strong message about the government's financial objectives, and restricts its ability to allow expediency to dictate aggregate revenue and spending levels.

The budget targets used in Member countries can be grouped into three categories. Some countries rely on two or more of the practices described below to influence budgetary developments. The categories are as follows:

- a *ratio* usually expressed as a percentage of GDP or some other indicator of aggregate economic activity; the ratio may relate to the level of public debt, budget balance or government borrowing, revenue or expenditure, or a combination of these factors;
- a *rate of change:* a common guideline has been zero real growth over the stated period, although targets have also been expressed as some allowed rate of increase or required rate of decrease in real expenditure;

alternatively, targets have also been expressed in nominal terms, published alongside target ratios for the budget balance or the revenue burden;
- an *absolute value in nominal terms:* targets in cash terms are typically expressed as either the future level of expenditure or deficit, or as the amount of desired change from some baseline level.

Table 3 summarises the nature of high-level targets currently announced by countries. (It is important to note the simplifications implicit in the table. It merely summarises the form of target that a government highlights in its public statements of budgetary objectives. It does not summarise all the targets that are operative in a government's budgeting process – in some senses, an entry could be made for many countries in all the columns).

A related and significant approach adopted by some OECD Countries (*e.g.* Australia, Canada, Denmark) has been to establish expenditure norms or frames for individual ministries and agencies. This approach lightens the burden of identifying expenditure trade-offs on the Budget Ministers and the Prime Minister by involving individual spending ministers in this task. This can be most important politically, and the devolution involved can also lead to better-informed choices.

Multi-year budgeting (MYB) is the bridge between aggregate medium-term targets and annual budgets, and has become an instrument of financial management in a number of OECD countries. Under MYB, aggregate budget targets are typically expressed for several years ahead. This multi-year dimension is essential in providing clear parameters within which current decisions must be made. Also, bringing the budget into line with acceptable fiscal targets must typically be done in stages, with each year's budget progressing toward the stated target.

As originally conceived, MYB was a planning device, a means of identifying programme initiatives and setting aside funds for them in future budgets for their orderly implementation. MYB was itself an engine of expansion as departments and agencies saw the plans as future entitlements to increases in budgetary resources. But as the rate of public sector growth becomes unsustainable, this aspect of MYB has increasingly been viewed as inappropriate.

OECD countries have generally reoriented their MYB arrangements from instruments of programme expansion to constraints on future spending. In some, such as the United Kingdom, this reorientation was signalled by a switch from planning in volume terms to cash planning. In others, it was reflected in rules requiring that estimates of future spending be based on unchanged policy – estimating the future cost of existing programmes without making any provision for new initiatives – or even requiring that outlays be reduced to produce a required bottom line budget result (surplus/deficit). In some countries (Netherlands, Sweden, United States) this baseline has

Table 3. **Synopsis of current announced budgetary medium-term objectives**

	Ratio to GDP of			Growth rate of expenditure		Money level of	
	Deficit [1]	Expenditure	Revenue	Real	Nominal	Expenditure	Deficit [1]
Australia	X	X	X				
Belgium	X		X				
Canada	X				X		X
Denmark	X			X			
Finland	X			X			
France	X						
Germany					X		X
Greece	X						
Ireland	X	X	X			X	
Italy	X		X			X	X
Japan							X [2]
Netherlands	X		X				
Norway [3]							
Portugal	X	X				X	
Spain	X	X	X			X	X
Sweden	X		X				
Turkey					X		X
United Kingdom	X	X				X	
United States							X

1. Deficit or borrowing requirement or accumulated public debt.
2. The objective in Japan is not formulated as a specific numerical target.
3. Norway does not formulate medium-term targets.

become the starting point for work on the budget. Whatever the baseline, it conveys a powerful message: that the built-in momentum of existing programmes has already claimed all future resources and that there is no margin for new spending schemes; in other words, all new proposals would have to compete with existing programmes for funds.

Although governments always reserve the right to change policies in response to unforeseen circumstances, such budget guidelines can involve a measure of agreement regarding resources for as much as three years ahead, and possibly some modest flexibility to shift operational resources among years.

MYB does not generally involve multi-year legal appropriations: it almost always operates within a one-year budgeting framework. But decisions on the annual budget are taken in full knowledge of their impact on out-years and the achievement of out-year targets. A medium-term planning framework thus has the advantage that it forces governments to focus on the out-year implications of policy changes. Otherwise, there is always a risk that savings are achieved simply by deferring expenditure and that new policies that initially cost very little are adopted without full cognizance of their medium-term expenditure implications.

Greater transparency, providing the public with much better information on budget targets and results, greatly assists improved budgeting. Maintaining tight expenditure restraint is not easy when faced with pressure from various interest groups – governments need allies. The general public can be expected to provide such support only if it is furnished with sufficient information to be able to assess properly the nature of the choices that need to be made. Publishing the forward estimates of the cost of existing policy reinforces expenditure restraint by forcing governments to declare where and by how much its decisions on new policy have added or subtracted from outlays and their impact on future budget balances.

Efforts to improve fiscal management through greater public disclosure of fiscal trends and performance are probably most advanced in New Zealand. The Fiscal Responsibility Act 1994 requires all governments, current and future, to keep New Zealanders regularly informed of the true state of public finances. The key new elements of fiscal disclosure mandated by the legislation include the following:

- all fiscal reporting to be prepared in line with generally accepted accounting practice so as to be more consistent with private sector practice and provide better information on the government's assets and liabilities;
- an annual statement of the government's fiscal objectives and the methods by which those objectives are to be achieved, covering notably government spending, revenue, the fiscal balance, and public debt over a ten-year period;
- six-monthly economic and fiscal updates including three-year forecasts;
- disclosure of all items with a reasonably certain fiscal cost or gain, and identification of potential ''fiscal risks'' involving items where costs or gains are likely but timing and amount are uncertain;
- economic and fiscal updates prior to elections.

Devolution: letting managers manage

Devolution is the significant strategy underpinning the philosophy of ''letting managers manage''. It involves a shift from detailed regulations, *ex ante* controls, and emphasis on compliance management to increased discretion and initiative for operational managers in achieving performance targets, defined in terms of outputs and outcomes in relation to inputs. In some cases, it has involved the creation of new autonomous agencies or units (Canada, Denmark, France, United Kingdom). An important objective has been to provide managers of programmes and activities with the information, incentives, and flexibility to focus on the economy, efficiency, and effectiveness of programmes, and on service quality, *i.e.* on performance. This shift in emphasis is also seen as offering more fulfilling working conditions for managers.

Devolution is a frequently misunderstood aspect of the reforms. It involves devolution of decision-making authority, both from central to line agencies and within agencies to individual managers and regions. It also involves a reduction in prescriptive rules or controls, giving managers greater freedom to use their own judgement, albeit in many cases in accordance with some overall guidelines. Both aspects, increased delegation and removal of prescriptive requirements, involve giving greater authority and flexibility to individual managers.

Devolution goes hand in hand with accountability. Managers cannot be held accountable for performance or results if they lack the authority to make decisions that are part of producing those results. It is this very authority that makes managers accountable: to put it in everyday terms, they have no excuses to hide behind. Yet controls and accountability are frequently discussed as if they were synonymous. In fact, they are opposites: the more controls the less accountability, the fewer the controls the greater the accountability.

In practice, in most countries devolution has been restricted to operational decisions, rather than policy, strategic, or political decisions. Indeed, one of the elements of the reforms has been to remove detailed transaction controls precisely so that senior managers and central bodies are able to concentrate on policy or strategic issues. For example, reforms to the budget process have partly been aimed at eliminating discussion about detailed input requirements to focus on strategic issues of programme priorities and effectiveness (Australia). Senior managers and ministers are, at least in theory, able to devote more time to assessing the overall effectiveness of programmes, considering the level of service to be provided, and generally establishing the policy and quality frameworks within which the programmes are to be delivered. To the extent that such frameworks did not exist in the past, and local officials had discretion on policy matters, officials are becoming more accountable for their actions, not less so. This explains complaints in some cases that the performance management approach has increased "centralisation" of decision-making, or increased "control".

Devolution is pursued on the assumption that it will improve performance. First, it is argued that decisions made lower down the organisational structure or closer to their point of impact will be more effective because they are made with better knowledge of their impact. Second, decisions will be made faster and reduce costs in time for managers and customers as well as other transaction costs. Third, devolution accompanied by guidelines and *ex post* review may be a more effective way of achieving certain types of behaviour or decisions. Fourth, many central controls may not achieve the desired result: as perceived problems or difficulties arise, there is a tendency to erect new controls without sufficient thought given to whether they will achieve their objective. Finally, there is a tendency for central controls to lose their currency over time and to become ends in themselves. As such, a regular culling of central controls is needed.

The question of how much devolution is enough or what should be devolved is a matter of judgement or balance, which in principle is best resolved by an analysis of the costs and benefits of the higher-level controls or detailed prescriptions. This is clearly difficult in practice. The experience of those governments that have relaxed central controls is that few, if any, benefits have been lost, and that in view of the efficiency gains made, neither the central nor the line agencies wish to return to the previous system (Australia, Canada, Denmark, New Zealand, Sweden, United Kingdom).

A number of countries, particularly at the political level, have been reluctant to embrace devolution. First, such changes may be perceived by ministers, legislators, and the public as giving too much power to officials at the expense of elected representatives. Second, they may be perceived as opening up too many possibilities for improper or inappropriate behaviour. Third, they may lead to different decisions being made by different officials in similar cases, *i.e.* lack of standardization.

However there are strong countervailing arguments that governments have advanced in promoting devolution:

- Detailed central controls do not, in any event, guarantee the protection of citizens' rights and the prevention of improper behaviour. Decision-makers at higher levels may be too overwhelmed by the sheer volume of decisions to make appropriate decisions on such matters.
- Appropriate reporting mechanisms can ensure the transparency of the exercise of this devolved authority for *ex post* review agencies. Thus, if officials are freed from a requirement for public tendering of purchases in certain cases, probity can still be safeguarded by a requirement to report and justify all such cases so that conformity with guidelines can be assessed. Review agencies, such as external auditors and administrative appeal institutions, can play an important role in reviewing such decisions. Such transparency should be coupled with appropriate penalties for breaches of requirements.
- Standardization of approach is not necessarily a desirable goal and, in any case, central controls may not achieve standardization.

It is clear, nevertheless, that devolution has not advanced very far in some countries. In some cases, this reflects political desires for political involvement in operating decisions, even at the possible expense of policy decisions. Although the boundary between political and administrative decisions must be politically determined (*i.e.* ministers are entitled to decide what decisions they, as opposed to civil servants, will make), the arguments made above in support of devolution remain relevant.

A reluctance to pursue devolution may also reflect beliefs that compliance issues are more important than performance issues. To put it another way, probity takes priority over effectiveness or efficiency. This attitude may be reinforced by the stance taken by review agencies such as auditors or legislative committees. This is a matter of values or opinions as to what is important. It may also reflect the fact that measuring compliance is easier than measuring performance. The reforms are based on the need for a greater emphasis on performance issues. This is not to the exclusion of compliance, and is only at the expense of compliance inasmuch as it reduces the number and detail of rules to be complied with.

All governments have faced the issue of which comes first, devolution or accountability structures. Should devolution be deferred until performance measurement and other accountability mechanisms are fully developed, or should devolution be implemented early in order to create the conditions for improved performance? Different approaches have been adopted by different countries. In some cases devolution has been introduced as a matter of principle (New Zealand, United Kingdom). In others, increased devolution has been used as a reward for agencies that have improved their performance (Denmark). Successful devolution requires an element of trust in the ability and willingness of lower levels to perform adequately. It also depends on the existence of an information system under which the performance at lower levels can be regularly and reliably monitored by higher levels.

Thus, deciding on the appropriate level of devolution or flexibility involves an assessment of the risks of fraud, citizens' rights being ignored, or other improper behaviour compared with the potential efficiency gains. The decision is one of risk management. This involves assessing risk, not ignoring it. It is essential to understanding the move from a compliance to a performance approach.

Risk management is intrinsic to devolution and a performance management operating environment. It requires or encourages managers to adopt control practices that adequately weigh the possible costs from a lower level of control (*e.g.* the risks involved in not checking all payments) against the costs of 100 per cent verification. Such risk management decisions are not new and are faced every day by officials in many types of decisions: what goods should a customs inspector physically inspect, how much checking of a tax return is required, how many checks are needed to authorize an account for payment.

Changes in budgetary systems

Against this background, governments have shown a renewed willingness to re-examine systems of central budget control. The trend to provide managers with the incentives and flexibility to manage resources to achieve greater efficiency and effectiveness is strongly in evidence. Institutional incentives have been expanded. Within organisations, more discretion is given to operational managers in the selection of inputs, the timing of expenditures, the reallocation of funds among programmes or activities, user charging and the use of the proceeds. Savings beyond centrally determined limits are left with the institutions and not automatically reappropriated by the budget office.

Flexibility in administrative expenditure

The consolidation of detailed appropriation items and the devolution of resource allocation decisions, especially for salaries and administrative expenditures, have been common elements of the devolution strategy outlined above. Such arrangements aim to induce managers to accept responsibility for achieving results by providing them with the flexibility to achieve those results. The consolidation of numerous appropriation items into a single item gives departmental managers the freedom to decide on the mix of resource inputs in the pursuit of desired outputs, and to adapt more flexibly to changing priorities, without having to refer back to the central budget agency. In some countries, flexibility has been extended to include the abolition of separate staff number controls in favour of a single monetary control over expenditure – either for total running costs or salaries.

Because of their inherent greater flexibility, consolidated appropriations, or running costs as they have been commonly termed, have made adherence to global fiscal constraints both more practicable and more acceptable to ministries. Establishing firm bases for running costs has also enabled the government, the budget agency, and ministries to give greater attention to major expenditure programmes, and not be bogged down in the detail of relatively minor changes in running costs. It is important to note that such arrangements as have been introduced are not perceived to have led to any weakening of aggregate expenditure control. A changed basis of control has been the order of the day. Freed of the day-to-day application and enforcement of detailed input controls, both central budget agencies and spending departments and agencies are able to concentrate on arguably more important policy and implementation questions concerning the efficiency and effectiveness of public programmes and activities. Controls are at a higher, more strategic level; are enforced differently; and are arguably more effective. Budget scrutiny has become more relevant to the key decisions of government.

This flexibility has usually been accompanied by two other changes. In return for the increased within-year flexibility, the allocations are strictly cash limited, *i.e.* no supplement is provided except in clearly defined and limited circumstances. Correspondingly, the amounts will not normally be reduced within the year, thus providing some certainty within years.

The increased organisational efficiency resulting from such arrangements – as distinct from those resulting from better programme management and a more systematic focus on performance – should not be underestimated. Administering systems of detailed input controls, which achieved little in terms of greater overall control, involved significant dead-weight costs in terms of managers' time and energy.

Medium-term planning

In some countries, arrangements have been developed that substantially modify the tradition of annuality in budgeting. As outlined above, multi-year budgeting has been introduced to promote the effective use of public monies and encourage responsiveness and innovation. Multi-year frames – giving indicative financial allocations up to three years in advance in some cases – have been adopted, particularly for administrative and operational expenditures. Such arrangements reflect the awareness that, in addition to flexibility to choose the best resource mix, managers need some stability to plan expenditures over the medium term.

Strict annuality, as traditionally applied, provided little incentive to managers to economise resources or plan expenditures in an orderly fashion with a focus on results. Funds remaining unspent at year's end, whether resulting from enhanced efficiency or unforeseen circumstances, were usually "captured' by the central budget agency. In most cases they were viewed as demonstrating provision in excess of need. Allocations for future years were reduced accordingly. Efficient managers were thus penalised under this arrangement. Conversely, inefficiency went unsanctioned. The logical response, therefore, tended to be higher spending at the end of the financial year, simply to avoid losing funds and to guarantee the base for future spending allocations. Financial management was seen in terms of process, neither under-spending nor over-spending, rather than performance (economy, efficiency, effectiveness, and service quality).

Indicative multi-year spending allocations have been directed at avoiding such behaviour. By providing a degree of certainty in the level of funding over time, they aim to lift the sights of both managers in spending agencies and central budget offices to more strategic questions of the best resource allocation mix and the most appropriate timing of expenditure in pursuing programme objectives. These arrangements have generally been supported by the additional flexibility to shift funding among years, either by borrowing from future years' allocations or carrying over unspent funds to future years. These medium-term commitments to funding have, however, been qualified to some extent to enable governments to retain some flexibility to respond to changing priorities and uncertainties. Most countries that have adapted such arrangements have limited them to operational expenditure, and have not extended them to the much larger programme outlays.

As discussed below, the quid pro quo of additional certainty and flexibility in administrative and operational spending has generally been a requirement for improved performance and managing within reduced funding. Under multi-year budget frames, managers have the incentive to pursue efficiency gains in the use of administrative resources, since part of any gains may accrue directly to programme managers and agencies. Most governments that have introduced a multi-year budget frame have required that at least some efficiency gains be retained to assist the overall budget and thereby provide enhanced scope for the government to reorder *its* priorities.

This is sometimes effected by requiring that administrative and operating costs be reduced by an enforced productivity gain or efficiency dividend, so that programme managers are required to achieve at least a minimum target for improved productivity. This reduction is also reflected in the estimates for the forward years. In some countries (Denmark, Sweden), these productivity targets are negotiated for individual agencies or programmes and reflect assessments of the scope for such gains using performance measures and other reviews. In other countries (Australia, United States), a more across-the-board approach is adopted, because of the difficult judgements and political sensitivity of distinguishing the relative scope for increased efficiency among different agencies.

In most countries, it is left to individual managers to determine how best to achieve the targeted efficiency gains, as is consistent with the emphasis on devolution. Central agencies have, however, provided advice and training. In some countries there have been specific reviews, such as the efficiency scrutinies in the United Kingdom and Australia, that have been promoted and overseen by a central agency. Where the savings from such reviews are substantial, there has usually been a negotiated sharing of the proceeds between the budget office and the spending agency, but for relatively small savings it has been usual to allow the spending agency to retain them or to use them as a contribution towards the achievement of its efficiency dividend.

Arrangements in Ireland and Sweden probably best typify how these multi-year frames for administrative budgets are being applied in countries and the broader objectives that such arrangements are meant to further.

The introduction in 1991 of three-year administrative budgets in Ireland was aimed at delegating greater authority to line departments (and within departments to line managers) for administrative expenditure and related matters. Each participating department negotiates a three-year agreement with the Minister for Finance. This agreement states the total expenditure to be available (in constant terms) in each of the three years, specifies the circumstances (if any) under which these amounts will be changed, allows the transfer of resources among items (but not among appropriation votes), allows some carry-over of resources from one financial year to another, and arranges for monitoring the agreement and resolving any difficulties that arise. Each department is required to reduce its running costs by two per cent in real terms in each of the second and third years. To ensure that the devolution extends to operating levels, each department must prepare a plan for internal delegation of authority over administrative expenditure. During the 1991-93 period, three-year agreements covered departments employing 80 per cent of the civil service and covered expenditure of some IR£ 560 million in 1991 terms. A new cycle of administrative budgeting was introduced in 1994; it covers expenditure of some Ir£ 650 million in 1994 terms.

Sweden's three-year budget frames for agencies' administrative costs has been in place since 1989. Although funds are still appropriated one year at a time, agencies can carry forward savings in one year to the next and, within strict limits, draw in advance on future appropriations. The three-year frames are applied to administrative expenditure, which has been subject to extended downward pressure for more than a decade.

Under three-year frames, agencies go through a more elaborate process in formulating their budgets. At the start, they receive both general and special directives, the former issued by the government or the Ministry of Finance, the latter by the ministry in their area of operation. The general directives in Sweden require agencies to report on performance for the past five years, assess current objectives and arrangements, and develop measurable targets for the work to be done and results to be achieved over the next three years. These directives also call upon agencies to apply the productivity measures developed in recent years, to show whether they are becoming more or less efficient. The directives also ask agencies to measure productive versus non-productive (direct versus indirect) costs. The special directives are tailored to each agency's circumstances and pertain to the evaluations to be undertaken, priorities, and the policy options to be considered. The evaluations look back at past results, and the policy options look ahead to future accomplishments.

The process extends to programme objectives and expenditures as well as administrative costs. That is, agencies are called upon to assess their total performance and to justify the full range of activities for the next three years. In effect, the government is offering increased flexibility over administrative matters as an inducement for agencies to make a broad, probing assessment of their overall performance.

It may appear curious that the reforms outlined above are focused on a vital but (in most countries) relatively small slice of the budget – namely, administrative or running costs. However, there is a certain logic to this focus. Although it has been subject to tight controls, administrative spending has generally crept upwards over the years, and there is evidence that productivity gains in OECD governments have lagged behind comparable trends in the private sector.

Moreover, administrative costs loom large in the everyday operations of agencies. The rules and procedures governing these expenditures influence the behaviour and performance of managers. If the rules are highly process-oriented, it is argued, managers give priority to the legalities of control and care less about results. They cannot be held accountable for performance because they lack a genuine voice in how funds are to be applied, and they are prevented or discouraged from shifting resources from less to more productive uses. Managers cannot manage if they must repeatedly seek approval from others before spending funds, or if their requests to shift resources are denied by external controllers.

Stimulating commercial and competitive approaches

In addition to institutional incentives for managers to pursue efficiency savings, attempts are being made to simulate a market-determined approach to resource allocation for a number of public sector activities. These are discussed in detail in Chapter 15. However, changes to budget arrangements are important elements of this strategy and are briefly discussed here.

Traditionally, budget-funded agencies have been provided with many services, such as property, printing, government cars, and legal advice, by a central agency at no cost. Consequently, the consuming agency had no incentive to economise in terms of either quality or quantity, while the service provider was happy to lobby the budget office for funding on behalf of its clients. The supply of such services was effectively rationed by the budget office limiting the funds available to the supplier, and sometimes it also controlled standards in order to limit expenditure. Recent reforms have transformed this system: now, service providers operate on a commercial basis. They charge for their services, and the supply is governed by the amount the consuming agencies are prepared to pay for out of their own budget allocations. The supplier retains the revenue but must meet financial performance targets.

Further benefits can accrue from commercialisation, where such structural changes are accompanied by increased competition. This is more obviously accomplished by market testing and/or contracting out. Sometimes the service provider subcontracts, arranging the leases of privately owned property for other government agencies, for example. Alternatively, individual government agencies deal directly with private suppliers by calling for competitive tenders.

Commercialisation along these lines also involves a significant improvement in asset management. The major assets owned by the general government sector (such as real estate and cars) are vested in the commercialised agencies, which operate to financial targets based on full cost recovery. These agencies can then be given the flexibility to make commercial decisions as to when to invest in new assets and retire existing assets. For other, less significant assets, ownership can be vested in individual spending agencies, with the incentive to improve management being the retention of all or part of the proceeds of any sale.

Countries have also been experimenting with increased user charging for goods and services provided directly to the public. Charges for services to external users are used to strengthen market signals and thus improve resource allocation decisions in the public sector. Many goods and services produced in the public sector (*e.g.* statistical publications, mapping services) present considerable private benefits to the user. Free provision gives users no incentive to economise in consumption, nor does it provide any indication of the effective demand for such services.

Under external charging arrangements, the supply of goods and services to which charges apply need no longer depend solely upon a fixed budget allocation to the supplier. Supply becomes a function of, and dependent upon, users' willingness to pay. Thus, a user charging regime can, of itself, generate pressure for greater efficiency and effectiveness in service provision, particularly in conjunction with financial targets set for the supplier. Consumers of public services will generally demand value for money if they have to pay for a public service.

Increasing reliance upon a market approach through external user charging (where possible and appropriate) is also seen to have the significant advantage of loosening structural rigidities in the public sector. It facilitates the measurement of operational efficiency and effectiveness of government programmes and a more explicit choice between public and private provision.

Countries that have more systematically applied user charging have also favoured the concurrent adoption of revenue retention arrangements through net appropriations or "net budgeting" for such services. Net budgeting refers to arrangements where revenues raised from a particular expenditure activity are offset against related expenditure appropriations, such that entities receive and are accountable for the net amount only. Thus, agencies are permitted to use revenues from outside sources without formal appropriating authority.

Net budgeting arrangements create an incentive for managers to generate revenues in order to benefit from a possible higher level of expenditures, but also because if there is a risk of deficit the net appropriation may be supplemented by these revenues. Similarly, programme managers have greater flexibility in delivering services: increases in demand requiring additional expenditure can be met, at least in part, by the increased revenues generated. In this sense, user charging is entirely consistent with making and letting managers manage.

Under arrangements requiring specific levels of cost recovery, net budgeting implicitly imposes a requirement for managers to regularly review and justify rates of charge. In the case of user charging within government, more accurate identification of programme costs is facilitated by the requirement to attribute to benefiting programmes the costs of services provided by other programmes.

Countries that have introduced commercialisation, and associated user charging are concerned to ensure that charges reflect as closely as possible full resource costs, as opposed to cash costs alone. This has often led to the introduction of some form of accrual accounting.

Accrual accounting seeks to match the costs incurred during a particular accounting period with the benefits received, and revenues with goods or services provided. The relating of revenues and expenses enables the determination of profit in the case of business-oriented activities and permits the assessment of the net cost of providing services in the case of non-profit organisations. The accrual basis of reporting is seen as useful in providing information on matters such as the resources controlled by an entity, the full cost of service provision, and the assessment of the efficiency or economy of operations. It is essential to measuring supplier performance and to comparing costs with those of alternative private sector suppliers. It is an underlying feature of most charging regimes.

More recently, a number of countries have extended, or announced proposals to extend, the use of accrual accounting to core elements of the public sector as part of broader goals of enhancing managerial decision-making and accountability for performance (Australia, Iceland, New Zealand, United Kingdom and United States).

Moves to apply accrual accounting to core public sector activities are consistent with the objectives of public sector management reforms in general, which emphasize the cost-effectiveness of activities, and which incorporate a range of incentives to manage better, provide greater flexibility in the allocation of total resources and adopt a focus on value for money. Within this framework, financial accounting and reporting systems are seen to have an important role to play in providing the necessary information to support decision-making and to reflect accountability in value-for-money terms.

The objectives of financial reporting in the public sector encompass the provision of information required to assess: the stewardship of resources and compliance with legal requirements; the state of finances; performance in terms of economy, efficiency, and results; and economic impact. The accounting bases underlying accounting and financial reporting systems have important implications for the nature of the information they provide and, thus, the extent to which these objectives can be met.

The value of cash accounting in assessing the macroeconomic impact of public sector activity and in informing judgements about the relationship between fiscal and monetary policy is unquestioned. The additional benefits that accrual accounting can provide for public sector entities include the ability to: enhance the accountability basis for the new flexibility provided to public sectormanagers; underpin objectives for a more competitive approach to public sector provision; facilitate more efficient and effective resource management; improve accountability by extending the notion of performance beyond the focus on cash flows; and provide a focus on the long-term effects of government and management decisions.

The nature of accountability within the public sector has shifted from a relatively narrow focus on compliance with spending limits to a broader perspective encompassing the following elements: accountability for the outputs, efficiency and results of activities; concerns with total resource management reflected in full costs of operations; and long-term obligations and overall financial condition. Some form of accrual accounting is recognised as increasingly necessary to reflect and provide the information needed to support decision-making.

Recent efforts to apply accrual accounting to the public sector are thus not being undertaken for their own sake, on the basis of a belief in the superiority of this form of accounting. Rather, they aim to arrive at the best mix of cash- and accrual-based financial information for use as an additional management tool to stimulate and reflectetter, more results-oriented public sector performance. Accrual accounting is viewed as a means rather than an end.

Making managers manage: accountability for performance

To improve performance, managers need greater autonomy and flexibility. But autonomy, although necessary, is not sufficient. In return for relaxing highly prescriptive and detailed central controls, managers must focus on performance and be held accountable for results.

A systematic approach to performance management

It is useful to use the term ''performance management'' to describe the systematic approach to performance being encouraged by Member countries. Such approaches, described variously as programme management or results-oriented management, have generally involved the encouragement or mandating of a regular management cycle in which:

- performance objectives and targets are determined for programmes (and in many cases made public);
- managers responsible for each programme have the freedom to implement processes to achieve these objectives and targets;
- the actual level of performance against targets is measured and reported;
- the performance level achieved feeds into decisions about future programme funding, changes to programme content or design and the provision of organisational or personal rewards or penalties;
- the information is also provided to *ex post* review bodies such as legislative committees and the external auditor (depending on the latter's performance audit mandate), whose views may also feed into the decisions referred to above.

This systematic approach to performance management clearly involves mechanisms, such as corporate planning, under which the organisation's and programmes' objectives are determined. The budgetary process, linked with the corporate planning process, is the most important vehicle for the reforms. This is reflected in the fact that, in many governments, the performance management reforms are led or managed by the central budget office. The processes may also involve other mechanisms, such as divisional work plans, purchasing plans, personal performance improvement plans, etc. These are all articulated with the budgetary and corporate planning processes, but subsidiary to them.

A performance orientation

A performance or results orientation involves focusing on:

- the achievement of programme results, which includes cost-effectiveness and generally encompasses quality of service;
- operating efficiently and with due regard to economy.

Some governments, particularly New Zealand and the United Kingdom, distinguish two aspects of performance: accountability for outcomes (what is achieved by the programme) and accountability for outputs (what is actually done under the programme). Ministers are perceived as accountable for outcomes but officials, only for outputs. Others, while accepting the distinction, do not consider that accountability can be so clearly defined (Australia).

A number of governments have recently emphasized quality of service to consumers as a major part of performance (Belgium, France, Portugal, Spain, United Kingdom). In some countries, the concept of service standards relates mainly to issues of quality of service rather than to outcomes. Elsewhere, it is more broadly defined to cover other significant aspects of programme effectiveness. In general, the pursuit of quality issues is consistent with greater efficiency and effectiveness, but there may be occasions where a trade-off between the interests of consumers and taxpayers is involved. For example, an ineffective or poorly targeted programme may provide services that are timely, accurate, and accessible, just as ineffective programmes can be efficiently run.

Responsibility for performance will be different at different levels of the organisation. Clearly, the responsibilities of ministers are broader than those of chief executives, which, in turn, are different from those of divisional or programme managers. Determining the boundaries of each person's responsibility, and thus accountability, is a complex but fundamental issue. In particular, the accountability of officials for programme effectiveness (outcomes) as opposed to efficiency (outputs) appears to be a matter of debate and to be regarded differently in different countries. Likewise, accountability lines or relationships are also frequently debated. For example, the accountability of officials to the legislature appears to be an unresolved issue in some "Westminster"-type governments (Australia, United Kingdom).

Performance measurement

The reforms place considerable emphasis on performance measurement. In the public sector this involves some difficulties and subjectivity. For example, defining operational objectives is difficult. There may be conflicting or multiple objectives. How are these conflicts to be resolved and different objectives weighted? How are multiple outputs to be combined or ranked? In actually measuring results, it may be difficult to determine cause-effect relationships, *i.e.* did something happen because of a programme or despite it?

Performance measurement has two main elements: performance indicators and programme analysis or evaluation. Performance indicators are quantitative measures of performance, often expressed as ratios, such as cost per unit of output. They cover effectiveness (outcomes), efficiency (outputs) and may be quality-of-service indicators expressing timeliness, accuracy, accessibility, continuity, etc. They provide a *prima facie* indication of whether a programme's performance is adequate or on target, but not of reasons or cause-effect relationships. A poor level of performance as shown in performance indicators is a signal for more detailed analysis so that corrective action or other decisions can be taken.

Most governments have put considerable emphasis on requiring agencies to develop performance indicators, and many of their published budget documents, annual reports, and other material contain an extensive range of indicators. In developing such indicators it is important to focus on key indicators and to keep the process simple, rather than attempt to cover every aspect of a programme's performance. There has been a tendency in many countries to develop excessive numbers of indicators, without an adequate understanding of their interrelationships or of how the information might be used. On the other hand, the performance measures must be sufficiently comprehensive to cover all significant aspects of performance. It is important that programme managers also perceive any reported indicators as relevant to their own management and use them for this purpose. In addition, performance indicators must be carefully chosen so as not to bring about dysfunctional behaviour by managers.

Programme analysis or evaluation involves an in-depth assessment of performance in terms of programme effectiveness, or whether a programme is meeting its objectives. It seeks to identify cause-effect relationships or reasons for a particular level of performance, and to assist in deciding whether a programme should continue, be expanded, terminated, or otherwise modified. In this sense, it involves going beyond the performance indicators.

Many governments have taken steps to formalize requirements for programme evaluation usually as part of reforms to the budgetary process (Australia, Netherlands). While evaluation is perceived as primarily the responsibility of individual agencies and managers, selective programme evaluations may be undertaken by central budget offices or by external auditors, depending on the scope of the latter's mandate. In some cases, such as in Australia, the results of internal evaluations must be reported externally and be accessible by external review agencies such as legislative committees.

Performance measurement is not an exact science, and the use of performance information therefore requires judgement. Most governments have recognised that all performance measurement must be undertaken with the knowledge of its conceptual (methodological) and practical (data) limitations. Performance measurement in the general government sector is used to get a better feel for performance to assist in decision-making rather than to measure some precise bottom line. This point has not always been understood by legislators and even ministers, who may make uncritical use of performance information based on a belief that all performance can be fully and precisely quantified.

In evaluating performance levels, it must be recognised that a performance measure is relative, and must be evaluated by reference to some base. While actual performance will be compared to budget or targets, these can be set at tight or achievable levels and, in turn, be based on past performance or performance of other comparable organisations.

Performance reporting and monitoring

Performance information must "count". It must be used for decision-making. Performance is not simply measured for its own sake. For it to count, it must be reported to the person who will use it. Thus, the appropriate determination of relative responsibilities at all levels is crucial to performance management and will determine what is reported to whom. While performance information has a role in determining sanctions and rewards, its principal role is in performance improvement. In this sense, it is a positive, not a negative, instrument. It should not be used primarily for assigning blame in cases of inadequate performance, but rather for taking corrective action to enhance performance.

Performance information is reported in different forms at different levels of the organisation and the government, reflecting responsibilities at different levels. Ministers, for example, will wish to monitor the performance of programmes for which they are responsible so as to esnure that corrective action is taken, if necessary, as well as to form judgements about future programme design, funding, and priorities. Chief executives and managers within the organisation will have roughly similar needs, but at a greater level of operational detail, and at lower levels will focus more on efficiency than on effectiveness. Service quality issues will be important at all levels. The legislature may also use performance information to form broad judgements about the performance of particular ministers, as well as to decide whether to support particular funding levels for particular programmes or to press for the termination or expansion of certain programmes.

The role of external review agencies such as auditors may be enhanced under performance management reforms. Apart from carrying out performance reviews (UK National Audit Office and US General Accounting Office), they may have a role in reviewing the quality of performance information. In principle, any published claims about performance should be subject to some form of external independent audit, as is the case with published financial information. Only a few governments (Finland, Sweden, New Zealand) have a formalized requirement for the attestation of performance results. The external auditor may also review and evaluate the general adequacy of internal performance measurement and monitoring mechanisms, such as under the comprehensive auditing approach adopted in a number of jurisdictions (Australia and Canada).

Performance contracting

Performance management is increasingly carried out through formal or semiformal contractual arrangements under which one party undertakes to achieve a particular level of performance in return for agreed funding levels and/or prescribed managerial flexibilities. Such arrangements must clearly specify who has authority to contract with whom, and about what, *i.e.* relative responsibilities. This point is particularly relevant to the respective roles of the legislature, ministers, and officials. The existence of contractual arrangements reflects a view that the formalization of requirements and mutual undertakings, which will usually include a reference to rewards and sanctions, helps to reinforce a greater focus on performance issues. The range of such agreements developed in countries encompasses the following:

- Agreements between the central budget office and agencies that financial allocations are provided in return for an agreed level of performance. These have no legal status, but are a formalized part of budgetary negotiations between the two parties. Sanctions or rewards in terms of budget alterations may be set out. The term resource agreements is sometimes used for such arrangements. They may extend to only parts of an agency. For example, an agreement under net budgeting arrangements may relate to what type and proportion of receipts may be offset against an appropriation, or how any surplus or shortfall is to be handled. Or, an agreement may relate to funding for a major capital item, with corresponding staff savings or efficiency gains being deducted from the agencies' base funding. The Australian system of resource agreements illustrates this approach.
- Formal legislative appropriations being made on the basis of the agency producing an agreed level of outputs (as in New Zealand). Although performance against targets will be reviewed, it may not be clear what sanctions or rewards may apply.
- Formal performance agreements between a minister and an agency on the services to be delivered by the agency and the level of performance to be achieved. The annual performance agreements for United Kingdom Executive Agencies reflect this approach. Sanctions and rewards will be expressed in institutional terms. The agreement will also indicate funding provisions and the managerial freedoms to be granted to the agency.
- Formal performance agreements between senior management or chief executives of agencies and either the minister or the central personnel agency. These relate to the specific agreed responsibilities of the chief executive *vis-à-vis* the minister and thus are likely to encompass those activities of the agency for which the chief executive and officials can be held responsible. They may focus on processes and tasks to be completed, as well as on performance issues. The corporate plan may often be the source of the agreement. Sanctions and rewards are usually prescribed in terms of tenure and remuneration. The interests of the chief executive and the agency are assumed to be synonymous, as is their performance. An appropriate medium-term period for such agreements is necessary in order to discourage dysfunctional short-term behaviour by the chief executive.

– Performance agreements between the chief executive and senior managers. These are now common in a number of governments, and commonly relate divisional objectives to corporate objectives through the corporate planning process. These may pertain to task completion and behaviour as well as to prescribed levels of performance. Again, the performance of divisional managers and their divisions are assumed to be synonymous, and sanctions and rewards relate to tenure and remuneration.

To the extent that more than one of the these mechanisms are present, they must obviously be consistent and be derived from the same corporate planning base.

Such a contractual approach can be an important aspect of making the managers manage. However, a number of issues arise concerning all such agreements. These include determining an appropriate time frame, an adequate resourcing level for the agreement to be realistic, provision for review within the period, and provision for dialogue on the interpretation of results. The need for independent verification of the actual level of performance may also be necessary. Without appropriate provision for these, the contract may not elicit the type of behaviour required. This may also be a problem if it is not truly a contract between equals, with each having access to the relevant information and each obliged to adhere to their commitments.

In the first two types of agreement, it may be difficult to establish a direct link between the level of performance and the budget. Apart from resource agreements, a number of countries aim to establish performance measurement more firmly in the budgetary process, by focusing the budget dialogue on past and planned performance. *Results budgeting* is a term commonly used to describe this process. Experience suggests that decisions on resourcing take into account a number of factors other than performance, including political considerations. Thus, the link between performance and budgeting tends to be indirect rather than direct. In addition, there are the methodological and practical limitations on performance measurement above.

Who is accountable to whom for what?

The earlier discussion referred to the importance of this issue in performance reporting and performance management generally, and as a major issue in devolution. Without a clear answer to this question, accountability is blurred.

Within individual agencies the relative responsibilities are fairly clear if the organisational structure is hierarchical in nature, the chief executive being ultimately accountable for the actions of his subordinates. It may become blurred if the organisational structure involves matrix management arrangements, as in the case of programmes that have national programme managers at the central office but that are delivered by regional managers responsible for delivering a range of programmes. Determining appropriate accountability in such a system may involve issues similar to the responsibility for outcomes as opposed to outputs. The issue of matrix management also arises in the private sector, where it is considered to engender complexities, but not insurmountable problems.

In the public sector, particular questions present themselves regarding:
– the relationship between ministries and subsidiary agencies;
– the relationship between officials and ministers on the one handand the legislature on the other.

The first question relates mainly to the accountability of the subsidiary agency to the minister. To what extent is this through the ministry or is there a direct accountability link to the minister? The relative responsibilities of the ministry head and the agency head may not be clearly defined in some cases. In other cases, the signing of a performance agreement between the agency head and the minister, with the ministry advising the minister on negotiations on the agreement, suggests direct accountability of agencies to the minister (United Kingdom).

The second question is whether officials are responsible and thus accountable only to the minister, or whether they are accountable also, or for some specific matters, to the legislature. This is the same issue as the responsibility of ministers to the legislature, which appears to be of particular concern in Westminister-style governments. (In many other countries, officials are not considered in any way answerable or accountable to the legislature.) Is the minister responsible and thus accountable for everything his officials do? There is strong conventional support for the view that officials are not accountable to the legislature and that ministers *are* responsible for everything that officials do (United Kingdom). But some legislatures have expressed a different view (Australia). Resolution of the issue is complicated by the informal arrangements under which officials frequently appear before legislative committees.

The practice of granting agencies substantial operational autonomy and clearly designating them as responsible for outputs may suggest some changes to the traditional notion of ministerial accountability. It may suggest, for example, that the agency head, not the minister, is accountable to the legislature for particular aspects of performance, or at least that the minister's accountability is lessened.

Both of these unresolved issues have a parallel in some countries in respect of the responsibilities of the boards of statutory corporations or government business enterprises. Given the board's substantial autonomy and, in some cases, responsibilities set out in legislation, there is direct accountability of the board to the legislature rather than only to the minister(s) as the shareholder(s).

Evaluation of the reforms

Strengthening aggregate expenditure control

The evidence suggests that the reforms have assisted rather than detracted from aggregate expenditure control. Budget targets are not self-executing, nor is it always within the grasp of the government to meet them, no matter how strong its determination. In pursuing stated fiscal norms, governments must be sensitive to the short-term performance of the economy. When recessions occur, fiscal targets will likely yield to the realities of economic conditions. Other shocks can force governments to retreat from carefully crafted fiscal objectives (the unification of Germany and the enormous cost of rebuilding and integrating the eastern sector is a prominent example). Much also depends on the short-term control exercised by the government over key variables such as interest rates, and the cost of demand-driven entitlements programmes.

OECD countries have differed substantially in their fiscal performance measured against the targets they set for themselves. Leaving aside the recession that unfolded in the early 1990s and had not yet fully run its course in all countries when the present study was prepared, some countries out-performed their targets and some did significantly worse. Japan and the Netherlands were among the countries in the first category; Italy and the United States were in the second. The message about the need for belt-tightening in hard times may lose effectiveness in repetition. By the early 1990s, global targets were institutionalised in the budget practices of many OECD countries, but they were somewhat less influential as guideposts to budget policy and actions than they had been in the mid 1980s. It should be expected, however, that as the current recession takes its toll on budget balances, the subsequent recovery will bring renewed emphasis on stringent targets as a means of fiscal consolidation.

The real issue here is the extent to which the reforms have contributed to strengthening aggregate expenditure control. There seems no evidence to suggest that they have weakened it. The experiences suggest rather that they have:

- helped bring about a greater focus on medium-term aggregate budget targets;
- helped in ensuring that micro or programme decisions are consistent with or made in the knowledge of their impact on achieving these targets;
- helped to achieve budgetary control at agency level, through cash limiting arrangements;
- given managers additional tools with which to achieve these targets, particularly flexibility.

Improving Performance

No detailed assessment has yet been made of performance improvement resulting from the reforms. Such an assessment would, in any case, require some broad assumptions about cause-effect relationships. Nevertheless, there is considerable evidence of individual agencies successfully "doing more with less" and of significant improvements in efficiency and service quality. Making broad assessments on improvements in programme effectiveness is clearly more difficult. In the case of some commercialised organisations, there are relatively clear indications of performance improvements covering all aspects. Where once they required regular injections of central budget funds to support operations, this is no longer the case and some have become profitable enough to allow them to return dividends (see box for example of Australian Department of Administrative Services).*

The rationale for incentives has been virtually the same in all countries, although relative emphases have differed. The translation of increased managerial freedom into permanent changes in management practices and better performance rests on two key assumptions.

---

* This and other examples are discussed in more detail in *Internal Markets,* Occasional Papers on Public Management, Market-Type Mechanisms Series No. 6, OECD, 1993.

Australian Department of Administrative Services (DAS)

Prior to 1987, the DAS provided a large range of services to other government departments (printing, property, transport, etc.). A process of commercialisation beginning in 1987 included devolution of funding to client agencies, the release of agencies from obligatory use of DAS services and the restructuring of DAS services into separate units operating with clear commercial objectives (such as full cost charging, and profitability and rate of return objectives).

As part of early evaluation of results, DAS commissioned a reconstructed financial history" of its businesses on a consistent basis for the period 1987-88 to 1990-91 inclusive. It indicated:

- an imputed financial operating loss of A$120 million on turnover of A$1.2 billion was reduced to near break-even level over the period;
- a reduction in staffing levels of some 34 per cent, with further reduction planned;
- increased real revenue per employee at a weighted annual average of around 5 per cent p.a. (against an estimate for the Public Service as a whole of 3 per cent p.a.)

While most of the businesses have yet to earn a fully satisfactory "rate of return" on funds employed, no budgetary appropriations have yet been required to subsidise operations.

Assumption 1: Incentives (both positive and negative) will improve performance

This assumption is in broad agreement with the considerable amount of research done in management over the last two decades, which suggests that the organisational climate or corporate culture has a profound impact on performance, in virtually every type of institution. This implies that the clearer, results-oriented accountability implicit in the reforms is a move in the right direction.

It is also generally accepted that "climate" and "organisational culture" need concrete manifestations in terms of rewarding appropriate behaviour. The recent interest shown by countries in supplementing institutional with personal incentives demonstrates a view that institutional incentives may be insufficient to achieve the desired objectives.

The significance of recent experience as an indicator of the success of incentives and performance improvement cannot be regarded as wholly conclusive at this stage. This results from:

- the difficulty of drawing valid conclusions about performance mainly or solely from expenditure performance; and
- the possible lack of sufficient signals/incentives that reinforce the risk management approach inherent in a focus on performance.

On the relationships between expenditure reduction and performance improvement, a key government objective has been to reduce or contain public expenditure. Savings achieved through increased performance (efficiency and effectiveness) are clearly the most desirable reductions. Efficiency gains, as opposed to reductions in outputs, are the least likely to encounter organised resistance within the electorate. This means that there is considerable pressure to achieve expenditure reduction through increased efficiency. In practice, institutional incentives are geared to both objectives. However, setting targets strictly in terms of expenditure reductions (as occurs in most cases), with only limited performance indicators available to measure changes in efficiency, results in expenditure reductions being the dominant objective. Nevertheless, a causal relationship has been postulated between expenditure reduction and efficiency (productivity) improvements. While this relationship cannot be rigorously supported, it is likely that institutional incentives have helped to implement expenditure reductions primarily by making full use of the superior knowledge of operational managers in identifying the cuts in least necessary or low priority inputs, or the least unacceptable cuts in outputs.

On the relationship between risk and incentives, there has been a tendency for line departments and agencies to be slow to relax internally the tight controls and regulations central budget offices have been moving away from. These developments might reflect prudent and rational responses to new responsibilities that are unaccompanied by an appropriate sanction and reward system. For instance, if a manager's performance is judged on the grounds of unfortunate accidents (*e.g.* "horses on the payroll", "bills paid twice") rather than on overall performance, the avoidance of risk through the institution of costly "fool-proof" procedures is a rational strategy for an individual manager, however undesirable it could be overall. Key public control mechanisms (parliamentary auditor, legislative committees, etc.) mainly focus on these kinds of errors.

Increased freedom for managers also entails increased risk, all other things being equal. The reforms require that risks be managed rather than ignored. If institutional incentives are expected to lead to more innovative managerial behaviour, it could follow that the additional risks should be allowed for in assessing performance. Taking risks into account reinforces the case for complementing institutional incentives by individual ones. However, if the allotment of rewards and penalties is based on criteria other than those promoted by the budget office, managers may end up receiving conflicting signals.

Expanding the use of incentives requires both progress in refining performance indicators, so that changed levels of performance are more transparent, and their use by other important elements of the system (*e.g.* auditors, parliamentary committees, personnel appraisal systems).

Assumption 2: Devolution will improve performance by reducing dead-weight losses associated with central controls

Regulations become outdated (*e.g.* financial limits which have been overtaken by inflation), or redundant (paper vs. computer controls). More importantly, their accumulated, combined weight can be such that nobody is really expected to know them all. (The US Government's much discussed 10 000 page Personnel Management Manual may be a good illustration.) While such dead-weight costs have not been systematically measured, their significance is widely recognised. The clear view of line managers and budget officials alike is that devolution and the removal of unnecessary prescriptive controls have reduced (or will reduce) dead-weight losses, and that this would represent a significant improvement in the use of managers' skills and time.

Conclusions and future directions

A brief summary of conclusions can be formulated as follows:
- No country is proposing any major change in the direction of budgetary and performance management reforms. However it is acknowledged by many that a compliance orientation will remain or quickly return in the absence of appropriate signals and incentives to maintain the pace of reforms.
- Short- and medium-term success has been achieved in containing or reducing administrative expenditures without a major negative impact on programmes, without extensive use of precise productivity measurements, and with limited use of individual incentives.
- The main incentives have been institutional ones that consist in relaxing controls on operational managers and allowing their organisations in some cases to retain a portion of the resources freed by increased productivity or reduced output.
- There remains some reluctance to embrace devolution, because of the perceived risks involved.
- Managers have been given the responsibility for achieving planned reduction of administrative expenditures; there is clear evidence of many individual agencies successfully doing more with less, although in the absence of fully refined performance measurement, the extent to which overall reductions result from output reduction as opposed to increases in efficiency is unclear.
- All governments have complemented the mix of top-down limits and partial deregulation with strategies to foster a more performance-oriented managerial climate, while recognising that this is necessarily a long-term process.
- Better performance measurement is essential to building confidence in a performance management approach; however, it will be as much a result of the new climate as a contributory factor.

Additional changes are probably required if the momentum is to be maintained and if the targeted structural changes are to be realised. The accumulated experience with incentives is short and, consequently, most of the conclusions are tentative. The following appear to be critical elements of strategies to further embed a performance-oriented management culture.

Finishing the job of devolution and flexibility

Constraints on operational managers remain tight in some cases. They include separate controls on manpower and salary funds; rigid barriers between current and capital expenditures; low caps on carry-overs; and continuing state-monopoly suppliers. If the basic intention of creating a managerial environment where managers have appropriate autonomy to achieve results is to be realised, the process of devolution and de-control needs rounding out. It is clear that further persuasion is necessary for some governments and legislatures to loosen the system.

Making performance count

The sanctions for bad organisational performance remain weak. The appropriate response may be the refinement of performance indicators and improved individual incentives. Nevertheless, it is important to recognise that countries have come a long way in, at least, not sending the wrong institutional signals. Efficiency is no longer penalised by reductions in future budgets.

As regards incentives, it may be illusory to expect great changes from institutional incentives alone: all the more so since those incentives are of immediate relevance only to the very top managers. On the other hand, the costs in terms of money and time of introducing monetary rewards can be high. In addition, public sector experiences with various forms of individual incentives are inconclusive as yet, and research in the private sector has cast some doubts on the capacity of monetary rewards to shape behaviour (see Chapter 16).

Improving performance measurement

Significant conceptual and practical difficulties remain in the way of adequately measuring performance. Performance information must therefore be used carefully in forming judgements, and, in particular, in a positive way (fixing a problem) rather than a negative way (assigning blame). The proper use of indicators that are necessarily imperfect requires caution and judgement.

Given these difficulties and recognising that there will always be limitations on performance measurement in the public sector, it could be fruitful: *i)* to give more importance to indicators arrived at by consensus; *ii)* to experiment with the assessment of organisational strengths and weaknesses when performance measures are ambiguous or unattainable. Nevertheless, developing performance information in which all parties can have reasonable confidence is a key to directing the public sector away from compliance towards performance. It is particularly important in reorienting external reviewers such as auditors and legislative committees, who may otherwise encourage a return to a compliance-dominated approach and the retention of detailed central controls within agencies.

In measuring performance in terms of effectiveness, the limitations on the number of programme evaluations that can be realistically carried out and effectively used may make it preferable, in countries that do not have an institutionalised system for regular evaluations, to conduct them on a selective basis, with an opportunistic approach and with customised incentives.

Selectivity in budget targets

In most of the countries studied, expenditure reduction targets have been uniformly applied. It is generally recognised that uniformity penalises the already efficient, thereby running the risk of generating perverse incentives. So far, this problem has been considered minor. In the future, given the unfolding of changes in managerial behaviour and climate, it may not remain so. This reinforces the case for both individual incentives and the use of a wider array of performance indicators, since both provide for increased selectivity.

Chapter 15

MARKET-TYPE MECHANISMS ASSESSED

Introduction[1]

Market-type mechanisms (MTMs) encompass all arrangements where at least one significant characteristic of markets is present (competition, pricing, dispersed decision-making, monetary incentives, and so on). This definition excludes the two polar cases of traditional public service delivery and complete privatisation. MTMs are mixed strategies where a substantial amount of collective decision-making and management remains alongside markets elements.

MTMs are key instruments in OECD countries' efforts to change public sector management. The objectives pursued with MTMs, as with other instruments, include raising productivity to better control public expenditures, improving accountability relationships, and increasing flexibility and responsiveness. Levels of effort, emphasis, and priorities differ markedly among countries.

Yet differences among countries' reform strategies are perhaps greatest when it comes to MTMs. Some countries have placed systematic use of MTMs at the heart of their reforms. Other countries are still studying the extent to which they want to use them. Still others are implementing significant changes that involve a *de facto* expansion of MTM but without reference to an explicit market model.

The most common instruments mentioned in current discussions of MTMs include: user charges, internal pricing, internal markets, contracting out, vouchers and their equivalents, the creation or modification of property rights, intergovernmental contracts and joint public/private financing of infrastructure. This list is not exhaustive, but it covers the bulk of the arrangements for producing goods and delivering services that can be classified as MTMs and illustrates their heterogeneity.

Moreover, every item on this list refers to arrangements that could replace traditional public service delivery either with an almost pure market structure or with a system that barely modifies traditional practices. An example of the first case is contracting out all in-house building maintenance to private firms. For this, the only key decision not governed by the market is the desired level of service. An example of the second approach is contracting out the provision of X-ray services with stipulations such as uniform prices, the regulated use of specific equipment and types of personnel (with prescribed salaries and conditions), the assignment of patients to specific providers, and so on. These two MTM examples cannot be expected to generate identical outcomes.

Similarly, charging users full costs for passports and nautical charts would produce quite different results. In the first case, a monopoly exists: the MTM is hardly likely to modify the quantum of resources allocated to that activity. In the second case, customer demand will ultimately decide the quantities produced, and the level of activity and its competitive structure will be affected.

This diversity in arrangements and objectives of instruments that can be legitimately included under the MTM banner reflects the fact that each example implicitly refers to a different set of characteristics of market arrangements: competition, private ownership, profits, entry, monetary incentives, prices (their role and relationship to costs), decentralised decision-making or organisational structure.

The same diversity is evident in the rationale governing MTM use. For example, user charges are a very old device for generating revenue, rationing demand, increasing allocative efficiency, and removing some decisions from the political arena, or for attaining these ends simultaneously. In some countries, MTMs are being used within the context of an overall readjustment of the respective roles of the state and the private sector; in others, they are seen purely as techniques for improving efficiency and flexibility in an otherwise unchanged balance between the public and private sectors. Systematic contracting-out policies are an example of the first case, although they are sometimes also used as industrial policy instruments. And some quite innovative MTMs, such as the modification of property rights in fisheries or telecommunications, have been introduced as sectoral responses to technological changes or the deficiencies of previous policies.

Issues

The potential of MTMs may be ignored because of fears about some of their outcomes (*e.g.* a negative impact on equity) or because of a tendency to oversell their merits as general cures. Uncertainty surrounds several aspects of MTMs: the outcomes to be expected from introducing elements of market arrangements into the public sector; whether increasing the use of MTMs means reducing the role of the state; and the particular types of MTM arrangements and their outcomes. The value of MTMs for improving public management has to be judged by three sets of criteria: efficiency, feasibility/compatibility, and equity.

Efficiency

Their potential to enhance efficiency has prompted much of the interest in MTMs. This potential is based on the belief that mixed strategies such as MTMs can replicate efficient markets, and that the closer they resemble them, the greater the efficiency gains. However, the notion that market arrangements are inherently more efficient than non-market arrangements has been shown to be rather naive.[2] Indeed, if market arrangements were always more efficient, large and successful firms would not manage their affairs as many do now, handling the bulk of their activities in-house.

There may be considerable potential for increasing efficiency by applying MTM arrangements found in the private sector. That assertion is based on solid observations. Unfortunately, such well-grounded knowledge is limited to how certain MTMs work in very specific circumstances.

For example, the contracting out of relatively simple activities has been the subject of repeated and well-analysed experiences. At the same time, the management requirements and effects of complex forms of contracting out (sometimes entailing delicate risk-sharing among the parties involved, high costs where changing suppliers is necessary, or the threat of losing strategic expertise in administrations) are not very well known. For instance, subcontracting computer system development could prove cheaper than in-house development but result in a serious deterioration in the organisation's capacity to control and adapt its systems in the long run. In this case, one activity is handled more efficiently, but the long-term efficiency of the overall organisation is reduced.

Moreover, few empirical studies have been made of the vast domain of MTMs such as the creation of markets in rights (relating to the environment, transportation, telecommunications, or fishing), vouchers (for housing, education, or social services) and emulations of business or market practices in the delivery of public sector services, such as health, where commitments to collective responsibility are not questioned and where measures of efficiency are primitive or difficult to interpret.

Feasibility/compatibility

Implementing MTMs may involve substantial organisational changes. What these changes will be and how they will help or hinder the achievement of benefits are more difficult to predict than the behaviour of prices or other standard economic indicators. Nevertheless, the capacity to obtain desired results from MTMs will depend in part on the organisational dynamics involved. Convincing examples to this effect can be found in the complex set of reactions of actors in fields as diverse as film conservation, water management, hospital budgeting, etc., as well as in the history of contracting out under directive A-76 in the US (see Occasional Papers on Public Management, Market-Type Mechnisms Series No. 1 and 2). In all these cases, the implementation of MTM proved as important as their design, if not more important, in leading to improved performance.

As for compatibility with other policies, the main question on the agenda virtually everywhere is to what extent MTMs can further efficiency without impairing the realisation of such objectives as equal access to services (health, social insurance and services), integrity, and transmission of values (education). The key concern in this regard is equity.

Equity

It is difficult to judge whether the distributive concerns raised by the expansion of most MTMs are important in reality or only symbolically. An exception is the obvious issue of the rights of staff adversely affected, for example, by the opening-up to competition of previously protected public sector monopolies.

The rather scarce evidence to date on cases similar to MTMs, such as the marketisation of postal systems, the deregulation of airlines, and user charges in airports and telecommunications, would indicate that most of these measures had a neutral or progressive effect on income distribution. One of the key issues in the debate over the equity effects of MTMs is to distinguish between, on the one hand, claims made under the banner of equity by parties with a vested interest in the status quo and, on the other, the real, measured impacts on income distribution (and ways to alleviate them if they are regressive). Methods for carrying out these assessments are not well developed and will have to be improved. The considerable body of knowledge already available on taxation, investment evaluation, and regulation offers a good starting point.

Results of PUMA studies

The results described here are those of the studies carried out within the PUMA programme of work on MTMs. Three general conclusions for MTMs as a whole are described in the paragraphs that follow. Results relevant to specific MTMs are then set out in subsequent sections.

In designing MTMs, the deliberate inclusion of as many basic features of competitive markets as possible is likely to maximise efficiency gains. This is the case when prices reflect costs, when quantity adjustments are allowed, when information-seeking and decision-making are left to those whose interests are immediately at stake, when prices have a significant influence on output, and when forms of contract and organisation can adapt to circumstances.

Opting for MTMs that closely resemble market arrangements is a less risky strategy than grafting on only a few aspects of market arrangements or private sector practices. That is not surprising, whether in terms of economic theory or of managerial common sense. Market outcomes are predictable, generally speaking, but not when isolated elements of private practices are incorporated into a large public organisation.

Obtaining improvements through the use of MTMs is never automatic, fast, or painless. Even in the clear circumstances described above, implementation requires time and resources. Business-style behaviour cannot be distilled into a few instant recipes. Training has proven to be crucial. Learning how to operate internal markets takes time. Markets do not just emerge; they are social arrangements whose creation takes place in a political arena and whose "technical features" are complex and require negotiation. Pressures for change in other parts of the system are bound to arise, as in the case of accounting practices at both extremes of the range of MTMs studied ("open" internal markets and hospitals); the same holds for complex contracting out *vis-à-vis* contract regulation.

The distributive effects of MTMs are probably less marked than feared in terms of income/wealth groups.[3] None of the PUMA studies revealed any significant regressivity. However, fears of adverse distributive impacts can threaten the viability of MTM projects. The design and implementation of MTMs can both reduce opposition to them and ensure fairness and efficiency by providing for compensation and mitigation. Even at that limited level, establishing who gets hurt and by how much is not a trivial operation: claims by self-proclaimed "victims" can be misleading (as evidenced in the case of pollution and fishing rights). Such measurements are nevertheless both necessary and feasible.

Vouchers

There were few formal voucher systems appropriate for study given their recent launching (*e.g.* in education and training). However, numerous government funding schemes are vouchers in all but name (*e.g.* student loans and scholarships at university level, on-site training subsidies, the explicit calculation of housing allowances within welfare payments). The PUMA study highlighted the key features of a well-established instrument which, in the above-mentioned cases, is no longer a subject of controversy.

The US housing voucher programme is regarded as an unequivocal success. The programme structure is simple: the funds are appropriated annually by Congress (for a five-year period), allocated to the various housing markets and administered by local authorities. Applicants are listed according to rent burden, level of income and quality of housing, with those worst off heading the list. The available funds are then distributed according to need until the appropriation has been spent. The value of the voucher equals the difference between 30 per cent of income and an estimate of the cost of adequate housing in a particular market. Provided the selected lodgings are deemed adequate by the authorities, recipients are entitled to the voucher for five years, subject to annual verification of income. They do not have to spend all their additional income from vouchers on housing nor restrict their choice to lodgings whose rent is at or below the ceiling, nor do they have to change residence.

Designed to help low-income earners, the programme has reached the target population as well as, or better than, the supply-side or rent supplement alternatives, and has done so at lower administrative cost and with greater real income benefits to the recipients. Total outlays under the programme have been tightly controlled, its

113

scope is being expanded, and fears that subsidies would end up in landlords' pockets through price increases have not materialised. Difficulties experienced by recipients in finding appropriate accommodation have been limited to a few markets where regulatory rigidities are considerable.

The vouchers, in providing an incentive to look for accommodation and negotiate with landlords, make recipients responsible for functions they can perform more efficiently than administrations – especially when they exercise freedom of choice in competitive markets. The mix of controls and the tenant's freedom of choice act as incentives to maintaining and upgrading the housing supply, on both the landlord and tenant sides. Housing vouchers are not a universal right nor an entitlement; the annual appropriation remains discretionary, facilitating tight budgetary control.

The UK quasi-voucher scheme formed an integral part of the Income Support System. Under the scheme, funds were provided as a means-tested allowance for people in residential care and nursing homes, leaving the private sector to perform the key role of meeting the demand for facilities. The amount of the quasi-voucher, frequently revised over time, was influenced by the level of care and services provided. The scheme, which began in 1985, was replaced in 1993 for new residents by a scheme that included an assessment of need as well as an assessment of means. The old system still applies for people who were living in registered homes on 31 March 1993, immediately before the Community Care programme came into effect.

On one side, quasi-vouchers for people in residential accommodation produced some of the results expected from that type of instrument as market providers quickly expanded to meet demand. On the other side, it proved difficult to control total costs and distortions appeared in terms of meeting both the preferences and needs of recipients. This had the effect of encouraging residential care as opposed to domiciliary care.

The cost control problem arose from three sources:

– being part and parcel of the income support system, the voucher was an entitlement, the only constraints being the number of requests by people satisfying the means threshold and the number of places available;
– the very dynamism of the expanding industry catering to these needs meant that publicity stimulated demand;
– a ratchet effect seems to have operated: once a recipient was in a home, it proved politically impossible to stop or reduce the subsidy and extremely difficult to resist pressures for improved quality or cost increases.

Distortions in meeting the preferences and needs of the elderly arose because, by its very nature, the programme provided assistance *only* for meeting the costs of nursing homes and residential homes and not for possible alternatives such as sheltered housing and domiciliary care. The two problems are linked insofar as nursing and residential homes are the most expensive of the options available.

As a means of empowering consumers of publicly funded services, and of thereby stimulating supply-side improvements in the quantity and quality of these services, vouchers can be expected to do the following:

– Lead to rapid supply adjustments, except in cases where barriers to entry or expansion continue to exist (regulations that distort prices and quantity, monopolies, key proprietary technology, and so on). Gauging the importance of such obstacles entails little more than applying established analytical techniques borrowed from industrial organisation.
– Increase total expenditure if vouchers embody new entitlements. This effect is not to be attributed to the use of vouchers *per se,* but to the new entitlement character of the benefits, since changes in their cost are difficult to predict in almost any situation.
– Allow recipients to search more efficiently for the services they want than is the case with traditional public supply, provided reasonably competitive markets exist or can be expected to develop. They are also likely to generate positive income effects, all the more so if vouchers are means tested.
– Reduce administrative expenses (*e.g.* cost of search for accommodation, allocation of clients) and the cost of implementing relevant policies.

Internal markets

Internal markets refer to the systematic emulation of market conditions in the provision of services produced by and for central administrations, such as printing, fleet and real estate management, consulting and legal services. The difference between internal markets and contracting out is that public employees continue to operate the service using public sector capital, instead of their activities being assigned to outside contractors. The PUMA study focused on cases where the supplying units no longer enjoyed general budgetary appropriations and were at least partly exposed to outside competition, and where customers and suppliers enjoyed substantial managerial and purchasing autonomy.

The main benefits of this type of MTM are significant productivity increases and substantial changes in the amounts and composition of services purchased. Together, these result in a reduction in overall expenditure. There remains some uncertainty as to the exact amount saved, chiefly because of the following difficulties: adequately circumscribing the costs associated with a new system based on different accounting principles; taking transition costs into account; and clearly separating productivity gains from the savings attributable to changes in the quantity or structure of consumption.

Internal markets can be seen as an extension of the general trend towards the devolution of authority within administrations. To some extent, internal markets offer an alternative, and in some cases a complement, to performance measurements. It is very difficult to measure performance or productivity in activities such as consulting, legal services, and fleet management. Subjecting these operations to market discipline provides crude but robust bottom-line indicators and facilitates adjustments and the redeployment of the resources devoted to them.

Full internal markets can constitute a stable solution or a useful intermediate step towards full contracting out, depending on policy preferences. The fact, too, that explicit internal contracts are increasingly being used as a general mode of ensuring the accountability of managers is further evidence of the wider scope for internal markets.

The commercialisation process calls for a number of reforms:

- substantial investment in training, for both the supplier and the customer (efficient commercial practices differ from the simplified images that sometimes prevail in administrations);
- a revamping of accounting practices to ensure fairness compared to private sector suppliers (charges for the use of capital, taxes) and proper costing and control of in-house units established to supply services to departments;
- a clear distinction between commercial activities and those performed for other purposes at the request of the government (met by specific appropriations);
- the establishment of a proper capital base and financial structure;
- substantial reductions in personnel arising from increased productivity.

The potential efficiency gains of internal markets are appreciable. Moreover, the rationale for internal markets as a mode of operation within the public sector is the same as the one underlying the widespread reforms of the status and control of public enterprises in a large number of countries over the last decade.

Markets in property rights

The PUMA study focused in particular on the use of markets in property rights in fisheries in Australia, Canada, Iceland, and New Zealand. The design of this MTM is simple in the case of fisheries. The government determines the total allowable catch and parcels it (through grants to fishermen) into Individual Tradeable Quotas (ITQs), *i.e.* rights to catch a percentage of the total. Although the maintenance of the state's prerogatives over common resources makes these rights slightly less absolute than property rights, individual holders can sell or lease them, partly or completely, with a minimum of administrative fuss. The enforcement of catch limits relies on reporting by ITQ holders, backed up by controls at dockside and at processing plants.

The main achievements of creating markets for fishing rights have been:

- a reduction in the number of fishermen and vessels in an industry where excess capacity had been endemic, which was both a cause and a consequence of the previous regulatory regime;
- no increase, and in some cases a reduction, in the costs and difficulties of policing total catch limits, as compared to previous arrangements;
- a decrease in administrative and programme costs, largely through the reduction in excess capacity;
- a substantial rise in the resource rent accruing to fishermen, meaning they earn higher incomes from their activity.

ITQ systems are successful – compared to the regulation of activity and effort (vessel size, equipment, area, length of season, and so on) – because they eliminate the perverse incentives of this type of regulation. For instance, global limits on catch size were an incentive to overinvest: since no fisherman could know in advance when he would be told to stop, it was rational for him to maximise his equipment and activity. Shortening the season exacerbated this phenomenon. The rent from the resource was dissipated and the claims for protection and subsidies increased. ITQs, on the other hand, allow fishermen to behave like rational firms. There is no intention in the countries studied to abandon ITQs and return to the previous regime.

Although the experience with them is much less extensive than with ITQs in fisheries, property right markets in pollution control (essentially under the guise of tradeable emission rights) seem able to deliver similar benefits. They are systematically superior to command regulations in terms of encouraging adaptation, minimising transitional disruption and costs to firms and the economy, and ensuring fairness. However, they involve rather complex institution-building and legal frameworks.

Markets in property rights are a highly promising device, in spite of their apparent novelty in most contexts. This is especially so in the management of common goods (fisheries, the environment, radio frequencies, and so on) and state-controlled assets (such as airports and forests). Their main virtue is their contribution to bringing about structural adjustment, since they provide a self-correcting mechanism eliminates the need to create additional regulations (or expenditure programmes) because the industry has "adapted" to the existing regime, or because the regulations have been overtaken by technology or innovative operators.

In this respect, the way in which they bring about efficiency gains is akin to that pertaining to housing vouchers: it is much easier for the state to obtain desired results when the people involved are asked to act in their own interest and when the incentives systems are such that collective and individual objectives can be pursued simultaneously.

Complex contracting out: information technology

One of the most striking features as regards contracting out information technology (IT) is that systematic cost comparisons between in-house and contracted-out activities are rare. This situation can be ascribed to the cost and difficulty of establishing valid points of comparison for non-repetitive operations, and to differences between public and private accounting systems. When faced with complex non-recurrent tasks, such as major investments in system development or a need for very specialised skills over limited periods, the real choice for IT managers in the public sector is not between contracting out and doing the work in-house, but between contracting out and not getting the job done.

Several factors account for this. First, the rapid and continuous expansion of the IT industry generated relentless upward pressure on remuneration for specialised skills; the inherent rigidities of wage determination in the public sector resulted in persistent problems in recruiting and keeping the required skills. Second, a major upgrading programme or systems development project typically constitutes an investment which is both labour/ skills intensive and of a limited duration that is often difficult to predict. The difficulties that all public services face in handling such demands, whether in the early stage of expanding resources or at the later stage of running them down, have encouraged the systematic use of outsourcing. In that respect, IT is not very different from large construction projects or military procurement.

When large system development is contracted out, the issues seen to play a significant role in the management of contracts are the same as those identified in the literature on the economics of organisation and on transaction costs. The main problems and opportunities concern:

– the contractual structures capable of handling risk satisfactorily, both the technical risks and those arising from the differing interests of the parties to the contract;
– the management implications of such contractual structures;
– the crucial importance of perspective, which shows up in the definition of critical or strategic systems and which greatly influences which activities are to be contracted out.

Within the same government there are sometimes significant variations in the policies on contracting out of different departments, even as regards activities with confirmed potential for efficiency improvements. This suggests that rigidities and turf protection play a role in artificially reducing the amount of contracting out and that the instrument is underutilised when not powerfully supported by the centre.

As regards contractual structures for handling risks, the constraints surrounding the public sector's traditional contracting procedures appear to deprive it of some of the main methods used by the private sector for handling risk efficiently. In the private sector, contractual relationships run the gamut from "pure market" to partnership with suppliers. "Pure market" involves arm's length transactions for very specific jobs, making repeated and maximum use of competition to obtain the best prices. Partnerships involve a great deal of trust, sophisticated harmonization procedures, wide sharing of information, and relatively long-term commitments cemented by client-specific investments or mutual shareholdings.

Standard public sector procedures in most countries tend to locate the options of contract managers at the "pure market" end of the spectrum, although experiments with various forms of partnership are being carried out. Traditional public sector control in favour of error avoidance and strict compliance with regulations reinforces the tendency towards trying to shift all risks onto the contractor. This considerably limits the possibilities of benefiting from the various forms of partnership, the potential of which is corroborated by its extensive and growing use in the private sector.

This situation seems to go hand in hand with findings regarding the management of contracts: not only are public sector IT managers more restrained than their private sector counterparts but the tradition of rigid market relationships seems to have led to an underestimate of the time, resources, and skills needed in complex contract management.

On the question of perspective, the evidence suggests that contracting out IT challenges central authorities directly. It is received wisdom, and observed behaviour in the private sector, that critical activities are not contracted out. However, what constitutes a strategic activity is more difficult to ascertain in the public sector, and legitimate differences of appreciation are probably unavoidable between those judging the critical nature of activities from a government-wide perspective and, for instance, local management and IT managers. If the strategic activity is vital to the survival of the organisation, it is inevitable that in some cases the organisation will be unwilling to contract it out, even if it would be desirable to do so from the standpoint of the public sector as a whole. This applies both to the complex activities discussed here and to the entire public sector.

In general, contracting out IT operations has demonstrated the potential for economies in the public sector. There is also evidence indicating that contracting out may impose clearer discipline on managers, forcing them to plan and control resource use more rigorously. However, in order to exploit fully the potential of this MTM, there seems to be a need for more flexibility in regulatory regimes and practices.

Emulation of markets in hospitals

In the countries studied (Belgium, France, Germany, UK), the public nature of the health sector is regarded as sacrosanct. That is not the case of other areas in which similar MTMs are applied, such as the creation of internal markets in administrations responsible for printing, consulting, or building management. As regards these types of internal market, deciding whether to replace them by contracting out or privatisation depends largely on results.

In the absence of reliable output measures and prices that reflect relative scarcity, the hospital sector and the health system in general have to be analysed on the basis of producers' activities and of their internal logic. The term ''efficiency'' has unavoidably different meanings according to actors and perspectives. For the rational hospital manager, no matter how good, to be efficient can easily mean something different from what budget offices, the health ministry, or the government considers to be efficient. For example, it could mean ensuring that the hospital's doctors are well known in the community, that the hospital has the most sophisticated equipment, that its budget is adequate and increasing appropriately.

MTMs observed in hospitals included business practices similar to those used in the private sector (Belgium, France, Germany) and the explicit introduction of competition among hospitals (UK).

Private sector practices

Included in this category of market emulation are the following:

- investments in management know-how and techniques;
- the structuring of establishments on the model of cost and profit centres;
- the introduction of detailed analytical accounting methods capable of reflecting the consumption patterns of hospital service;
- the formulation of strategic plans by establishments or departments; and
- the abandonment of detailed, centralised budgetary controls in favour of making establishments and their managers accountable for internal resources allocation.

The reasons for introducing these practices were, first, to improve expenditure control and, second, to enhance the flexibility and efficiency of institutions. The underlying rationale is the division of tasks: professional managers are given responsibility for economising resources, while the medical profession devotes itself to patient care. The object of the exercise is to ensure that the expansionist (and inflationary) rationale of a management guided solely by medical imperatives is counterbalanced by a professional management that is as cost-conscious as in a private firm and speaks the same language as the supervisory authority. Strengthening local management techniques and expertise is particularly important insofar as the supervisory authorities cannot or will not exercise close control from a distance and have adopted some form of global budget.

Most of these changes are still taking place. For instance, as regards the introduction of cost accounting by diagnostic group, the practices studied are in the course of being developed.

The main example of this type of MTM is the recent UK health reform. This explicitly established competition among hospitals as a decentralised mechanism for reallocating resources. It created a market-type link between the loads and effectiveness of a hospital and its access to public funds. An internal market was created within the health service by transforming local health authorities and general practitioner groups into purchasers of hospital services on behalf of their patients. Since the notion of profit does not apply, it is replaced by incentives linked to the size and growth of the establishment, its prestige, and the performance of its managers and professional staff. Hospitals are given the possibility of enjoying a very large degree of autonomy as regards the techniques and approach they adopt for the management of all their resources.

This market is purely internal. It is designed to guide the allocation of resources within the system and not to regulate the total volume of resources allotted to the health service or even to the hospital sub-system. The prices that hospitals charge their customers act as the markers for reallocating business among different suppliers of hospital services. The prices must reflect all the relative costs of the different establishments, including capital charges. The equivalents in the market economy are internal transfer prices within large business groups, when those are allowed to reflect costs, as in the auction system utilised by General Motors for choosing the factory in which a particular model will be produced.

At first sight, reforms that give priority to practices borrowed from private firms differ markedly from those in which competition among hospitals predominates. However, they may yield similar end results. In the case of adopting practices of private firms, hospitals can be subjected to real market-type controls to varying degrees, depending on the use the supervisory authorities make of the signals transmitted. The same applies to the UK regime, where the outcome depends on the extent to which the authorities allow ''automatic'', decentralised reallocation mechanisms to operate through the competitive process they have established.

The paradox is only apparent. For example, in a regime like that in France, in which very sophisticated indicators of costs already exist or are being put in place within a framework of managerial autonomy for hospitals and global budgets, political decisions about the total volume of resources allotted to the sector could be dissociated from decisions about the allocation of resources within the sector. That would call for a system of local spending limits under which managers are penalised for breaches.

In that kind of framework, it is perfectly conceivable that the allocation of funds among establishments may be entirely and automatically determined by relative cost indicators – taking into account, of course, the limits imposed by the capacity and location of each establishment. Such a regime of market emulation could, in theory, produce results akin to those pursued by the UK reforms, since it is driven by similar competitive forces.

When all is said and done, the divergences observed relate less to the potential of the MTMs used than to how they are used. These observations clearly illustrate the real significance, potential, and limits of MTMs in a public health service.

The introduction of private sector techniques and expertise alone made a very modest direct contribution within the framework of reforms aimed above all at controlling costs. Borrowing the methods of the private sector can also go against the goal sought, at least in the short term. That is not necessarily surprising, since it is quickly appreciated that supervisory authorities and political decision-makers must be ''managed'' as particularly important ''clients''. Hence, it is only natural that the management experts brought in have also used their skills to circumvent supervisory constraints, have demonstrated a certain aptitude for playing local politics, and have encouraged and exploited the complexity of cost calculations (at which they are extremely proficient).

Private sector practices can contribute to efficiency and probably enable the system to adapt more readily to evolving needs and technologies, in the medium and long term. However, their effects on expenditure control are less certain. That might also be true, to some extent, of the MTMs that entail the creation of internal markets, as in the UK. Unlike normal markets, they do not operate as a self-regulating mechanism over the total resources available to the sector. Preliminary evidence suggests, nevertheless, that they do have considerable potential for allocating available resources more efficiently among establishments, for generating productivity gains, and for improving capacity utilisation. The size of this potential of efficiency gain, however, remains largely unknown.

Consequently, the effects of the MTMs studied (importing business practices into establishments and creating an internal market among hospitals) cannot be predicted with confidence until it is known how authorities will use the signals that these MTMs generate. However, the encouraging results already achieved could be interpreted as good omens for the future.

Concluding remarks

The results of the studies confirmed for more novel MTMs what was known for more classic market-type instruments. MTMs are useful tools: they economise resources, serve as benchmarks for performance, and facilitate change. Their adverse distributive effects appear very limited, when they exist at all. Indeed, it is striking that MTMs are being used successfully in delivery of programmes to the poor.

They are also demanding tools whose application should be considered as investment and, therefore, require the same skills in design and implementation, and the same care for adequate funding, as any major institutional investment requires. MTMs are certainly not magic recipes.

A glimpse into the future

It is not yet possible to assess statistically the extent of use of MTMs in OECD countries. The impressions gathered in PUMA work are that they are not as uniformly discussed and used as were the commercialisation and privatisation of state-owned enterprises over the last decade. The explanation for this slower expansion provides some indications of the obstacles to be overcome for their maximum use:

- questions about the efficiency contributions of mixed strategies such as MTMs;
- concerns about the compatibility of MTMs with other objectives of state intervention, such as equity, social integration, community life;
- the power of vested interests operating in protected environments, including groups within the public sector (vouchers opposed by teacher unions; markets in property rights opposed by firms believing that they could enjoy preferential treatment under a regulatory regime and by traditional regulatory bodies; competition being depicted as antiprofessional by the medical and social professions; market testing or contracting out opposed systematically by insiders; etc.);
- the novelty of many MTMs, and the attendant perceived risk, as well as the conceptual and institutional innovations that are often needed to combine both the political and markets mode of decision.

MTMs are tools, not goals. Their attraction stems from their capacity to help reach key targets such as responsiveness, economy, flexibility, and self-correction of systems for public services. If the capacity of markets generally has been increasingly recognised, it is only in a few countries that their legitimacy as a mode of providing public services (all or in part) has been sufficiently strong to enable a systematic attempt to expand MTM use in a continuous fashion, by appeal to efficiency, equity, and choice. In other countries, the introduction of MTMs has been driven by fiscal restraint and sectoral problems where other solutions have proved ineffective.

Overall, it is unlikely that this pattern will change much in the near future, although the reduction in the perceived and real risks of innovative MTMs could encourage expansion in their use.

Air transport deregulation, the opening-up of telecommunications to competition, the erosion of postal monopolies, were all daring experiments a few years ago, in a handful of countries. They are now accepted ways of achieving public policy objectives. The daring MTMs of today (private provision of infrastructures, vouchers, systematic market testing or internal markets) could very well become the standard procedures of tomorrow.

NOTES

1. This chapter is based on a PUMA study of MTMs that focused on assessing instruments that could be considered innovative in a substantial number of countries, while having solid track records in others. Two of the most frequently encountered MTMs, user charges and simple contracting out, were not covered, since there was already a solid body of knowledge on the efficiency gains they yield and the conditions for achieving them. The overall findings are reported in *Managing with Market-type Mechanisms,* OECD, 1993. The assessment approach of the study is set out in an annex to the chapter.

2. See, for example, Coase, 1960 and Williamson, 1990.

3. That is, in terms of negatively affecting the poor; this of course does not mean that groups such as employees of public monopolies would not be affected.

PUMA WORK ON MTMS: ASSESSMENT APPROACH

The general approach to the PUMA examination of MTMs involved the following three steps, illustrated in Figure 4:

– Identifying the specific design, environmental and implementation conditions of an MTM (the OBSERVED MTM box).
– Specifying the characteristics of market arrangements whose outcomes are predictable; the relevant ones here are those which would prevail if arrangements as close as possible to pure market arrangements had been put in place instead of the mixed strategy of the observed MTM (the MARKET BENCHMARKS box).
– Using observation to explain the differences between the observed and expected results. This involves knowing how MTMs have evolved through time and why it was necessary to modify their design or implementation (the DIFFERENCES box).

This series of steps forces the specification of the relevant benchmark market arrangements and clarifies the rationale of the MTM involved. It indicates on what grounds the MTM was expected to generate specific outcomes and on what known properties and conditions of market arrangements it was based. The differences between the predicted outcomes and the observed outcomes have then to be explained. The differences may be attributed to the environment in which the shift to MTMs took place (*e.g.* if the markets involved are non-competitive); some specific characteristic of the design of the MTM (*e.g.* the absence of price or quality competition); or techniques used or obstacles overlooked in their implementation (*e.g.* the high transition costs of contracting out or the behaviour and power of front-line managers).

Figure 4. **Framework for assessing the potential
of market-type mechanisms**

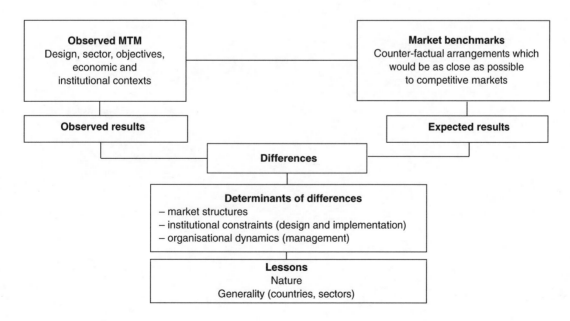

Source: OECD.

When applied to MTMs introduced essentially to obtain efficiency gains, this approach is quite simple: it amounts to determining whether and to what extent the conditions existed for an MTM to produce close to market results. The first line of the DETERMINANTS OF DIFFERENCES box refers to this operation. The empirical findings are likely to support generalisation.

The second and third lines of the same box (DETERMINANTS OF DIFFERENCES) refer to more complex questions. As mentioned above, managerial and implementation dynamics have still not been modelled precisely. This is true also of the influence of what are known as institutional constraints. These can range from rigidities in pay policy or the power of vested interests leading to biases in the design or implementation of MTMs, to the multipurpose nature of some MTM initiatives (*e.g.* better services to all or certain groups combined with lower costs and more challenging working conditions for employees).

The programme sought to take account of these sets of rather "soft" factors, although they make the generalisation of findings more delicate. If those factors were avoided the result would be to highlight what is clear at the expense of what is important. The efforts now being made in so many countries to improve public management through the use of MTMs do involve risk and uncertainty and do face such messy realities as the simultaneous interplay of economic, managerial, institutional, and political factors.

The last step in the approach was to establish the extent to which the findings could be generalised. This entailed dealing with two dimensions: international and intersectoral. With regard to intersectoral transferability, the limits depend on how well the characteristics of those sectors not specifically covered by the programme are known. For instance, how can the lessons learned from modifications of property rights in fisheries be applied to telecommunications, transportation, or forestry? With respect to the international transferability of the lessons learned, the programme assumed that such evaluations were best left to the public sector managers who have an intimate knowledge of how their national conditions differ or resemble those where the experiments took place. The contribution of the PUMA work in that respect was to distinguish reliably between replicable market features and conditions, on the one hand, and institutional idiosyncrasies, on the other.

Chapter 16

CHANGING PRACTICES FOR MANAGING PEOPLE

Introduction

This chapter provides an overview of recent and current changes affecting human resource management (HRM) in the public sector, focusing mainly on central government organisations. It seeks to identify the main reform trends, to compare and contrast approaches to reform in different countries, and, to the extent possible, to assess the impacts of changes in HRM. The point of departure for the analysis is the broad agenda of structural and managerial reform that OECD governments are pursuing in the public sector: the central questions addressed concern the implications of this reform agenda for the management of people; whether HRM policies and practices are changing in ways that are consistent with the aim of building a more productive, performance-oriented, and responsive public service; and whether these reforms are having the desired effects.

The discussion is based on information collected and analysed over the past several years as part of the Public Management Committee's programme of work on public sector human resource management. An important source of information has been an assessment of HRM reforms undertaken by PUMA in 1993-94.* To the extent that this assessment has not been completed at the time of writing, the analysis may be somewhat partial in places. There is also some unevenness in the coverage given to different countries as a result of the varying amounts of information at the Secretariat's disposal. Every effort has been made, nevertheless, to give a balanced account of reform trends.

The chapter is structured as follows: the next section discusses the implications of public management reforms for HRM and identifies other influences; following this, the main reform trends and strategies are examined; subsequent sections provide an analysis of the main developments in HRM, focusing on devolution, accountability and performance, the development of skills and abilities, and pay and employment practices; the final section draws some conclusions concerning progress with HRM reforms and outlines how OECD countries see their priorities in this area in the coming years.

The term "human resource management" or "HRM" is used throughout this chapter to cover the entire range of policies and practices for managing people. The choice of this term, rather than "personnel management", is intended to signal that many of the changes being pursued in the public sector appear to imply a more strategic approach to the management of people, a focus on changing cultures and values, and the introduction of systems and practices that have much in common with HRM practices that have been widely adopted in the private sector since the 1980s.

The term "public service" is used here to refer to departments, agencies and other organisations of central government administrations, thereby excluding state and local government and other parts of the public sector. In practice, of course, the composition of the public service varies considerably among countries.

The implications of public management reforms for HRM

A move from centralised to decentralised management environments and a closer focus on results are two crucial ingredients of the new approach to public management. Typical elements of reforms include a greater focus on performance; increased value for money; enhanced managerial flexibility; strengthened accountability; a client- and service-oriented public sector; a strengthened capacity for developing strategy and policy; a positive

---

* The assessment is based on a questionnaire to all OECD countries and case studies in selected departments and agencies in nine countries (Australia, Canada, Denmark, France, Netherlands, New Zealand, Spain, Sweden and the United Kingdom).

impact on economic efficiency; and changed relationships with other levels of government. Other analysts have identified similar themes in public sector reform agendas (*cf.* Hood, 1991).

Many of these reform trends have important implications for the way people are managed in the public service, and they will provide the framework for much of the discussion in this chapter. In particular, they imply:

– increased devolution of responsibility for HRM to line departments and agencies and to line managers within departments and agencies, in accordance with the commitment to more decentralised management environments and increased managerial flexibility;
– HRM policies and practices that contribute to the development of the desired focus on results and that include accountability mechanisms appropriate to a decentralised management environment – for example, performance management systems and improvement of the skills and abilities of staff;
– the development of pay systems, conditions of employment and working practices that are consistent with the quest for increased managerial flexibility and value for money, and a focus on performance;
– the use of HRM instruments to build a stronger client/service orientation – for example, building this orientation into staff training and development and performance management systems, and moving responsibility for managing people closer to the point of delivery of services;
– a change in the role of central management bodies from detailed regulation and control of HRM to a focus on policy and strategy.

Private sector management techniques have been a major source of influence on the public sector. Characteristics of the approach to HRM that has gained prominence in the private sector since the late 1970s include: policies driven by top management but delivered by line managers; the integration of HRM strategies with business strategies; a comprehensive and coherent approach to employment policies and practices; an emphasis on organisational culture and values and on the attitudes and behaviour of employees; rewards differentiated according to performance, competence, or skill; employee relations unitarist rather than pluralist, individual rather than collective, and high trust rather than low trust; organic and decentralised organising principles, with flexible roles and emphasis on team work (Armstrong, 1992, pp. 22-23). There are evident parallels between the elements included in this model of HRM and the HRM measures implied by the public management reform agenda.

While public management reforms have important implications for the management of people, other factors are also influential. Labour market pressures, demographic factors, considerations of equity and social justice, and the need to hold down public expenditure all impinge on HRM policies. The public sector, like the private sector, is having to adapt its employment practices to ensure that it can recruit and retain a skilled workforce as the population structure ages. In addition, all OECD governments subscribe to the principle of providing equal employment opportunities (EEO) in the public service. Finally, budget constraints create a continuing pressure to cut costs, of which staffing costs are a major element.

HRM reform trends and strategies

Annex 1 provides an overview of the main HRM reforms undertaken in OECD countries since 1980. With a few exceptions, reforms have been implemented mainly since the late 1980s and are continuing in the 1990s. Countries where the current reform process was initiated in the first half of the 1980s include Australia, Denmark, and the Netherlands. Canada and the United States also implemented important reforms in the early 1980s and late 1970s, respectively, but these were not part of a continuous process, and new reform phases have been initiated in both countries in the early 1990s. Most countries have adopted a gradualist approach to reform: often there has been a series of changes at intervals of several years and implementation is in many cases ongoing. An exception to this pattern is New Zealand, where the strategy has been one of radical and rapid change.

Established systems of public service employment and pay, existing practices for managing people, and the industrial relations context, among other factors, will inevitably exert an important influence on reform priorities and choices, as will the broader economic and political contexts within different countries. The analysis in Part A of this report demonstrates that there are, nevertheless, some clearly identifiable public management reform objectives and trends common to many OECD countries. There have similarly been a number of common trends in respect of HRM reform.

The devolution of responsibility for HRM from central management bodies to line departments and agencies, accompanied by devolution within departments and agencies to line managers, was cited by half of OECD countries in the PUMA comparative study as one of the key reforms of the recent period. However, as will be discussed later, the extent of devolution has varied greatly among countries. It is also important to note that in some countries devolution does not appear to be on the agenda to any great extent. The introduction of devolved budgeting arrangements for line departments and agencies, involving the consolidation of salary costs and administrative expenditures, has been a crucial element in devolution of HRM by enabling the substitution of an overall budgetary control for detailed controls over staff numbers, classification, and, in some cases, pay. Changes affecting pay systems have figured prominently, with an emphasis on gaining greater flexibility and relating pay determination more closely to productivity, performance, and recruitment and retention needs. Here again, reforms have varied greatly in extent, ranging from quite radical changes in some countries to more marginal adjustments in others. In a number of countries important changes have also been made to job classification structures and industrial relations systems. Other areas frequently targeted for reform have been staffing policies and processes and employment practices: systems of recruitment, promotion, and deployment, and arrangements for terminating employment have been rationalised and made more flexible in many countries; appeal and grievance procedures have been streamlined; more flexible working arrangements have been introduced; and the use of contract employment has been expanded, including in several countries the introduction of contract arrangements for senior public servants.

While the HRM reforms set out in Annex 1 reflect, to varying extents, the new approaches to public management, there are important differences in scope and strategy. In only a handful of countries have changes in HRM been an integral part of the overall public management reform strategy from the outset and the underlying reform principles applied consistently to the management of people. This is most evident in Westminster-type administrative systems (Australia, Canada, New Zealand, the United Kingdom, but less so Ireland) and, to a somewhat lesser extent, in the Nordic countries and the United States. Reforms in many continental European countries also reflect objectives such as increased managerial flexibility and a stronger performance orientation, but, in general, changes in HRM have been less comprehensive and less consistently integrated in reform programmes. In some countries, for example Germany and Japan, the influence of new management ideas on public service HRM appears to have been marginal and HRM has not been a priority area for reform. A detailed exploration of cross-national variations in reforms cannot be made in the space of this chapter, but some examples will illustrate different reform patterns.

Australia and New Zealand are perhaps the best examples of a highly integrated approach to HRM reform: in both countries, HRM has been treated as an integral part of a comprehensive public management reform agenda; HRM reforms have been pursued consistently over a period of years; and a wide range of interrelated HRM changes has been implemented, comprising many of the public management elements identified in the previous section of this chapter. At the same time, there are some crucial differences in the reform strategies pursued in these two countries, especially in terms of the way devolution of HRM has been handled.

HRM has also occupied a prominent position in the public sector reform strategy in Sweden, with the highly decentralised nature of the administration providing a framework for significant devolution to agencies and other state institutions. Labour market pressures and, recently, the severe economic crisis have exerted a strong influence on the reforms, resulting in a focus on pay reform and, recently, methods of reducing public sector employment. By contrast, some other aspects of HRM, such as performance management, have received less attention. Denmark and the Netherlands have also integrated HRM into their reform programmes from the start, focusing particularly on the devolution of responsibility to line management; however, the reforms to date have been less comprehensive than in the three countries just discussed.

Although Canada has also given HRM reforms a high profile since the early 1980s, the measures implemented have not been part of a consistent programme of public management reform and they have often been undermined by cost-cutting exercises. The Public Service 2000 programme, launched in 1989, signals a more coherent reform strategy involving a range of HRM initiatives, although implementation has encountered some difficulties. A more structured approach has also been adopted recently in Finland and Norway in the context of public management reform programmes launched in the early 1990s, and comprehensive changes in HRM systems are being made with the aim of moving to a more devolved and flexible management environment.

The United Kingdom has adopted a different approach to HRM reforms. Although a fundamental transformation of public service management has been in progress since the early 1980s, changes in HRM have been seen more as an inevitable consequence of structural and financial management reforms than as an integral part of the reform strategy from the outset. As a result, although significant HRM reforms have been implemented, they have come later in the reform process. Moreover, while the aim of increasing managerial efficiency and effectiveness has led to the introduction of more flexible, performance-oriented pay and personnel systems, the high priority attached to reducing public expenditure has meant that the flexibilities have been tightly controlled. For this reason, the devolution of HRM to Departments and Executive Agencies has been approached with caution, although a more comprehensive devolution of pay and other HRM matters has recently occurred.

In many countries, HRM reforms have been a series of separate or only loosely connected measures taken over time. The changes have been more partial and more *ad hoc* than those outlined in the preceding paragraphs, with the main impetus often coming from pressures or dysfunctions in existing systems. Nevertheless, the objective of moving to a more efficient, results-oriented administration is also generally a theme in the reform efforts. For example, although HRM occupies a central position in the public service modernisation programme launched in France in 1989, the aim is not a complete revision of the HRM regime; instead, the focus is on training and development, more effective planning of personnel and skills requirements, and encouraging departments to involve their staff in service improvement projects as a way of motivating them and developing more effective work practices. A reform of the public service pay grid, begun in 1990, was motivated primarily by the need to correct imbalances that had gradually appeared in pay structures for some groups rather than by the objectives of the modernisation programme.

In Spain, the transfer of responsibilities from central to regional and local governments, efforts to modernise the old bureaucratic structures, and public finance constraints have been the main factors shaping HRM reforms. This has led to a concentration on the following issues: improving staff mobility; rationalising grading, career, and pay structures; establishing structures for union representation within the public service; and stricter controls on hiring and wages. The task of modernising the administration is seen as requiring time and a step-by-step approach rather than sudden, radical change. The situation in Spain, and in Portugal, Greece, and a number of other countries, illustrates clearly that there is no single, ideal path to reform. A major challenge for these countries has been to replace complex and often fragmented pay and personnel systems with more transparent, uniform rules and standards. In some important respects, therefore, increasing the efficiency and effectiveness of the public service is seen as requiring more, not less, standardization and centrally defined rules and procedures. Consequently, although ministries and agencies are being given more freedom in HRM, devolution tends to be much more circumscribed than in some of the countries discussed earlier.

Other examples of a more limited approach to reform are provided by a number of countries: the United States, where the main preoccupations until recently have been the performance management system and reforming the federal pay system; Ireland and Italy, where the need to put the public finances on a sounder footing led to a concentration on staff reduction measures, although a number of managerial initiatives have been launched since 1990 in both countries; Belgium, where an improved personnel planning system and training of personnel have been seen as key ingredients in building a more efficient, target-oriented administration; and Austria, where efforts have concentrated on mobility and motivation of staff. In Japan, the emphasis has been on reduction of public service employment and working-time reforms. For Germany, the main concern recently has been incorporating the new Eastern *Länder* into the public service system.

Some general aspects of these different reform patterns are worth commenting on briefly. The existence of a comprehensive plan for the reform of public sector management clearly increases the likelihood that a high priority will be attached to changes in HRM and that such changes will be pursued in an integrated way. However, this is not a sufficient condition, as evidenced by the United Kingdom, where much more importance was attached initially to financial management reforms. Strong and sustained support at a high level is an essential condition for effecting change. While public servants have in many cases demonstrated a willingness to embrace reforms, there are often powerful forces for inertia, which can undermine reform efforts and impede the underlying transformation in the public service culture. In the countries where most change has occurred in HRM there has been continuing high-level political support for reform, bolstered by an influential unit or agency within the public service.

The strength of public sector unions and their stance on reforms is another important element. For example, in the Nordic countries the high level of unionisation and strong tradition of seeking consensus has meant that gaining union support and involving them in the reform process have been essential. For some other countries, such as the Netherlands and Spain, one of the aims of the reforms has been to give the unions a negotiating rather than a consultative role concerning pay and conditions of employment, thereby bringing industrial relations in the public service more into line with private sector practice and binding the unions to the reform process. In New Zealand and the United Kingdom, less importance has been attached to gaining the support of the unions; indeed, a reduction in the role of collective bargaining has been viewed as important for increasing managerial flexibility.

Altering the terms and conditions of employment of public servants where these are laid down by statute clearly poses considerable problems in some countries, although for others legislative change appears to present less difficulty. The reform process may be more straightforward where the situation of public servants is not defined by statute.

Although the preferred strategy in many cases has been to apply reforms to the public service as a whole, particularly where legislative change is involved, some countries have chosen to undertake pilot studies in selected departments or agencies before generalising the reforms. This has been done, for example, in Austria and France, where selected departments have developed new approaches to HRM on an experimental basis, and in the United States, where "demonstration projects" have been run in a number of agencies. An additional aspect of strategy is whether reforms have been imposed from the centre or whether they have depended more on the voluntary involvement of departments and agencies. Although there has been a mixture of the two approaches in many countries, central imposition has tended to dominate. An exception is France, where the modernisation plan firmly places the emphasis on mobilising management and staff to develop local initiatives for improving HRM on a voluntary basis. There also tends to be more reliance on persuasion in countries where the public service has traditionally been less monolithic, and central HRM bodies consequently less powerful, as in the Nordic countries and the Netherlands.

Analysis of main developments in HRM

Devolution of responsibility for human resource management

Although the principle of managerial devolution has been espoused in varying measures by many countries, its application to the management of human resources has been quite uneven, both in terms of the aspects of HRM that have been devolved and the extent of devolution in different countries (see Annex 2). The variations observed can be attributed to the place of HRM in the overall scheme of public management reforms, to concerns about the impacts of devolving responsibility for certain aspects of HRM, and to competing HRM reform objectives.

Concerns about control over personnel costs and, for many countries, a wish to maintain some degree of unity and uniformity in the public service weigh heavily in decisions about devolution. Consequently, pay determination and decisions concerning staff numbers and job classifications are often kept under the control of central management bodies, or are devolved later and less fully than other aspects of HRM. Other matters that tend to be subject to greater control from the centre include codes of conduct and disciplinary procedures, redundancy arrangements, basic terms and conditions of employment, and equal employment opportunities.

For the most part, devolution has concerned the operational aspects of HRM, with responsibility for determining policy retained by central management bodies. What this means in practice depends on how detailed the policy framework is. The management of people within the public service has traditionally been highly regulated in most countries. The simplification of rules and procedures and the introduction of more flexible policies are an important corollary of devolution. Notions as to what the appropriate balance is between managerial flexibility and regulation will, of course, vary from one public service to another. However, in many countries the emphasis is shifting from detailed controls to providing looser guidelines and defining basic standards that must be observed in managing people. At the same time, efforts are being made to develop a more strategic role for central management bodies.

Even where formal devolution of authority is limited, the development of more flexible HRM policies and less cumbersome procedures can be important in providing managers with increased room for man16vre. For example, although pay determination has remained centralised in most countries, in an increasing number of public services various types of pay flexibilities are provided to departments and agencies. There is also a trend in many countries to introduce more flexible policies in areas such as recruitment, termination of employment, and grading and classification.

Common features

Some common features of the devolution of HRM can be observed in OECD countries. Devolved budgetary frameworks that provide single running-cost appropriations for salary costs and other administrative expenditures have provided an essential underpinning for the relaxation of central controls over key aspects of HRM such as staff numbers, classification and grading, and pay. Such frameworks generally contain some provision for the carry-over of funds, which can provide important flexibility in managing staffing levels. Even with devolved budgeting, most countries have preferred to maintain central control over pay. Only in Australia, New Zealand, Sweden, and the United Kingdom has pay determination been devolved to any significant extent, and in these countries, at a minimum, an overall limit is applied on pay expenditures. This may be bolstered by some involvement of central management bodies in pay negotiations, as in New Zealand, in setting negotiating parameters, as in the United Kingdom, or in negotiating basic pay increases against a service-wide pay and grading structure, as in Australia.

The most extensive devolution of HRM has occurred in New Zealand and Sweden. In New Zealand, the 1988 State Sector Act made heads of government departments individually accountable and transferred to them the role of employer, with responsibility for most aspects of HRM policy and practice. The Act also obliges them to be "good employers", requiring them, for example, to appoint staff impartially, to provide opportunities for staff development, and to develop and implement an Equal Employment Opportunity (EEO) programme. The State Services Commission (SSC), which formerly held all HRM authorities, has retained an important operational role only in relation to the employment of top management and pay determination. Since 1992, authority for negotiating pay and other conditions of employment has been delegated. The SSC remains the agent of government in this regard, laying down broad policy parameters, participating in negotiations, and approving departmental agreements.

In Sweden, agencies and boards control most aspects of their HRM policies and operations since 1985, with very little intervention by central bodies. The Ministry of Finance sets the salaries of directors general of agencies and advises on the recruitment of these officials. A service-wide system of pay and grading was abolished in 1990, leaving agencies free to determine their own pay structures and to set pay individually for their employees. Devolution has progressed to the stage where, from 1994, agencies are free to decide the balance between centralised and decentralised negotiations and whether they wish to be represented by the National Agency for Government Employers. Wage developments are controlled only through an overall budget constraint fixed by the Ministry of Finance.

In Australia, the responsibility for most HRM operations has been transferred to heads of government departments since 1987, in the context of a central policy framework and certain legislative requirements. Central control over pay and conditions of service, employment structures, classification standards and base grade recruitment reflect a concern to maintain a common, service-wide core. In general, however, the focus from the centre has shifted from detailed controls to looser guidelines and defining basic standards on policy direction, key values and service-wide principles that must be observed while leaving individual departments with much room to man16vre. The restructuring of pay awards and a reform of the classification system have contributed to providing departmental managers with more flexibility. Since 1992, a system of workplace bargaining by departments and agencies has been implemented.

In Denmark, government departments are responsible for most aspects of their HRM, and there has been a concerted effort in recent years to achieve further devolution from departments to service delivery agencies. Pay determination remains largely centralised for the time being. In the United Kingdom, devolution of HRM was, until recently, carried out agency by agency rather than across the service as a whole. Legislation passed in 1992 provides for a more comprehensive approach, enabling the delegation to departments and agencies of authority for determining terms and conditions of employment. From 1994, the responsibility for pay determination has been devolved to larger executive agencies (covering more than half the civil service).

Canada has also pursued a more active policy of devolution recently, and a concerted effort is being made to replace central rules with guidelines. The introduction of operating budgets for departments in 1993 enabled the removal of centralised controls over staffing levels. In the Netherlands, a policy of managerial devolution has been pursued since 1984, and there has been a considerable shift of authority to departments. Central control has, however, been maintained over staff numbers, the determination of pay and conditions of employment, and some aspects of classification and grading. With the introduction of running-cost budgets from 1994, controls of staff numbers are due to be removed in 1995. Since 1993, pay determination has been decentralised to eight sub-sectors within the public sector, of which the civil service is one; negotiations for the civil service remain centralised under the control of the Ministry for Home Affairs. Devolution in other countries has been on a more limited scale.

In all countries there is a continued involvement of central bodies in the appointment, pay, and classification of top public service positions and in managing the performance of top officials. Often this also applies to senior management positions below the top level. In addition, there is usually some involvement of the government in top-level appointments. Such arrangements are dictated by several factors, apart from the obvious wish to maintain control over the filling of top and senior positions:

– there is an important element of accountability;
– in most cases, there is a desire to maintain a degree of cohesion at senior management levels and to ensure that a collective public service perspective is not lost as a result of increased devolution;
– there may be a wish to manage mobility and deployment of the senior group;
– usually, some central involvement in management development is considered desirable in order to ensure that senior managers possess certain common skills and abilities and as a way of inculcating a core of common values; and
– often, there is a wish to separate the senior group from the rest of the public service for purposes of pay fixing and to establish individualised pay arrangements.

The devolution of HRM does not give managers a totally free hand in matters such as hiring, firing, determining employment conditions, and so on. There are always laws or collective agreements that set basic standards and procedures that must be observed, although, as noted earlier, there are important variations among countries in the degree of regulation. Usually, central management bodies maintain an oversight responsibility in areas such as equal employment opportunity, health and safety, "good employer" requirements, and so on, although, again, there are significant cross-national variations in the content and exercise of such responsibilities. The interviews carried out in selected departments and agencies in several countries in the context of the PUMA assessment of HRM reforms suggest that, for the most part, managers do not find "good employer" requirements unduly restrictive. Rather more concern was expressed about regulations and controls affecting recruitment, termination of employment, classification and pay; even in some of the countries where there has been extensive devolution of these matters, it was felt that procedures could be simplified and made less time-consuming. This was especially the case with procedures for terminating employment.

Where there has been significant devolution, the size of central management bodies has diminished appreciably. In Australia and New Zealand, the number of staff in central bodies concerned with HRM has been halved. There has also been a significant reduction in Sweden and the United Kingdom and some reduction in the Netherlands. Elsewhere, there appears, as yet, to have been little change.

As noted earlier, an expected corollary of managerial devolution is that central bodies take on a more strategic role in relation to HRM. Some of the developments just discussed in terms of oversight responsibilities and ensuring that broad parameters for pay developments are applied represent a transition from detailed control to broader strategic concerns. However, the extent to which central bodies have developed their strategic role varies greatly among countries. This has perhaps received most attention in Australia, where the Public Service Commission has been committed to the development of an integrated HRM framework that can assist departments and agencies to manage their staff more effectively and to ensure the dissemination of an agreed set of managerial values throughout the public service. High priority has been given to strengthening strategic management from the centre in Canada and New Zealand, and this is also a concern in the Netherlands, Finland, and the United States. The Danish Ministry of Finance has recently published a White Paper setting out a general HRM policy for central government, intended to provide a basis for policy development in departments and agencies. Less attention has been devoted to this issue in many other countries. This is of particular interest in the case of Sweden and the United Kingdom, given the extensive devolution that has occurred. Current developments in both countries suggest that the public service will become more fragmented in the future, and that the role of the centre will be primarily concerned with ensuring that public expenditure and performance targets are met, and with identifying and disseminating advice and best practice, rather than with formulating strategies for the management of people.

Experience with devolution

Where line departments and agencies have gained extensive freedom from central control there has, in turn, been a significant shift of authority for HRM to line managers. Devolution appears, on the whole, to have been pushed further down the line in Australia, New Zealand, and Sweden than in other countries. HRM practices in these three countries, as well as in Denmark, the Netherlands, and the United Kingdom, are in striking contrast to those in force prior to the reforms, although the situation varies from one organisation to another within countries. In Canada, because many of the changes are so recent, it is more difficult to judge their effects.

The more limited devolution from central management bodies in other countries means that line managers have not gained as much freedom. Nevertheless, many countries report an increase in managerial flexibility compared to the situation several years ago, as a result of a reduction of central involvement in areas such as classification, control of staff numbers, and recruitment. The spread of performance appraisal and flexible pay arrangements administered by line managers has also contributed to giving them a more active role in managing their staff, although the degree of discretion built into pay and appraisal systems varies considerably among countries (*Private Pay for Public Work,* OECD, 1993).

The assumption underlying the devolution of HRM to departments and agencies is that it will enable them to manage their staff actively to improve individual and organisational performance, rather than simply applying given rules and regulations. This implies a much closer integration of HRM with organisational goals and strategies than has been typical of public service organisations in the past. In all countries involved in the PUMA case study, the organisations examined acknowledged the importance of integrating HRM with corporate strategy; this concern is also evident in the reforms being undertaken in many other countries. Equally, however, most organisations felt they still had some way to go in achieving a satisfactory level of integration.

The case studies revealed extensive programmes of reorganisation of departments and agencies in many of the countries covered, in response to the pressures to increase efficiency and to improve service to clients. Many of the organisations studied had recently implemented major structural and managerial reforms, or were in the process of so doing. The flexibilities available in HRM have been important in enabling organisations to tailor their reforms to their particular needs, and distinctive organisational cultures have begun to emerge. In most cases, key aspects of the reforms have been flatter structures, reorganisation of the way work is done, simplified and more flexible job descriptions, and major efforts in training staff. Less has generally been done in terms of altering pay and grading systems, although departments and agencies in New Zealand, Sweden, and the United Kingdom have begun to take advantage of the freedom available to them in this area. Where rigorous performance and accountability frameworks have been established for heads of agencies, as in New Zealand and the United Kingdom, this has created an incentive to use HRM flexibilities more actively in an effort to improve the agencies' performance.

Although restructuring has provided opportunities for the use of HRM flexibilities, it has also put considerable pressure on both line managers and HRM specialists and has, in some respects, diverted attention from HRM. As reorganisations have generally involved staff reductions, much energy has had to be channelled into managing redeployment and redundancy. This has meant that managers have focused less on other aspects of HRM and that staff have tended to be unreceptive to HRM initiatives. In many of the organisations examined, the only other aspect of HRM that had received consistent attention was training and development of staff to adapt to new working methods. Ongoing pressure on departments and agencies to deliver efficiency gains has also had a mixed effect on the use of HRM flexibilities, often creating a tendency to focus on cost-cutting measures and a reluctance to invest resources in developing new HRM policies. Nevertheless, where reorganisations had been completed and there had been time for changes to become established, attention was turning to other aspects of HRM and a more comprehensive, strategic approach was gradually taking hold.

Corporate planning systems are in operation in most of the case study organisations, although in many instances this is a recent development and in several countries (*e.g.* France, Spain) it is by no means generalised across the public service. HRM usually features in corporate plans; at a minimum, this involves planning staffing needs in the light of organisational objectives, including the training and development needed to ensure that the necessary skills are available in organisations. Actions aimed at achieving a stronger client focus and improving standards of service are a common feature of corporate plans, and where such objectives are articulated they usually provide a basis for a statement of associated training activities. With the exception of Australia, New Zealand, and the United Kingdom, other aspects of HRM are less frequently addressed in corporate plans and less clearly integrated with corporate strategy, and even in these three countries the situation varies greatly among organisations. The extent to which HRM objectives are translated into specific targets and strategies that are then followed through in business planning and performance planning systems is also highly variable.

Performance management systems are key instruments for linking the management of people to organisational goals and strategies. Yet, in many cases, they are not used to their full potential in this context. The most highly developed system is in New Zealand, where the system of purchase contract agreements between departments and the government makes it imperative that departmental outputs are tightly managed and that the work of employees contributes to the desired outputs and only to these outputs. The logic of the system is that there is a chain of performance agreements, with specified performance targets derived from corporate objectives, from the chief executive downwards through senior management to middle management and staff. In practice, departments have found that it takes a considerable length of time to establish performance management systems and that achieving the desired linkage between individual, unit, and corporate target-setting is far from easy. Nevertheless, the attention of both management and staff has generally been brought to focus much more clearly on the achievement of specified outputs and on service standards.

Performance management systems have also been developed across the public service in Australia, Canada, and the United Kingdom; however, senior management in the organisations studied felt, in many cases, that the linkages between individual and organisational performance objectives were not strong enough, and merited further investment of time and effort. Performance management is much less developed in the other countries studied, although a number of departments in the Netherlands have recently established systems whereby senior and middle managers have performance contracts based on corporate goals. Some of the organisations examined in France and Spain have also put similar systems in place.

Problems affecting devolution

The devolution of HRM has not been without its problems. In all of the case study countries, both line organisations and central management bodies felt that managers had often been slow to take full advantage of new flexibilities. There appear to be a number of reasons for this. HRM tends to be viewed by managers as more complex and time-consuming than financial management, and there is often a tendency to push problems back to the centre of the organisation. Technical managers in particular are slow to accept HRM responsibilities, seeing their role more in terms of their specialist skills. In many cases, line managers lack the competence to deal with HRM; new skills are required, but training in HRM has not always accompanied managerial devolution. This has been identified as a serious shortcoming in many of the organisations studied. Managers may also be reluctant to accept HRM responsibilities if their delegation has been partial, feeling that they cannot successfully tackle some aspects while others are outside their control. The extent to which managers are held accountable for their performance of HRM functions can have an important influence on their handling of these functions.

Corporate HRM services have also had to adapt to the new situation. Where there has been genuine devolution to line managers, central HRM units within departments and agencies have been reduced in size and their role has shifted towards planning and policy development, setting guidelines, advising line units, monitoring, and developing HRM strategy. However, these new roles are not always being performed adequately: for example, monitoring has in some cases been hampered by a failure to develop management information systems; line managers complain of a lack of clear and easy-to-apply guidelines; the development of a more strategic role has often received insufficient attention; and there are some concerns that HRM expertise has been lost at the corporate centre without being replaced at the line management level.

For large departments and agencies in particular, devolution raises the issue of the loss of an overall HRM focus and the concept of a core, mobile, professional public service. This issue emerged, for example, in some organisations in New Zealand and Sweden where there had been extensive devolution to line units. In New Zealand, there was also a concern in some departments to ensure that the degree of independence given to line units did not jeopardise the accountability of the chief executive for the department as a whole. Such concerns have directed attention to the need for corporate management structures to ensure the oversight and co-ordination of HRM and for guidelines within which line units can operate flexibly. This said, different organisations have very different conceptions of what the appropriate degree of independence is for their line units.

Central management bodies have also expressed some concerns. While there is no wish to draw back from the devolution of HRM, most countries wish to ensure that increased devolution does not result in the loss of a service-wide perspective or a dilution of principles and values that are considered fundamental to the public service. There are also concerns about whether line departments and agencies are held sufficiently accountable for their performance of HRM functions, and about the capacity of central bodies to monitor compliance with service-wide requirements in areas such as "good employer" practices and equal employment opportunities. Reaching a balance in practice between devolution and due attention to service-wide goals and values is difficult, and in all countries the balance between control and devolution continues to evolve.

Benefits of devolution

Countries that have implemented significant devolution of HRM are generally very positive about its value. Advantages reported by central management bodies include the following:

- it permits the implementation of organisational change and a greater diversity of practice between departments;
- it enables departments to recruit and retain staff more easily and to manage their people efficiently;
- it has increased the responsibility and accountability of managers and enables them to manage their resources more actively;
- it has contributed to a sharper focus on efficiency and effectiveness, with positive impacts on service delivery and responsiveness;
- it has improved the link between policy and execution.

Positive assessments of the impacts of devolution are generally borne out by the experience of line departments and agencies, as discussed above, although none of the organisations examined had undertaken a formal evaluation of HRM reforms. Neither management nor unions (where the opinions of union representatives were sought) wished to return to the previous situation of centralised control. Concerns centred on the appropriate degree of devolution rather than the principle (in general, line departments and agencies wanted more freedom), the ability of line managers to carry out their new responsibilities and the adequacy of the training and support they were given in their new role.

Accountability and performance

HRM policies and practices have an important role to play, both in the accountability mechanisms needed in a devolved management environment and in building the desired focus on results and performance in the public

131

service. Performance management systems and accountability arrangements applying to senior managers are key factors in this context. Measures to improve the skills and abilities of staff, which are discussed in the next section, are also crucial.

The most highly developed system for holding top managers personally accountable for their own performance and that of their organisations is found in New Zealand. Chief executives of government departments are appointed on five-year contracts; have detailed annual agreements covering personal performance, departmental outputs and general management obligations; and are subject to an annual performance appraisal. A 1991 review of reforms found that this model is proving reasonably robust and effective, although it is taking time to become firmly established, and some problems have been encountered with the specification, measurement and reporting of performance (New Zealand State Services Commission, 1991). In principle, the system includes rewards for good performance in the form of performance-related pay and penalties for poor performance in the form of provisions for termination or non-renewal of contracts. In practice, performance pay has been hindered by budgetary constraints; only one chief executive's contract has not been renewed and no chief executive has been dismissed. Senior managers are also employed on five-year contracts, have performance agreements with their chief executives, and are subject to performance appraisal and performance pay.

A system of five-year employment contracts for heads of departments has been established in Australia. It is aimed at strengthening accountability, clarifying performance requirements, providing for the penalty of dismissal, or non-renewal in the case of unsatisfactory performance, and introducing more flexibility in the recruitment of top managers. The contracts do not include any provision for performance pay, although there is a loading of up to 20 per cent above the basic rate to compensate for loss of tenure. The possibility of introducing fixed-term contracts for senior managers is under review. In the United Kingdom, chief executives of executive agencies (but not usually heads of departments) are recruited on fixed-term contracts through open competition, and their pay is linked to their own performance and that of their agencies. Heads of departments in Canada are not appointed on contract, but they can be moved and removed from office at the discretion of the government. They are also subject to performance appraisal and performance pay, although it is felt that the link between the performance review and appraisal system and organisational goals needs strengthening. Sweden and Ireland are the only other countries where top managers (heads of agencies) are systematically subject to fixed-term employment contracts; and, although these systems provide for individual pay fixing, they do not include formal performance agreements, performance review, or performance pay. In Ireland, heads of departments are appointed on fixed-term contracts. However, performance pay does not apply to such appointments.

The use of performance management techniques that were originally developed in the private sector (involving individual agreements on performance objectives and development needs, and monitoring and review of performance against the agreement) has spread in the public service in recent years. Up to two-thirds of OECD countries have introduced at least some elements of performance management in the public service, although in many cases the systems are partial and still in their infancy. Formal systems of performance review and appraisal linked to performance agreements are most developed in English-speaking countries. Elsewhere, the approach tends to be less formalized and, indeed, there appears to be a view in some countries that highly developed and formalized performance management techniques are inimical to the public service culture.

Performance pay systems have been in use in the public service in Canada and the United States since the early 1980s, and have been adopted in Australia, Ireland, New Zealand and the United Kingdom at varying times since the late 1980s. In most of these countries the main focus is on managers; performance management systems for non-managerial staff are less well developed, although such systems are being developed down through departments and agencies in New Zealand and the United Kingdom. The extent to which these systems link individual objective-setting and performance review to organisational goals and service standards is highly variable. The departments examined in New Zealand had made major changes to their performance management systems, so that individual performance agreements and staff development plans are clearly geared to the achievement of corporate objectives. Several departments felt they still had some way to go in achieving the desired level of integration. Agencies in the United Kingdom also appear in many cases to have focused their systems much more clearly on linking individual performance to organisational objectives and performance targets. In the other countries in this group, individual performance appraisal is, as yet, less well integrated with organisational planning and review systems.

There is not a strong tradition of performance management in the Nordic countries, and less formalized approaches are felt to be better suited to the public service culture. Several of these countries have introduced performance discussions between managers and staff, usually on a voluntary basis. The extent to which such discussions are held varies among organisations, as does the content: the focus is often on the development of individual skills and abilities rather than performance against set objectives. In Denmark, the introduction of a performance pay system has led to more emphasis on the definition and rewarding of results that contribute to the achievement of organisational objectives. Many agencies in Sweden have developed planning systems including goal specifications down to unit level, but these do not usually include individual goal-setting. The link to the individual level is more concerned with ensuring that agencies and their sub-units have the mix of personnel and the qualifications they need to achieve their specified goals, with a consequent focus on training and development and staffing policies rather than management of individual performance as such. In the Netherlands, departments are encouraged to hold performance discussions with staff, and here is a system of performance pay. Some departments have introduced more formalized systems of performance contracts and assessment for managers, linked to organisational goals.

Elsewhere, the development of performance management has been limited. Some departments in Spain have introduced performance evaluation systems since 1992 as a basis for productivity bonuses; however, the links to organisational performance are generally weak. An exception is the National Social Security Institute, which has developed a scheme including objective-setting, performance plans, individual appraisals, rewards/penalties and individual/group performance bonuses. In France, the service-wide system of performance grading is starting to be based on objective-setting and clear performance criteria; in addition, a few departments (Equipment, Education) have introduced their own schemes within the existing framework of regulations, focusing more on individual contributions to organisational goals. Austria is developing, initially on a pilot basis, a system of staff interviews covering objectives, performance, and development needs. Portugal introduced performance appraisal in the 1980s, and a system is currently being developed in Greece.

While performance-related pay is not an essential component of performance management, it has been introduced to varying extents in a number of public services, most notably in the English-speaking countries, the Netherlands and several Nordic countries. In Denmark, the Netherlands, and New Zealand, performance pay applies in principle to all levels in the public service, but in practice the spread of schemes across agencies has been uneven and there is a tendency to concentrate the available funds mainly on rewarding the more senior levels. In Australia, Canada, Ireland, and the United States, schemes are confined to senior managers. Only in Canada and New Zealand are heads of departments subject to performance pay; in the United Kingdom, the pay of chief executives of agencies is usually performance-related. In Canada, performance pay has been suspended for several years in the context of public service pay restraint measures; in New Zealand and the United States, the operation of schemes has been hampered by budget limitations.

A previous study by PUMA suggests that many performance pay schemes are not functioning effectively (*Private Pay for Public Work,* OECD, 1993). Common problems include the appraisal of performance for pay purposes, the poor management of performance appraisal ratings and the distribution of performance pay awards, excessive standardization of schemes and control by central bodies, and insufficient funding. As a result, those covered by schemes are often unclear or cynical about the relationship between performance and pay, and feel that awards are not sufficiently large to be worth the effort. Also, management often feel that the schemes do not provide them with sufficient flexibility and discretion.

The study found little evidence that departments and agencies were using performance pay to implement their corporate strategies or to shape the culture of their organisations. In countries with highly standardized schemes, such as Canada, the United Kingdom, and the United States, agencies had little flexibility to tailor schemes to their specific requirements. In countries such as the Netherlands and Denmark, where the schemes are more flexible, the involvement of unions in pay allocation decisions and a lack of highly developed corporate planning systems worked against the strategic use of performance pay. This may be changing, however. In the United Kingdom, the pay of all civil servants except heads of departments is usually performance-related; in the case of agency chief executives, a substantial proportion of their pay depends on the achievement of the agency's key targets. In Australia, several of the departments included in our case studies felt that the individual performance pay schemes introduced in 1991 for managers were at odds with the team-work culture that they were trying to promote; the introduction of workplace bargaining in 1992 was welcomed as providing more scope for tailoring pay arrangements to organisational needs. In the United States, agencies are encouraged to develop their own schemes following the demise of the service-wide scheme covering middle managers and supervisors. The case studies also revealed examples of individual and group bonus schemes in some agencies in Spain and Sweden, with rewards linked to the achievement of work unit goals derived from corporate goals.

Developing skills and abilities

The development of the skills and abilities of managers and staff has received increased attention and is widely targeted for continuing emphasis. Commonly cited reasons for this include: the need to invest managers with the necessary skills to handle newly delegated responsibilities; the increasing knowledge and skills required by public service jobs; to develop a client focus and improve standards of service delivery; to adapt to new technology and new working methods; and to address skill shortages. More generally, training and development programmes are seen as playing an important role in inculcating new values and bringing about desired cultural change.

Virtually all OECD countries have initiated new training and development measures in recent years. The emphasis is generally on requiring or encouraging departments and agencies to develop their own programmes (and, in some countries, to devote a specified level of resources to these programmes) so that they can tailor them to their specific needs. Several countries (Australia, Canada, Denmark, New Zealand, the United States) have also been anxious to establish service-wide frameworks for human resource development, linked to the overall public service reform strategy. The development of managerial skills, especially at senior management levels, is a matter of high priority for many public services. This is generally regarded as an area in which central management bodies should take responsibility in order to ensure that all senior managers acquire the leadership and management skills that are considered essential to the success of public service reforms. In several countries (Australia, New Zealand, the United Kingdom) programmes are based on a set of core abilities that senior managers are expected to acquire. The competency-based approach is being developed across the entire Australian public service as a whole by a joint management-union training council as part of the government's national training reform agenda.

A major aim of training and development initiatives is to inculcate values and skills needed to reorientate the public service and public servants towards the provision of service to clients and concern with service standards. This emphasis is evident in many of the programmes launched in different countries in recent years. It was present in virtually all of the organisations included in the PUMA case studies, and was one of the areas where HRM was most evidently being incorporated in organisational strategies and planning processes. Line managers in these organisations were, for the most part, well aware of the importance of training and developing their staff in service skills.

More flexible, cost-effective pay and employment practices

Reforms of public service pay and employment practices are central to the aims of increasing managerial flexibility and obtaining better value for money. As noted earlier, in the discussion of reform trends, changes in these areas have figured prominently in HRM reforms in many countries.

Although details of pay reforms vary considerably across countries, a number of common reform objectives are evident. There have been efforts in many countries to gain tighter control over pay costs via changes in methods of determining general pay increases (*e.g.* the elimination of indexing; the reduction of the role of market comparisons; removal of pay linkages between different groups of public servants) and in the rules for individual pay progression (*e.g.* reducing the role of length of service as a criterion for pay progression). Some countries have linked pay increases more explicitly to increased productivity, via productivity bargaining, as in the Australian public service, or via a requirement for agencies to fund their own pay increases out of efficiency gains, as in recent pay rounds in New Zealand and the United Kingdom. Efforts to gain flexibility are reflected in provisions for greater individual variation in pay on the basis of performance, skills, or recruitment and retention considerations; flexibility for departments and agencies to reclassify positions; and variation in relation to labour market conditions for particular groups of employees or in different localities. There have also been moves in a number of countries to introduce separate pay arrangements and conditions of employment for senior managers that are more akin to those in the private sector (*e.g.* individual pay-setting, performance pay, fixed-term contracts).

While most countries have maintained unified, service-wide pay systems and centralised pay determination mechanisms, several have, as we have seen, moved to decentralised pay-fixing with the express aim of providing departments and agencies with greater flexibility to align their pay arrangements with their own operational needs and with the labour market segments in which they recruit, in the expectation that this will lead to greater efficiency. Such arrangements are spreading, although centralised pay determination seems likely to remain the norm for a majority of OECD countries. A crucial issue in this context is whether the increased managerial flexibility that undoubtedly results from giving departments and agencies more freedom to decide their own pay arrangements can be combined successfully with the control of pay costs. To date, all of the countries that have devolved pay-fixing have maintained some measure of centralised control over the total pay budget. Several have also limited the level of pay settlements.

Reforms of industrial relations systems have been undertaken in several countries (*e.g.* Italy, Netherlands, New Zealand, Spain) with the aim of bringing them into line with private sector practices and "normalizing" the conditions of employment of public servants. The New Zealand reforms, covering both the public and private sectors, removed the right of arbitration, abolished the special status in law of registered trade unions, introduced freedom of choice in industrial representation, and made the form and nature of bargaining a matter for negotiation between individual employers and employees.

More flexible and less complex job classification systems have been an important element of reforms in a number of public services. In Australia, a move to fewer, more broadly defined classifications, combined with a policy of multi-skilling, has helped to break down job demarcations, facilitate new working practices, and provide greater flexibility to redeploy staff. In Canada, a simplification of classifications is under way, with similar aims. France, New Zealand, and the United States have also undertaken reforms in this area.

There has been a range of changes in employment practices across different countries. Most common have been the introduction of more flexible working-time arrangements, measures to increase mobility, and provisions for easier redeployment. Recruitment arrangements have been simplified and made more flexible, and in a number of countries that previously operated closed career systems, open recruitment has been introduced. Flexible terms of employment, including contract employment, casual employment and part-time employment, have spread. Several countries have simplified provisions for terminating employment and laying off surplus staff, and there are moves in this direction in other countries.

In addition to undertaking HRM reforms, most countries have implemented cost-cutting measures involving reductions in the number of public service employees (via controls on recruitment or redundancy or both) and pay restraint measures.

Conclusions

New approaches to the management of people have gained ground in most OECD public services over the past decade, and especially since the late 1980s. The main impetus for change has been a recognition that improvements in the efficiency and effectiveness of the public service are closely linked to pay and employment practices, working methods, the performance and attitudes of staff, and other aspects of HRM. Increasingly, therefore, public employees are regarded as a key resource requiring careful and active management. This changing view is leading to an acceptance that managers need to be given more authority to manage their staff; that HRM should be adapted more closely to the particular circumstances of different organisations; and that more attention should be given to developing coherent HRM strategies, planning HRM needs, and developing and motivating staff.

While the extent and content of HRM reforms vary among countries, there are important points of convergence. Common features include:

- the devolution of responsibility for HRM from central bodies to line departments and agencies and to line managers;
- a greater focus on and new approaches to the management of senior public servants;
- increased emphasis on training and development and on performance management;
- the development of more flexible policies and practices in areas such as pay and conditions of employment, classification and grading, staffing, and working arrangements.

Reforms are generally aimed not only at providing managers with more discretion to manage their staff, but also at improving the skills of public servants and strengthening their commitment. Often, therefore, increased managerial flexibility is combined with measures such as greater involvement of staff in decisions affecting their work and working conditions, equal employment opportunity policies, and improved career structures. Cost-cutting measures such as pay restraint and efforts to cut public service employment have been an element in most countries, almost inevitably retarding or undermining other HRM reforms.

There are important differences among countries in terms of the degree of change that is being sought in HRM. At one end of the spectrum are countries such as Australia, New Zealand, Sweden, and the United Kingdom, where quite fundamental reforms are being pursued. At the other end are countries such as Germany and Japan, where changes have been few. Other countries are ranged at various points along this spectrum, with Canada, the Netherlands, Denmark, and Finland towards the more change-oriented end and many continental European countries towards the more conservative end. Thus, while the nature of public service employment is being radically transformed in some countries, in many others the changes are leaving the basic structures and principles relatively unchanged, at least for the present.

The influence of new public management ideas can be discerned in many countries; however, these ideas have, to date, been much more influential in the English-speaking and Nordic countries than elsewhere, and have tended to lead to more integrated programmes of HRM reform. The varying attachment to new management ideas is most apparent in the amount of decentralisation, devolution, and managerial flexibility that various countries appear willing to implement, and in the adoption of private sector management techniques, such as performance management. In most countries there is still a long way to go in terms of giving line managers authority to manage their staff. However, for some administrations, this may be a lower priority than bringing unwieldy bureaucratic structures and procedures under control and developing more transparent and rational systems for managing people.

In all countries that have devolved HRM, the balance between control and flexibility is still evolving. There are areas where central bodies are clearly unwilling to relinquish control completely; this applies especially to public sector pay, where devolved bargaining is usually combined with some mechanism for ensuring adherence to budgetary limits. There are also concerns about the balance between allowing departments and agencies the freedom to develop their own HRM practices, and maintaining some degree of unity and a collective perspective across the public service. Very few countries (Sweden and possibly the United Kingdom) appear willing to take the route of total fragmentation of the public service. Most appear committed to retaining a basic core of conditions that apply across the public service, although this may prove increasingly difficult as the effects of devolution take hold. Attempts to reinforce a collective perspective are reflected in centralised arrangements for the appointment and management of senior civil servants and efforts in a number of countries to develop a capacity in central agencies for the strategic planning of service-wide HRM policies.

Although the use of performance management techniques, especially performance review and appraisal, is spreading in the public service in many countries, such systems seem, with a few exceptions, to be underdeveloped. Linkages between individual goal-setting and performance review on the one hand, and organisational performance planning and targets on the other, are especially weak. However, managerial devolution is leading to a greater focus on this issue and, more generally, to efforts to forge a closer link between HRM and organisational goals and strategies. This is particularly evident in the increased attention being paid to the training and development of staff and to integrating training and development measures with organisational planning processes.

An issue raised at the outset in this chapter is the extent to which HRM reforms in the public service reflect the adoption of private sector approaches. Certainly, many of the elements that have been identified in private sector HRM are being adopted in the public sector, albeit to greatly varying extents in different countries. Elements such as the delivery of HRM by line managers; efforts to integrate HRM with organisational strategies; a greater emphasis on organisational culture and values; more differentiated, individualised reward systems; and a greater emphasis on team-work can all be identified in public service reforms. However, some other components of this HRM model, those relating to employee relations, are less in evidence. There is little indication in most countries of a move away from collective models of employee relations to more individualised systems. New Zealand and the United Kingdom are perhaps the most obvious proponents of a more individualised approach. However, despite legislative changes, collective relations have, for the present, remained the norm for most groups of public servants in both countries. Performance pay has often been seen as the exemplar of the adoption of private sector management methods in the public sector and as a logical component of reforms aimed at the more efficient and effective delivery of public services. Although performance pay schemes have spread, there are serious unresolved questions as to whether these schemes are operating effectively in many public service organisations.

There has been little in the way of systematic evaluation of HRM reforms. Australia and New Zealand have undertaken an assessment in the context of overall reviews of public service reforms; several other countries have conducted reviews of specific reforms. Information provided by central management bodies and line departments and agencies in the context of PUMA's assessment provides some further insight into impacts. However, many of the reforms are too recent for a full and balanced assessment, and, because the effects of some HRM reforms can take considerable time to work through the system, their impacts may not become apparent for a number of years.

The reviews in Australia and New Zealand concluded that the reforms had been well directed and had brought significant benefits that had outweighed their costs. The devolution of HRM and associated reforms in New Zealand were considered to have permitted more efficient recruitment, retention, and management of people and to have improved HRM overall in the public service. The responsibility and accountability for HRM placed upon chief executives were seen as critical in this context. In Australia, the working environment for staff had been improved by devolution, better job design, more participative approaches to work, and fairer HRM policies and practices. HRM reforms were seen by staff as critical to increasing the quality of service.

The case studies undertaken by PUMA in these two countries support this positive view of reforms. Although departments and agencies were not satisfied with all aspects of the reforms, none wished to return to the pre-reform situation, and all felt that the changes had given them much more ownership of their HRM policies, thereby enabling them to improve their efficiency. Managers were generally positive about the reforms; staff and unions, while generally supportive of the overall thrust of the reforms, had more mixed reactions. Factors such as organisational restructuring, redundancies, pay restraint, and, in some cases, a perception that line managers were not handling HRM issues competently had had a detrimental effect on staff morale and were, in the view of management, impeding the necessary cultural change. However, these problems were gradually being overcome and a service-wide survey of staff attitudes in Australia showed levels of job satisfaction and interest that compared favourably with other organisations.

Reviews by central management bodies in Denmark, Ireland, and Sweden have also been generally positive about the effects of reforms. In the United Kingdom, the fact that executive agencies have met or exceeded a large proportion of their performance targets is considered as evidence of the success of delegating HRM responsibilities.

This is not to deny that some problems have been encountered. Several issues have come to the fore in a number of countries:

- in countries where devolution has occurred on a relatively limited basis, a demand from departments and agencies for further freedoms and a perception that effective management is constrained by the limited powers available;
- a need for further devolution from the centres of line departments to agencies and regional offices;
- a concern that line managers are not making full use of the HRM flexibilities they have been given;
- concerns about line management competence and a perceived need for more training, support, and communication;
- a need for measures to hold line managers more accountable for their HRM responsibilities;
- a need for the effective monitoring of equal employment opportunities and other basic principles and standards, and a perception that this is not occurring in some countries;
- concerns that the devolution of HRM may impede staff mobility and erode the unity of the public service.

PUMA's assessment indicates that most OECD countries envisage growing emphasis on the reform of public service HRM in coming years. The most commonly identified priority is further emphasis on training and development, especially the development of management skills and abilities. Other priorities include the following:

- the development of strategic human resource management in departments and agencies;
- the need to improve the management and monitoring of the devolution of HRM and to attend to issues of co-ordination and central steering;
- securing increased mobility within the public service;
- greater flexibility and tailoring of human resource management to the needs of departments and agencies;
- more flexible pay and grading structures;
- workforce reduction and policies for exit from the public service.

These priorities indicate that the current thrust of reforms will be maintained and indeed intensified in the coming years.

MAIN HUMAN RESOURCE MANAGEMENT REFORMS 1980-1994

	Australia	Austria	Belgium
1982/3	**1983** White Paper on "Reforming the Australian Public Service".		
1984/5	**1984** Public Service Reform Act. Devolution of HRM started. SES established. **1985** Access and equity programme.		
1986/7	**1986** Staffing process devolved and streamlined. **1987** Most HRM operations devolved to departments and agencies. Public Service Board abolished. Public Service Commission established with responsibility for HRM policy. Major restructuring of classification plus job redesign.	**1986** Contract employment for senior staff.	**1986** Secretariat of State for Modernisation circulates modernisation strategy of high-priority actions. Creation of modernisation units in ministries and other public organisations.
1988/9	**1988-89** Wage restructuring linked to agreements on efficiency measures. **1989** Strategy announced to accelerate EEO.	**1988-91** Administrative Management project. **1989** EEO programme revised.	**1988** Individual appropriations to ministries for recruitment. **1989** Operation "logos": interactive process of meetings and interviews with senior civil servants to build momentum for modernisation.
1990/1	**1990** Joint APS Training Council established. **1991** Middle management development programme. SES classification structure broad-banded.	**1991** Pilot projects on personnel development and personnel efficiency.	**1990** Master training plans as management tools. Single statute introduced covering civil servants. Action plans to promote equality of opportunity. **1990-91** In-depth study of personnel requirements. **1991** New text of statute's general principles.

1991-92
Performance appraisal for SES and Senior Officer Grades.

1992/3	**1992** Workplace bargaining. Performance pay for SES and Senior Officer grades. Framework for integrated HRM. **1993** Strategic EEO plan for 1990s.	**1992** Human resource development concept launched in several agencies. Job exchange established to promote mobility. **1993** Federal Equality of Treatment Act.
1994		**1994** New classification structures to allow greater flexibility in remuneration and reduce the number of hierarchical levels.

	Canada	Denmark	Finland
1980/1	**1981** Management Category created.		
1982/3		**1983** Public Sector modernisation plan launched. First phase 1983-1985. Controls on numbers of posts in each ministry relaxed.	
1984/5	**1985** Reduction in public service personnel.		
1986/7	**1986** Increased Ministerial Authority and Accountability (IMAA).	**1986/87** Second phase of modernisation programme. Scheme for compulsory rotation of professional staff. **1987** Management training programmes. Equality of opportunity action plan.	**1987** Administrative development agency established.
1988/9	**1988** Canadian Centre for Management Development established. **1989** Public Service Reform initiative launched (PS 2000). Special Operating Agencies created.	**1988** Running cost budgets for departments and agencies. **1988-89** Third phase of modernisation programme. Emphasis on reducing public service personnel and further decentralisation. **1989-90** Flexible working arrangements. Flexible pay system.	**1988** Training programmes and consultancy projects established. Reform of pay system including productivity bonuses. **1989** Flexible working arrangements. Committee to reclassify grades. Reduction in number of personnel.
1990/1	**1990** Management Trainee Programme introduced. Human Resource Development Council established. **1991** Measures to streamline public service structures and classification levels. EEO programme. Wage freeze 1991/92. Performance-related pay for senior executives suspended.	**1990** Government management policy for the 1990s, including: performance-related pay for managers; management development; selection of managers; evaluation of managers; equal opportunity measures. **1991** New agreement on personnel mobility in ''free agency'' experiments. Further development of flexible pay system.	**1990** Results-oriented running cost budgets. Personnel Committee proposes reforms of personnel policy 1991-95. EEO plans for agencies. Personnel reduction measures. **1991** Decentralisation project launched. Taskforce on reform of legal status of public servants, to develop a uniform employment category and collective bargaining system. Performance management and management training programme introduced.

	France	Germany	Greece
			Reform of pensions system proposed. Plan to reduce number of posts in state administration by a further 5 per cent 1992-1995.
1992/3	**1992** Public service pension reform. Public Service Reform Act. Reduction in Public Service personnel. **1993** Operating budgets for departments, including personnel costs.	**1992** Performance evaluation for managers based on results.	**1992** Special personnel training project. Flexible working time. Reform of pay system 1992-95.
1994			**1994** Reform of collective bargaining.

	France	Germany	Greece
1982/3		**1983-86** Flexible working time measures, especially part-time work.	
1986/7			**1987** EEO policy.
1988/9	**1988** Decrees to widen promotion possibilities. **1989** Programme on public service modernisation launched, including more dynamic personnel management. Framework agreement with unions on continued training.	**1989** Further development of flexible working arrangements. Law to change working conditions of civil servants and judges.	**1989** Embargo on civil service recruitment.
1990/1	**1990** Agreement with unions on reforms of pay scales and qualifications, to be implemented over seven years. **1991** Deconcentration of interministerial training appropriations to regional prefects; deconcentration of some recruitment operations.	**1990** Major in-service training programme for new *Länder*.	**1990** Public sector personnel reduction plan 1990-92. Participation in training programmes compulsory for career development. **1990-92** Participation in training programmes compulsory for career development. **1991** Law on Modernisation of the Organisation and Functioning of the Public Administration and the Upgrading of Public Personnel. Recruitment suspended as part of drive to reduce public expenditure. New system of recruitment based on national competition.
1992/3	**1992** Renewal of framework agreement on continued training.		**1992** New promotion system. Performance appraisal introduced. New administrative hierarchy established. Pay freeze. **1993-95** Programme of Administrative Modernisation.

	Ireland	Italy	Japan
1980/1		**1980** Previous promotion and performance appraisals systems abolished.	
1982/3		**1983** Department of Public Service established to co-ordinate management of human resources.	
1984/5	**1985** White paper "Serving the Country Better".	**1984** Competitive examinations for promotion to managerial career group.	**1984** Management and Co-ordination Agency set up. **1985** New retirement age introduced.
1986/7	**1986** EEO policy and guidelines. **1987** Programme to relocate civil servants to regional centres. Embargo on recruitment and programme of early retirement.		**1986** Seventh staff reduction plan. EEO Law.
1988/9	**1989** Embargo on recruitment continued.	**1988** New law on staff mobility. **1989** Finance Act includes freeze on recruitment. Project to better identify staff needs launched.	**1988-89** Reduction in working hours.
1990/1	**1990** Performance-related pay for Assistant Secretary grade. Resumption of recruitment on a limited scale to fill essential posts. **1991** Flexible working arrangements. Staff reduction announced. 3-year administrative budgets for departments. **1991/93** Programme for Economic and Social Progress.	**1990** Project on "Functionality and Efficiency of the Public Administration" launched. New regulations governing right to strike in essential public services. **1991** Law on EEO.	**1991** Eighth personnel reduction plan.
1992/3	**1992** Training Initiatives Fund, introduced as vehicle for a more widespread promotion of training, needs analyses, and innovative training measures.	**1992** Reform of public service employment law; introduction of reforms aimed at controlling personnel expenditures. Freeze on new staff contracts, pay increases, and recruitment. **1993** Ordinance on rationalisation of public service departments and revision of employment regulations. Creation of agency for trade union relations of public administration.	**1992** Five-day working week system enforced. Child-care leave introduced. Special revision of compensation for employees working at headquarters of ministries and agencies.

	Luxembourg	Netherlands	New Zealand
1982/3	**1983** Administrative Training Institute created.		
1984/5		**1984** Decentralisation of public personnel policy.	**1984/92** Reduction in personnel numbers.
1986/7	**1986** Law on automatic promotion as a result of long service.	**1987** EEO policy.	**1987/88** Performance appraisal based on target-setting; performance management system; contract employment for chief executives and senior managers; formal job evaluation systems; corporate planning.
1988/9		**1988/89** Flexible salary system, including performance pay and market-related allowances. **1988/90** Reduction in personnel numbers. **1988** Management training programme. **1989** Protocol requiring agreement with unions on pay and employment conditions in place of former system of unilateral determination by employer. School of Public Administration founded for management training. Management Development Advice Centre established.	**1988** State Sector Act devolves responsibility for most human resource management functions to chief executives of departments. Performance pay introduced. **1989** State Services Commission restructured to focus on monitoring and developing government policy service-wide rather than detailed implementation of personnel policy. Decentralisation of collective bargaining begun. Public Finance Act clarifies responsibility of chief executives for outputs of their departments, and provides flexibility for input of resources, including staffing.
1990/1	**1990** Wage agreement between government and largest public service union, including modification of salary scales and bonuses.	**1991** Introduction of the concept of labour productivity in the public sector. Senior civil servant mobility scheme. Large- and small-scale efficiency operations launched. Further normalisation of status of government employees in line with private sector practices.	**1990** Public Service Code of Conduct issued. **1991** Employment Contracts Act creates new legal and institutional framework for industrial relations in public and private sectors. Major review of state sector reforms since 1987.
1992/3	**1992** Staff replacement pool created. Training courses revised. Re-entry programme for women.	**1993** Decentralisation of pay negotiations to eight sectors. **1993/94** Reassessment of rules governing personnel management – ''Towards more results-oriented management''.	**1992** Bargaining authority delegated to chief executives of departments. Bargaining authority devolved to chief executives of tertiary education institutions. Management development framework.
1994		**1994** Running cost budgets for ministries and agencies.	

	Norway	Portugal	Spain
1982/3		**1983** Performance appraisal introduced.	
1984/5			**1984** Law on Reform of Public Sector establishes basic jurisdictions and regulatory framework of every level of government for HRM.
1986/7	**1986** Policy of upward mobility – positions of adviser and project manager created. **1987** Programme of Public Management Improvement.	**1986** Secretariat for Administrative Modernisation set up.	**1986** Job evaluation systems introduced. **1987** Law regulating union representation and negotiation conditions.
1988/9	**1988** Women into Management project. Committee on proposal for new salary system.	**1988** Flexible working arrangements and EEO principle established. New recruitment and promotion arrangements. **1989** Comprehensive personnel reform programme. Reform of civil service pay system. Revision of statute of civil service senior management positions.	**1988** Rationalisation of structure of units and corps. Reform of career structure. EEO programme. **1989** Competitive entrance examinations extended to most civil service posts.
1990/1	**1990/93** Programme for Administrative Modernisation. **1990** Performance evaluation. **1991** Projects on the reorganisation and restructuring of the civil service. New, more flexible civil service pay system, top management removed from basic collective agreement.		**1990** Expansion of collective bargaining to cover annual pay increases and other matters. Manpower planning – central list of civil servic jobs. Decentralisation of HRM responsibilities to managers. Flexibility in recruitment practices. **1991** Management training plan. Pilot performance appraisal systems. Supplementary funds for improved remuneration. Government agreement includes collective bargaining.
1992/3	**1992** Increased emphasis on mobility including staff exchange schemes. Performance management introduced. Contract employment for senior staff. Flexible working arrangements. Training schemes. **1993** Readjustment and redeployment unit established.	**1992** New statute facilitating civil service mobility. Management development programmes.	**1992** Agreement with unions on modernisation of the administration and improvement of employment conditions. EEO plan. Development of medium- and long-term human resource planning. Amendment to selection procedures. Freeze on recruitment and remuneration Flexible working time. New management development programmes. **1993** EEO second plan.
1994			**1994** Employment plans to promote flexible and rational use of staff; early retirement incentives; phasing-out of tasks; greater use of part-time work.

	Sweden	Switzerland	Turkey
1982/3	**1983** Ministry of Public Administration established.		**1983** Programme of structural adjustment.
1984/5	**1985** Programme for renewal of public sector, including more flexible personnel policies. Experiment in 3-year budget frames for administrative costs. New, individual salary system for senior managers.	**1984/87** Project on increasing the efficiency of the Federal Administration aimed at saving 3 per cent of jobs and 5 per cent of working time over 3 years.	
1986/7	**1986** Management development for senior managers.	**1986** 42-hour working week as a result of efficiency project.	**1987** Directorate of Administrative Development created. Language achievement pay awards introduced. Number of hierarchical levels in administration halved.
1988/9	**1988/89** New instruction to agencies to decentralise. 3-year budget frames introduced. **1989** Flexible salary system and grading structure, flexibility in recruitment and mobility of senior executives.	**1989** Study on management control launched.	**1989** Performance evaluation introduced. In-service training increased.
1990/1	**1990** Programme to reduce national administration by 10 per cent over three years. **1991** Agreement on employment security as basis for structural reforms. Further decentralisation of HRM. Job classification system introduced as basis for individualised pay.	**1990** EEO Policy. **1991** Introduction of management control throughout federal administration.	**1990** Provision for employment of contract personnel in State Economic Enterprises. In-service training intensified. Job descriptions redefined. Retirement procedures simplified. **1991** Recruitment system centralised.
1992/3	**1992** New pension scheme for civil servants. National Institute for Civil Service Training and Development abolished. Flexible budget frames introduced, providing for increased decentralisation of HRM.	**1992/95** Pilot schemes on personnel exchanges and flexible working hours. **1992** Training and development programme, especially for managers. Directive on promotion of women.	**1992** Studies on comprehensive public personnel regime. Improvement of public service pensions.

Main human resource management reforms 1980-1994 *(cont'd)*

	United Kingdom	United States
1980/1	**1981** Civil Service Department disbanded.	
1982/3	**1982** Financial Management Initiative as first step in delegating financial and personnel management to line managers.	
1984/5	**1984** First programme of action for women.	**1984** Performance Management and Recognition System provides for performance pay for middle managers and supervisors.
1986/7	**1986** Running cost budgets. **1987** Long-term pay flexibility agreements. Performance-related pay.	
1988/9	**1988** Next Steps initiative to promote creation of executive agencies run by chief executives. **1989** 21 flexibilities for departments and agencies in fields of personnel management, pay and allowances. **1989/90** Measures to improve training of senior managers. New pay structures and frameworks for determining pay. Measures to develop more flexible framework for recruitment, management development and training.	
1990/1	**1990** Programme for Action for ethnic minority employees in the Civil Service. **1991** Treasury issues list of 40 flexibilities for departments and agencies in fields of personnel management, pay and allowances.	**1990** Federal Employees Pay Comparability Act. Human Resources Development Group established. Chief Financial Officers Act provides for increased managerial flexibility in using budgets. **1991** Compressed and flexible work schedules.
1992/3	**1992** New flexible pay agreements negotiated. Civil Service (Management Functions) Act to provide for increased delegation of HRM to line managers. New programme of action for women in the civil service. **1993** New civil service management code.	**1993** Personnel reduction plans launched. Performance Management and Recognition System discontinued.
1994	**1994** Delegation of pay bargaining to agencies. New Programme of Action for those with disabilities in the Civil Service.	

DEVOLUTION OF HUMAN RESOURCE MANAGEMENT AUTHORITIES
TO LINE DEPARTMENTS AND AGENCIES OF CENTRAL GOVERNMENT

	Policy of devolution	Salary costs [1]	Control of staff numbers	Classification/ grading [2]	Recruitment [3]	Pay determination
Australia	X	X	X	X	X	(X) [4]
Austria	X	(X)		(X) [5]	(X) [6]	
Belgium					X	
Canada	X	X	X	X		
Denmark	X	X [7]	X	X	X	(X) [8]
Finland	X	X	(X) [9]	X [10]	X	(X) [11]
France	(X) [12]				(X)	
Germany					X	
Greece						
Iceland						
Ireland	X	X	(X) [13]	X		
Italy					X	
Japan						
Luxembourg						
Netherlands	X	X [14]	(X) [15]	(X) [16]	X	
New Zealand	X	X	X	X	X	X
Norway	X				X	
Portugal					(X) [17]	
Spain					(X)	
Sweden	X	X	X	X	X	X
Switzerland					X	
Turkey					(X) [18]	
United Kingdom	X	X	X	(X) [19]	X	(X) [20]
United States	X			(X) [21]	X	

(X) = Limited devolution.

1. Salary costs included in single running cost budget appropriation.
2. With the exception of New Zealand and Sweden, service-wide grading structures and classification systems apply. In most cases, classification of senior positions has not been devolved.
3. Recruitment of senior officials generally not devolved.
4. Workplace bargaining in departments since 1992 on productivity increases but centralised determination of basic pay maintained.
5. Limited flexibility within overall system of central control.
6. Responsibility shared between Federal Chancellery and departments/agencies.
7. Ministry of Finance imposes limit on expenditure on pay.
8. Small proportion of pay budget set aside for local determination in departments and agencies.
9. Staff reduction plan to 1996 entails centralised control of overall staff numbers.
10. Ministries responsible for classification of employees with civil service status; agencies responsible for classification of other staff.
11. 1994 reform provides for increased devolution.
12. Policy is to retain existing centralised statutory rules and regulations, however, ministries are encouraged to devolve some operational aspects of HRM to their field services.
13. Up to middle management level.
14. Running cost budgets from 1994.
15. Some devolved freedom within limits set by Ministry of Home Affairs. Central controls to be removed in 1995.
16. Limited freedom to regrade staff within overall system of central control.
17. Recruitment above base grade devolved to departments and agencies.
18. Currently devolved but move to greater centralisation.
19. Departments and agencies may, with Treasury approval, determine own classifications. Delegation of pay bargaining to larger executive agencies from 1994 is intended to give greater freedom in grading.
20. Devolution to larger executive agencies (covering more than half the civil service) from 1994.
21. Responsibility devolved to departments and agencies under direction of Office of Personnel Management.

Chapter 17

CONTROLLING AND MANAGING REGULATION

Regulation in its many forms – from parliamentary law to ministerial orders to municipal by-law – is a key tool of government in OECD countries. Precisely because the quality of regulation is crucial for government effectiveness, regulatory reform will continue to be on the agenda of public sector managers in coming years. Although there is no accepted international definition, the term "regulation" is used broadly in this document to include the full range of formal legal instruments by which governing institutions, at all levels of government, impose obligations or constraints on citizens or private enterprises. Constitutions, parliamentary laws, international treaties, subordinate legislation, decrees, orders, norms, licenses, plans, and codes can all be considered as "regulation".

Regulatory managers from OECD countries, in a meeting at the OECD in May 1994, revealed a strong revival of interest in regulatory reform across the OECD membership, primarily fuelled by the current economic slump and unemployment concerns. Germany has initiated another effort to limit regulatory burdens on businesses. The United Kingdom is focusing on the employment effects of regulation. Sweden is attempting to improve domestic competition by removing outdated rules. Co-operation between the states and the Commonwealth in Australia is intended to remove regulatory barriers to the free movement of goods and services. In the EC Commission, subsidiarity and employment questions continue to focus attention on regulatory assessment and quality. In the United States, President Clinton signed a new Executive Order on regulatory quality. In Italy, the first steps are being taken to examine how the government can increase the flexibility and efficiency of its detailed and rigid legal system. Programmes are being initiated or expanded in France, Spain, and Canada. There was consensus that "regulatory inflation" is a serious problem that is not yet understood at the political level, and that more systematic attention is needed to regulatory quality in all its aspects.

As these activities demonstrate, governments have recognised that reform is not only a question of making improvements to the large stock of existing regulations, although this is an important and overdue step. Governments must go further: genuinely new and innovative styles of regulation are needed to respond to strong pressures in the broader governing environment:

- the performance of traditional regulatory approaches in reaching policy objectives has often proved disappointing to politicians and public alike;
- poor economic growth in the OECD area continues to focus attention on the impacts of government regulation on business development and trade, and weaknesses in macroeconomic tools for stimulating growth have led governments to turn to microeconomic strategies such as regulatory reform;
- regulatory inflation (the continuing growth in regulatory volume and complexity) has stimulated calls for relief from enterprises facing mounting competitive pressures in opening world markets;
- technological innovation in the financial, transport, and telecommunications areas, among others, have rendered many old regulatory regimes obsolete and even damaging to social and economic progress;
- fiscal strains are pushing governments to scrutinise regulatory administrations and enforcement programmes to find cost-savings;
- the globalisation and integration of regulatory systems at both international and subnational levels has led governments to review long-standing regulatory traditions and to seek new forms of co-operative regulation.

Two major regulatory failures

Two major weaknesses of regulations are particularly important with respect to the pressures described above. First, unlike the costs of programmes funded through budgeting systems from tax revenues, the costs of regulation are almost never calculated nor monitored, and hence are much less visible to the electorate. The underlying dynamic of regulation is that it benefits visible and vocal groups, and imposes costs on diffuse and unsuspecting groups (such as consumers). As a result, there is probably no easier way for a government to spend money than to regulate, particularly in the face of tight limits on public expenditure. In pluralist democratic systems, pressures for over-regulation are strong. Predictably, the governments of many OECD countries have complained of regulatory inflation in recent years.

Regulatory costs are no less real because they are less visible. In the United States, the only OECD country where an attempt has been made to calculate the full cost of regulation, annual aggregate costs of federal regulation falling directly on citizens, private enterprises, and local governments were estimated at up to US$500 billion in 1992, or about 10 per cent of GDP and one quarter of on-budget spending (Hopkins, 1992). Since costs to the government to administer these regulations were about US$9 billion, every dollar spent by the government on regulatory bureaucracies resulted in off-budget costs of US$55.

The costs of economic regulations are falling substantially in the United State as a result of deregulation, primarily in the telecommunications and transport sectors. A recent study estimated that deregulation in the United States is producing annual welfare benefits to consumers of US$32-43 billion, mostly through lower prices and better services, and benefits to producers of US$3 billion, through higher profit (Winston, 1993). Costs of social regulations in areas such as labor standards, health and safety, and environmental protection are projected to increase steadily in the future, to bring total off-budget regulatory costs to some US$660 billion by the year 2000.

Direct costs of this magnitude are significant for macroeconomic growth, job creation, and inflation, but they are not the whole story. Indirect costs may be as or more important. Many studies have suggested, for example, that some kinds of regulation tend to reduce innovation and productivity, and hence slow the speed of structural adjustment in opening world markets. In part, this is caused by the vulnerability of regulation to interest groups, which means that it can easily be used to block new products or processes that threaten the status quo. A recent survey of the cost of environmental regulation noted that, "Bizarre though it may seem, there are more examples of environmental standards being used to protect dirty old industries than to encourage new clean ones" (Cairncross, 1991). More recently, many governments have been concerned about the possible effects of regulation on international competitiveness. Given these broad and substantial impacts on economic and social values, the capacity of countries to absorb new regulations is clearly a limited resource that needs to be managed, just like any other resource.

What alternatives, and how?

The second major weakness of regulation is that it is inflexible and adapts more slowly than other kinds of policy instrument to the external pressures described above. This drawback is not inherent to the regulatory instrument, but is, rather, a consequence of regulatory traditions.

Innovation has come very late to the field of regulation in OECD countries. Governments still rely almost entirely on regulatory styles and designs – the so-called "command-and-control" (CAC) approach – that have been the mainstay of government for centuries. CAC regulation attempts to control behaviour by detailing how regulated entities should act, by relying on government inspectors to detect noncompliance, and by applying punitive sanctions such as fines. The CAC approach is preferred by regulatory administrators because it provides clarity, makes enforcement easier, and is perceived to be more equitable because everyone follows exactly the same rules.

However, several serious drawbacks to CAC regulation have been identified:

– CAC regulation is often *too* standardized and does not recognise diversity of conditions and capacities. By forcing all entities to behave in the same way, regardless of individual circumstances, it can substantially increase the costs of compliance.
– It is too rigid to adapt over time to new conditions and technologies, and easily becomes outdated. In fact, it can worsen problems by blocking economic and technological progress. In economies where competitiveness and structural adjustment are essential to maintaining quality of life in an open world market, regulations that block innovation can impose heavy costs in terms of growth and jobs. A notable example arises from current efforts in Europe to build an information superhighway and reduce telecommunications costs, considered by some to be crucial to the ability of European industries to compete. National regulations of telecommunication services have been identified as a major obstacle to progress.
– It is often ineffective because it concentrates on inputs rather than results. Regulated entities and officials find themselves focusing on the details of regulations rather than on accomplishing their objectives. As

PUMA has reported, studies of nursing home regulations have found that consistency and quality of care is higher in Australia, where regulations are flexible and performance-based, than in the United States, where regulations are detailed and focused on inputs.[1]

- It is vulnerable to abuse by producer groups and other commercial interests seeking to influence the details of regulatory prescriptions, compliance deadlines, and so forth, to their advantage.

In short, CAC regulation is a static and input-directed instrument of governance in an age that requires dynamic and results-oriented instruments. To avoid these problems, many governments are using a broad range of innovative policy instruments, both regulatory and non-regulatory to complement regulatory approaches. These innovative approaches can be more effective, less costly, more flexible than CAC regulation, and sometimes all three at the same time.

Several alternative approaches are under consideration in OECD countries, including information disclosure, economic incentives, tradeable property rights, voluntary agreements, self-regulation, risk-based liability, persuasion, and performance-based approaches. As the latter example suggests, the broader public sector movement towards a focus on results is also reflected in regulatory reform: performance-based regulation, with clear targets and performance measures, is receiving more attention throughout the OECD area. Brief discussions of these alternatives are presented in a box in Chapter 10.

PUMA case studies from several countries have shown that innovative approaches cannot be applied without careful attention to institutional settings.[2] Indeed, if the institutions responsible for carrying out the policy do not have the right incentives, outcomes can be perverse. One case study of the use of charges for water pollution in Denmark showed that local governments had incentives, not to reduce water pollution, but to increase it so as to pay off their investments in water treatment plants.

There is wide-spread agreement that governments must construct processes of systematic and open decision-making that use policy instruments more skilfully and creatively to achieve more efficient policy outcomes. Yet, it is difficult to win acceptance for new approaches within regulatory systems that, by design and habit, are built around command-and-control rules, particularly when new approaches are often complex in design and practice. The issue becomes highly political as interest groups tenaciously protect ''their'' regulations. Nor is it a matter of simply asking regulators to consider other approaches – fundamental change is needed in the ''logic of decision-making'' to improve the ways that problems are defined, and to create a broader vision of the role of government in society.

Major reform initiatives

The means and ends of regulatory reform stimulated much public controversy in the 1980s. ''Deregulation'', in particular, became an ideological symbol, promoted by those who wished to roll back the frontiers of what they saw as the bloated regulatory state, and opposed by critics who feared the return of untrammelled capitalism and the erosion of social protection. Behind the scenes, however, most OECD countries initiated a quieter set of reforms which, in the long term, are likely to be more influential in determining the role of regulation.

Specific reform actions vary widely among governments, but a gradual convergence can be detected: ''reform'' of regulation is developing into ''management'' of regulation. In most OECD countries, reform began as *ad hoc* efforts to correct problems caused by individual rules. It has become increasingly obvious, however, that the most pressing issues of regulation – the aggregate costs of multiple regulations, complexity and quantity, consistency among rules, legal clarity, accountability and openness, intrusion on private life – arise from the functioning and growth of the regulatory system as a whole, and that correcting these problems requires a long-term institutional view of how governments exercise their regulatory powers.

Governments have noted the importance of understanding the broader economic, democratic, and legal impacts of regulatory activity. In 1986, the United Kingdom warned that ''Many regulations seem relatively minor. But it is the cumulative effect of many regulations which weighs business down'' (Secretary of State for Employment, 1986, p. 4). In Germany, the State Secretary for Legal Simplification wrote in 1988, ''Our concept of a free, democratic society is not compatible with too many regulations, excessively complex stipulations, or bureaucratic obstacles and hurdles'' (Federal Ministry of Interior, 1988, p. 1). And in Norway, the regulatory system has been approached as an ''information system'' linking governments and citizens: ''Textual clarity, high consistency among the provisions, and a structure easy to understand and to which the user may relate, are the most important requirements'' a committee for improving the Norwegian legal system wrote in 1992 (Government of Norway, 1992, p. 8).

In grappling with such larger issues, governments have progressively widened the objectives of reform and strengthened regulatory disciplines and controls. In some countries, in fact, regulatory management has matured into a long-term and routine element of the central management functions of government. This development, which can be seen as a logical evolution of the regulatory state, is comparable to the adoption by governments earlier in this century of central management functions, such as modern budgeting agencies. These functions were intended to establish broad perspectives on related activities across government agencies, to co-ordinate interactive policies, and to improve administrative responsiveness to political direction. As the Swedish government pointed out in 1985, such reforms do not contradict the use of regulation to achieve public objectives, but, rather, improvements to policy instruments make the goals more attainable (Ministry of Public Administration, 1988, p. 2).

The centralisation of regulatory management may appear to be a counter-current to the decentralisation that has marked so many other areas of public management reform, but is probably best understood as a tardy recognition that governments must have capacities for general oversight and strategic planning of the regulatory function if they are to correct emerging problems. In that light, this trend is consistent with broader reforms toward more strategic government.

Regulatory interdependence

Regulatory management and reform are even more difficult today than before, because governments no longer act in isolation: internationalisation and decentralisation have profound impacts on how they use their regulatory powers.[3] There is relentless pressure for mutual action as economic, environmental, and social issues become increasingly intertwined:

- Markets create economic interdependence with the growth of global trade and capital movements; unless they resort to protectionist measures, governments have no choice but to follow. As the OECD has pointed out, "unless policy succeeds in sealing off substantially all channels for international exchange," governments will be forced to adjust to international integration (OECD, 1994a, p. 18).
- There is a growing perception of environmental and social linkages between trade and other policy areas, exemplified by charges of "social dumping". In co-ordinating such regulatory policies, governments are not controlling change as much as attempting to cope with it.
- Finally, there are substantial administrative advantages to be gained through varieties of regulatory co-operation ranging from information-sharing to concerted enforcement action.

One of the great challenges for contemporary government is the building of democratic institutions and processes within which governments can work confidently together to reap the benefits of mutual action. This does not suggest that government should be centralised at the international level. Rather, regulatory co-operation is occurring primarily through the regulatory institutions of national governments, who are linked formally and informally with their peers in other governments. If they are to deliver satisfactory results, these intergovernmental networks must work at least as well as do separate national institutions, notwithstanding the difficulties of managing and co-ordinating the actions of multiple partners.

Examples of co-operative activities and regulatory agreements among levels of government can be seen practically everywhere. These range from the supranational (for example, 22 000 EU regulations) to international multilateral agreements (NAFTA, GATT, Decisions of the OECD Council) to bilateral agreements (such as the Australia-New Zealand Closer Economic Relations Agreement) to national-local implementation arrangements to agreements among subnational governments (internal market negotiations among Canadian provinces). Seen in the aggregate, such arrangements can be visualised as a complex web of vertical and horizontal linkages extending from the lowest to the highest level of government (see Figure 3, Chapter 10).

Each of the many co-operative arrangements separately demands adjustment to governing capacities. Taken together, the impact on governments is considerable. Participation in such a multi-governmental regulatory system will profoundly affect administrative styles, governing cultures, and power relations within national governments themselves, as well as their capacities to protect and serve national values. How, for example, does a national government carry out regulatory policy when it has less control over its own actions, but more influence over the actions of others? Effects on the roles of the government, legislatures, and judiciary in establishing and overseeing laws and policy are only beginning to be perceived. It is not merely a question of implementation: underlying regulatory policies and objectives are also likely to change as problems and solutions are redefined, and as new opportunities for beneficial co-operation are recognised.

In brief, the old style of government – hierarchical, vertical, standardized, lodged firmly in the national-state structure – is not appropriate for a multi-layered regulatory system characterised by complex policy dependencies, diversity, and innovation. Difficult issues inherent in the long-term process of change now underway require innovative institutional responses. Concerns about trust and mutual confidence among countries, the erosion of national values, democratic accountability, national sovereignty, and the complexity of co-operative action must be addressed explicitly and resolutely if the public is to accept that co-operative action is in its long-term interests.

In establishing solid administrative foundations for regulatory co-operation, governments must focus on several key mangement issues. To work effectively in the new environment, national governments need to improve their capacities to manage complexity. Intergovernmental co-operation is often described as reducing regulatory discrepancies and harmonizing approaches. In reality, it has tended to amplify administrative complexity by introducing multiple actors and processes and adding new uncertainties about outcomes. Likewise, regulatory co-operation tends to greatly increase the amount and detail of regulation.

Nor is adjustment merely a matter of improving existing institutions: genuinely new governing strategies will be needed. For example, well-co-ordinated administrative networks are essential if governments are to carry out regulatory agreements. In many areas, such networks are already emerging: one example is the group of regulators from 144 countries who gather in Rome to determine food standards under the auspices of the FAO-WHO Codex Alimentarius Commission. An extraordinarily complex network is managed by the International Standards Organisation, which has a membership of 96 national standards bodies who work with 460 other international organisations through 2 678 technical committees to write international standards.

Such decentralised networks of regulatory administrators are difficult for national administrations to manage. They are often informal, responsibilities are diffuse, and issues are often technical. Information on what networks are doing is not always consistent or easily available. Frequently, it is not even clear who is involved in a network.

Governments are learning to develop management approaches for planning, organising, and overseeing network activities. The OECD itself offers several examples. The OECD Test Guidelines Programme for the mutual acceptance of data in the assessment of chemicals demonstrates the advantages of building personal contacts over time, of establishing a well-thought-out and transparent process of agreement, of maintaining flexibility, and of using a bottom-up process of consensus-building (see Chapter 6 in *Regulatory Co-operation for an Interdependent World,* OECD, 1994). Other areas have shown that subnational levels of government, often responsible for implementation, must be included more regularly in international regulatory networks.

As the number of actors and issues grows, co-ordination emerges as a major issue for managers. ''Top-down'' central co-ordinators and lengthy co-ordination processes may have to be replaced by ''bottom-up'' networks that are more tightly knit. The current efforts of pharmaceutical regulators from the United States, Japan, and the EC to arrive at consensus on requirements for drug testing and registration is a case in point. This informal and open process has made more progress toward improving drug standards and reducing testing costs than has been achieved by the time-consuming and formal national negotiating forum in the WHO.

Trust and mutual confidence are critical to the success of regulatory co-operation. Governments find it difficult to trust one another to carry out their respective duties in agreements. To some extent, this is realistic: many international agreements have not been respected. But it is also inherent in the intergovernmental process. Differences in administrative cultures, legal traditions (such as treatment of liability), capacities, values, and policy priorities undermine co-operative relationships.

Yet, trust is needed not only at the administrative level, but also at the political level and the level of the general public if co-operation is to be accepted. Pragmatically, too, trust reduces the need for costly hierarchical controls, excessive regulatory detail, and over-centralisation of decision-making. Ways have to be found to overcome differences in administrative culture, capacities, values, and policy priorities. Some prior convergence in administrative capacities may be a precondition for regulatory co-operation. In Canada, for example, success in harmonizing US-Canadian regulations as part of the Canada-US Free Trade Agreement seems to have been greatest where officials had already been consulting with their counterparts for years (see Chapter 4 in *Regulatory Co-operation for an Interdependent World,* OECD, 1994).

Concerns have been voiced about the impact of a multi-layered regulatory system on accountability and national sovereignty. In fact, the extent to which countries have already effectively surrendered legal authority to intergovernmental regulatory processes is probably not fully appreciated. Countries, particularly small countries, have become ''regulation-takers'' rather than ''regulation-makers'' in many areas. Traditions of intergovernmental processes such as closed negotiations, limited participation, and lack of public information on consequences and options have fuelled criticism. Improved information and communication offer ways to restore a degree of accountability. The analysis of benefits and costs, for example, can open up intergovernmental processes and improve the quality of public debate on important issues. Likewise, public consultation and participation, not well developed in processes of regulatory co-operation, could be strengthened.

Strategies of regulatory co-operation

In setting the stage for effective regulatory co-operation, it is clear that more understanding is needed of how various strategies that link regulations across legal and political borders actually work. Three strategies of regulatory co-operation, harmonization, mutual recognition, and co-ordination, are proliferating in the OECD area, touching almost every substantive policy area. These regulatory strategies are not simple in practice. On the contrary, their success requires sophisticated management approaches attuned to the specific regulatory environment and the roles of government institutions, including the judiciary. They must also take account of expected consumer and business responses.

One of the lessons that can be drawn from recent experience in OECD countries is that these strategies are complementary, not mutually exclusive. Harmonizsation, in particular, needs to be curtailed to cover only "essential" issues. On other issues, regulatory diversity is best protected through mutual recognition. This is the "new approach" adopted by the European Community in 1985, and it recognises that harmonisation imposes higher political and administrative costs than previously thought. Moreover, harmonization tends to "freeze" governments into a single regulatory approach, and reduces the potential for innovation and adaptation to new conditions that might arise from multiple competing approaches. It is evident from experience to date that a great deal can also be accomplished through informal processes of regulatory co-ordination. Formal and legalistic processes of mutual recognition and harmonization are not the only options.

Furthermore, the regulatory strategy needs to be adapted to the specific type of market failure being corrected. For example, mutual recognition is likely to be appropriate when the underlying market failure is insufficient information. Harmonization is more likely to be needed when the market failure is a negative externality such as trans-boundary pollution. Fitting the strategy to the market failure maximises the efficiency benefits of co-operation, while preventing unhealthy regulatory competition among jurisdictions in a "race to the bottom" in regulatory standards.

Disciplined mutual recognition, on the other hand, can establish the basis for beneficial regulatory competition. For the moment, more understanding is needed of how regulatory competition works, and the general rules by which it can be disciplined. Competition in regulation allows businesses and consumers to choose among alternative regulatory regimes. Theoretically, it expands consumer choice, increases efficiency, and rewards cost-effective regulatory approaches. The danger is that weaker standards "win out" over stronger standards (this is dangerous only if the "stronger" standards were in fact necessary), but experiences in car safety and financial securities markets shows that the opposite can also occur.

The implications of regulatory interdependence for the effective functioning of national governments needs to be further explored. There is a pressing need for a politically realistic framework of principles within which governments can adapt to the new environment. The central theme of such a framework should be balance – balance between stability and responsiveness to new conditions, between co-operation and sovereignty, between new fora for decision-making and accountability to legislatures and citizens, between complex agreements and simple government. Better information is needed on the dynamics and results of the multi-layered regulatory system. Co-operative efforts must be consistent with domestic policies of regulation or deregulation. Yet, while learning to be discriminating and selective in seeking to co-operate on regulation, governments should at the same time aggressively seek new opportunities to seize efficiency gains in intergovernmental arenas. The potential appears to be vast in many policy areas.

NOTES

1. The unfortunate US experience has been noted as an example of "ritualistic roller-coaster compliance". See *Improving Regulatory Compliance: Strategies and Practical Applications in OECD Countries, Occasional Paper on Public Management, Regulatory Management and Reform Series No. 3, OECD, 1993*.

2. Case studies include: "The Use of Voluntary Agreements for Consumer Product Safety in the United States, 1981-1993"; "Improving Flexibility and Responsiveness: A New Approach to Railway Safety Regulations in Canada"; "Innovation in Regulatory Enforcement: Contracting-out Inspections to Horizontal Bodies" (Iceland); "Self-regulation and Information Disclosure: The Cadbury Report on Financial Aspects of Corporate Governance" (United Kingdom). Documents not for general distribution.

3. The implications of regulatory interdependence for how governments use their regulatory authorities are discussed in detail in *Regulatory Co-Operation for an Interdependent World*, OECD, 1994.

GLOSSARY*

ACCOUNTABILITY exists where there is a hierarchical relationship within which one party accounts to the other (a person or body) for the performance of tasks or functions conferred. Accountability goes hand in hand with devolution and flexibility: managers are held accountable for results once they are given the authority to make decisions that are part of producing those results. The report also discusses other aspects of accountability such as the public accountability of those who govern to elected bodies and thence to the public at large.

CONTRACTING OUT – an arrangement whereby a department or agency enters into a commercial contract with an external supplier that provides services.

CORPORATISATION – the establishment of units with commercial functions as separate legal entities, similar to those operating in the private sector. It involves, among other things, identifying the property, rights, liabilities, and obligations of the business and establishing the capital structure and funding arrangements. Such state enterprises operate at arm's length from the ministers and parliament, within a framework of strategic objectives set by government.

COST-EFFECTIVENESS – the extent to which policy and programme objectives are achieved at minimum economic cost; synonymous with value-for-money.

DEPARTMENTS AND AGENCIES – used for line ministries and offices, distinguished from central management bodies such as the Ministry of Finance, the Budget Office, the Ministry of Public Administration, and the Prime Minister's Office.

DEVOLUTION – used in the report as a catch-all term for the granting of greater decision-making authority and autonomy:

   a) by central management bodies to line departments and agencies;
   b) by departments and agencies to their subordinate bodies;
   c) within departments and agencies to lower levels of management and to regional/local offices of central government; and
   d) by central government to lower levels of government.

A single term is used instead of several terms that have more precise meanings but that are used differently in different Member countries and can be a source of confusion in an international context (such as decentralisation, deconcentration, delegation, and devolution itself).

ECONOMIC EFFICIENCY – a situation is economically efficient if it is impossible by the reallocation of goods, services, and resources to make one person better off withouth making someone else worse off. This is a basic norm used by economists in analysing problems of economic policy and public sector management. The concept is more comprehensive than efficiency and cost- effectiveness in that it also includes the effects of public sector policies on other activities and sectors in the economy.

ECONOMY – This normally refers to obtaining inputs at less cost or reducing waste. An economical organisation acquires its resources in the right quantity and of a quality no higher than is needed for the job, at the appropriate time, at the lowest obtainable cost.

EFFECTIVENESS – the extent to which objectives (of an organisation, policy or programme) are achieved or the relationship between the intended and actual effect of outputs in the achievement of objectives (*e.g.* the extent to which the condition of hospital patients improves as result of treatment).

EFFICIENCY – the relationship between resources (inputs) used and outputs produced (*e.g.* nurse hours per occupied hospital bed day). An efficient activity maximises output for a given input or minimises input for a given output. Efficiency measures take the form of output/input ratios (productivity) and expenditure/output ratios (unit cost).

---

* The glossary describes how the terms are used in this report.

GOVERNANCE – the act of governing seen in a wide sense. The term covers public administration and the institutions, methods and instruments of governing. It further incorporates relationships between government and citizen (including business and other citizen groupings) and the role of the State.

INPUTS – the financial, human, and physical resources used to formulate and execute policy. An input to an activity may also be the output of an earlier activity; for example, hospital places are an output arising from the deployment of resources, but are also an input contributing to the final output of health care.

MARKET-TYPE MECHANISMS – all arrangements where at least one significant characteristic of markets is present (competition, choice, pricing, dispersed decision-making, monetary incentives, and so on). It excludes the two polar cases of traditional public delivery and complete privatisation.

MARKET TESTING – the subjecting to competition of activities currently performed within a department or agency. It can be compared to "make or buy" decisions in the private sector. In the market testing process there is a bid from those currently doing the work and that they are given an opportunity to change aspects of the way they do the work.

OUTCOMES – what is achieved in relation to objectives, to be distinguished from outputs, which measure what is produced or done. For example,using fewer resources compared with plans, previous performance or performance of other organisations. the outcome of a health publicity campaign might be a 5 per cent increase in awareness among those targeted.

OUTPUTS – the direct product of an organisation's activities in terms of goods or services (*e.g.* number of training person-days by type of training course). This says nothing about the actual outcome (*e.g.* skills absorbed, whether the skills helped gain long-term employment).

PERFORMANCE BUDGETING – budgeting organised around programmes and activities and linked to measurable performance goals. Under performance budgeting, the primary focus of the budget is on the level of output and how much that output costs. As with other forms of programme-related budgets, resources are allocated to sub-programmes and tasks rather than line items.

PERFORMANCE MANAGEMENT – the systematic approach to performance that generally involves the encouragement or mandating of a regular management cycle under which:
- programme performance objectives and targets are determined;
- managers have freedom over processes to achieve them;
- actual performance is measured and reported;
- this information feeds into decisions about programme funding and design and organisational or individual rewards or penalties; and
- the information is also provided to review bodies.

PERFORMANCE MEASUREMENT – the comparative assessment of policy outcomes, outputs, and inputs; performance measures are most useful when used for comparisons over time or among units performing similar work.

PERFORMANCE INDICATORS – proxy quantitative measures used when output or performance is not directly measurable. They do not necessarily cover all aspects of performance, but provide relevant information towards the assessment of performance (for example, qualifications obtained through a training scheme, hospital admission rates for infectious diseases).

PRIVATISATION – this report restricts use of the term to the transfer of more than 50 per cent of a public enterprise from State to private ownership. It is not used to refer to the introduction of market-type mechanisms such as contracting out, or the private provision of public infrastructure, or the growth of private alternatives to public sector provision.

PUBLIC SECTOR – central government departments and agencies (civil service), the wider public service (including defence forces, police, education, health), public enterprises, certain bodies funded from public monies, and subnational levels of government. The term corresponds roughly to the category of "general government" as defined in National Accounts statistics plus public enterprises.

QUALITY OF SERVICE – the extent to which the nature of the output and the delivery of the output meet user needs; quality of service may be directly measurable (for example, out-patient waiting time) or may need to be inferred from the results of customer surveys. Common aspects of quality are timeliness, accessibility, and accuracy of service.

REGULATION – includes the full range of legal instruments and decisions – constitutions, parliamentary laws, lower-level legislation, decrees, orders, norms, licenses, plans, codes, and often even "grey" regulations such as guidance and instructions – through which governments impose limits on the behaviour of citizens and enterprises. It should be noted that "laws" are a subset, although an important subset, of the set of regulations applied in a country.

REGULATORY SYSTEM – Regulations are product of the broad regulatory system, which includes the processes and institutions through which regulations are developed, enforced, and adjudicated. The regulatory system includes processes of public consultation, communication, and implementation. Regulatory systems in OECD countries encompass not only national rulemaking processes, but also regulatory processes at subnational levels of government (such as municipalities), and international regulatory processes (such as the GATT and the European Union).

RESPONSIVENESS – the quality of interaction between public administrations and their clients. It includes how far the needs of clients can be satisfied within the framework of policy, the comprehensibility and accessibility of administration, the openness of administration to client participation in decision-making, and the availability of redress.

SERVICE DELIVERY: the provision of a public service for a client (individual citizen, business, or other). The report distinguishes **direct provision** to the client by a public sector organisation from **indirect provision** to the client on behalf of a public sector organisation by a third party (*e.g.* a subcontractor).

STANDARD – usually an abbreviation for "minimum standard", indicating the level of performance (volume of output, quality, etc.) that an organisation commits itself to achieving.

STRUCTURAL ADJUSTMENT – the capacity of economies, institutions, and societies in general to adjust to changing circumstances, to create and exploit new opportunities, and, on that basis, to deploy and redeploy resources.

USER CHARGING – payment directly by the consumer for goods and services provided by the public sector to the private sector (whether for partial or total recovery of costs of provision) as well as the internal pricing of goods and services (*i.e.* user charges between public institutions and agencies).

VOUCHER – a form of payment or entitlement that can be used for the purchase of specific goods or services, to the stated value of the voucher, with benefits accruing only to the voucher recipient. The main feature of vouchers is that they restrict consumers in their choice of goods and services but allow them to choose suppliers.

SELECTED REFERENCES*

PUBLICATIONS OF THE PUBLIC MANAGEMENT COMMITTEE

Publications

Administration as Service: The Public as Client (1987).

The Control and Management of Government Expenditure (1987).

Flexible Personnel Management in the Public Service (1990).

Public Management Developments: Survey 1990 (1990).

Public Management Developments: Update 1991 (1991).

Public Management Developments: Update 1992 (1992).

Public Management Developments: Survey 1993 (1993).

Public Management Developments: Update 1994 (1994).

Private Pay for Public Work: Performance Related Pay Schemes for Public Sector Managers (1993).

Public Management: OECD Country Profiles (1993).

Pay Flexibility in the Public Sector (1993).

Managing with Market-Type Mechanisms (1993).

Regulatory Co-operation for an Interdependent World (1994).

Statistical Sources on Public Sector Employment (1994).

Occasional Papers on Public Management

Aspects of Managing the Centre of Government (1990).

Financing Public Expenditures through User Charges (1990).

Public Management and Private Enterprise: Administrative Responsiveness and the Needs of Small Firms (1990).

Performance Pay and Related Compensation Practices in Australian State Public Sector Organisations, A Summary of the Experience with Pay for Performance in the United States (1991).

Serving the Economy Better (1991).

Market-type Mechanisms Series:

No. 1. Issues and Strategy: Managerial Aspects (1992) [OCDE/GD(92)64].

No. 2. The United States Experience with Contracting Out under Circular A-76; User Charges for Prescription Drugs in Italy; Market-type Mechanisms and Health Services in the UK (1992) [OCDE/GD(91)205].

No. 3. Property Rights Modifications in Fisheries (1992) [OCDE/GD(92)132].

No. 4. Vouchers: Social Housing and Nursing Homes (1992) [OCDE/GD(92)133].

No. 5. Complex Contracting Out Information Technology Services (1992) [OCDE/GD(92)134].

No. 6. Internal Markets (1993) [OCDE/GD(93)135].

No. 7. Market Emulations in Hospitals (1993) [OCDE/GD(92)193].

No. 8. New Ways of Managing Infrastructure Provision. Occasional Paper 1994 No. 6 (1994).

---

* These references are a selective listing from a vast literature on public management. The listing is also restricted to references in the two official languages of the OECD.

Regulatory Management and Reform Series:

No. 1. Current Concerns in OECD Countries (1992) [OCDE/GD(92)58].

No. 2. Controlling Regulatory Costs: The Use of Regulatory Budgeting (1992) [OCDE/GD(92)176].

No. 3. Improving Regulatory Compliance: Strategies and Practical Applications in OECD Countries (1993) [OCDE/GD(93)63].

No. 4. The Design and Use of Regulatory Checklists in OECD Countries (1993) [OCDE/GD(93)181].

Value and Vision. Management Development in a Climate of Civil Service Change (1993) [OCDE/GD(92)186].

Internal Management Consultancy in Government (1993) [OCDE/GD(92)185].

Information Technology in Government: Management Challenges (1993) [OCDE/GD(92)194].

Accounting for What?: The Value of Accrual Accounting to the Public Sector (1993) [OCDE/GD(93)178].

Performance Appraisal: Practice, Problems and Issues (1993) [OCDE/GD(93)177].

Trends in Public Sector Pay: A Study on Nine OECD Countries 1985-1990. Occasional Paper 1994 No. 1 (1994).

Public Service Pay Determination and Pay Systems in OECD Countries. Occasional Paper 1994 No. 2 (1994).

Performance Management in Government: Performance Measurement and Results-Oriented Management. Occasional Paper 1994 No. 3 (1994).

Senior Civil Service Pay: A Study of Eleven OECD Countries 1980-1991. Occasional Paper 1994 No. 4 (1994).

Performance Measurement in Government: Issues and Illustrations. Occasional Paper 1994 No. 5 (1994).

GENERAL

ARMSTRONG, Michael (1992), *Human Resource Management: Strategy and Action,* London, Kogan Page (reprinted 1993).

AUCOIN, P. (1990), "Administrative Reform in Public Management: Paradigms, Principles, Paradoxes and Pendulums", *Governance,* Vol. 3, No. 2, April 1990, pp. 115-137.

BARZELAY, K. (1992), *Breaking through Bureaucracy,* University of California Press, Berkeley.

BOZEMAN, B. and J. D. STRAUSSMAN (1990), *Public Management Strategies: Guidelines for Managerial Effectiveness,* Jossey-Bass, San Francisco.

BRAIBANT, G. (1986), *Institutions administratives comparées: les structures; les contrôles,* Fondation nationale des sciences politiques, Paris.

CAIRNCROSS F. (1991), *Costing the Earth,* The Economist Books Ltd., London.

CHRISTENSEN, J.G. (1988), "Withdrawal of Government: a Critical Survey of an Administrative Problem in its Political Context", *International Review of Administrative Sciences,* Vol. 54, No. 1, March 1988, pp. 37-65.

CHUBB, J.E. and P.E. PETERSON (1989), *Can the Government Govern?,* The Brookings Institution, Washington DC.

CLAISSE, A. (1989), "La Transformation des relations entre l'administration et les usagers: Note de synthèse à partir d'exemples étrangers (Espagne, Grande-Bretagne, Italie, RFA)", Institut international d'administration publique, Paris.

COASE, R.H. (1960), "The Problem of Social Cost", *Journal of Law and Economics,* No. 1.

COMMON, R., N. FLYNN and E. MELLON (1992), *Managing Public Services: Competition and Decentralization,* Butterworth-Heinemann, Oxford.

CROZIER, M. (1987), *Etat Modeste, Etat Moderne: Stratégie pour un autre changement,* Fayard, Paris.

DROR, Y. (1988), *Policymaking Under Adversity,* Transaction Books, New Jersey.

DROR, Y. (1993), "School for Rulers", in Kenyon B. De Greene, ed. *A Systems-Based Approach to Policymaking,* Kluwer Academic Publisher, Boston, Chapter 5.

DUNLEAVY, P. and C. HOOD (1993), "From Old Public Administration to New Public Management", London School of Economics and Political Science, London.

FESLER, J. and KETTL D.F. (1991), *The Politics of the Administrative Process,* Chatham House, Chatham, New Jersey.

HAHN R. and J. HIRD (1991), "The Costs and Benefits of Regulation: Review and Synthesis", *Yale Journal of Regulation,* Vol. 8, No. 1.

HOPKINS T. (1992), "Cost of Regulation: Filling the Gaps", Report prepared for the US Regulatory Information Service Centre, Washington DC.

HOOD, C. (1991), "A Public Management for All Seasons?", *Public Administration,* Vol. 69, No. 1, Spring 1991, pp. 3-19.

JACKSON, P. and B. PALMER (1989), *First Steps in Measuring Performance in the Public Sector: A Management Guide,* Public Finance Foundation, London.

KEATING, Michael (1991), "Management of the Public Sector", Chapter 10 in J. Llewellyn and S.J. Potter (eds.), *Economic Policies for the 1990s,* Basil Blackwell, Oxford.

KETTL, Donald (1993), *Sharing Power: Public Governance and Private Markets,* The Brookings Institution, Washington DC.

KOOIMAN, J. (1993), *Modern Governance,* Sage, London.

LAN, Z. and D.H. ROSENBLOOM (1992), "Public Administration in Transition", *Public Administration Review,* Vol. 52, No. 6, November/December 1992, pp. 535-537.

LANE, J.E. (1993), *The Public Sector,* Sage, London.

LOVELL, R. (1992), "The Citizen's Charter: The Cultural Challenge", *Public Administration,* Vol. 70, No. 3, Autumn 1992, pp. 395-404.

LYBECK, Johan and Magnus HENREKSON, eds. (1988), *Explaining the Growth of Government,* North-Holland/Elsevier Publishers, Amsterdam.

MARTIN, Brendan (1993), *In the Public Interest? Privatization and Public Sector Reform,* Zed Books, Public Services International, Ferney-Voltaire, France.

MENY, Y. (1993), "La Cohérence et l'homogénéité de la prise de décision en France et en Italie", OECD Public Management Service, OECD, Paris.

METCALFE, L. and S. RICHARDS (1990), *Improving Public Management,* Sage Publications, London.

NORTH, Douglass (1990), *Institutions, Institutional Change and Economic Performance,* Cambridge University Press, Cambridge.

NORMANN, R. (1991), *Service Management: Strategy and Leadership in Service Business,* John Wiley and Sons, New York.

OECD (1990), *Progress in Structural Reform,* OECD, Paris.

OECD (1992a), *Progress in Structural Reform: An Overview,* OECD, Paris.

OECD (1992b), *Regulatory Reform, Privatisation and Competition Policy,* OECD, Paris.

OECD (1993a), "OECD Employment/Unemployment Study. Interim Report by the Secretary-General", [OCDE/GD(93)102] OECD, Paris.

OECD (1993b), "Reforming the Public Sector", *The OECD Observer,* October/November 1993, OECD, Paris.

OECD (1994a) *Assessing Structural Reform: Lessons for the Future,* OECD, Paris.

OECD (1994b) *OECD Economic Outlook,* No. 56, December 1994, OECD, Paris.

OXLEY, H., M. MAHER, J.P. MARTIN and G. NICOLETTI (1990), "The Public Sector: Issues for the 1990s", OECD Department of Economics and Statistics Working Paper No. 90, December, OECD, Paris.

OXLEY, H. and J.P. MARTIN (1991), "Controlling Government Spending and Deficits: Trends in the 1980s and Prospects for the 1990s", *OECD Economic Studies,* No. 17, Autumn 1991, pp. 145-189.

PAYE, J.C. (1992), "L'Encadrement institutionnel de l'économie de marché", *Revue française d'administration publique,* No. 61, janvier-mars 1992, pp. 19-23.

POLLITT, C. (1990), *Managerialism and the Public Service,* Basil Blackwell, Oxford.

POSNER, B.G. and L.R. ROTHSTEIN (1994), "Reinventing the Business of Government: An interview with change catalyst David Osborne", *Harvard Business Review,* Vol. 72, Iss. 3, May/June 1994, pp. 132-143.

PREMFORS, R. (1991), "The 'Swedish Model' and Public Sector Reform", *West European Politics,* 14, pp. 83-95.

PUBLIC POLICY FORUM (1993), "Private-Public Sector Cooperation as a Means of Improving a Country's Economic Performance", Ottawa.

PUBLIC SERVICES INTERNATIONAL (1993), "PSI Policy and Strategy on the Role of the Public Sector", Ferney-Voltaire, France.

PURCHASE, Bryne, ed. (1993), *Competitiveness and Size of Government,* School of Policy Studies (Queen's University), Kingston, Ontario.

REAGAN, M. D. (1988), *Regulation: The Politics of Policy,* Little, Brown and Company, Boston.

RHODES, R.A.W. (1991), "The New Public Management", Special edition of *Public Administration,* Spring 1991.

ROSELL, S.A. (1992), *Governing in an Information Society,* Institute for Research on Public Policy, Montreal.

ROSEN, E.D. (1993), *Improving Public Sector Productivity,* Sage, London.

ROWAT, DC (1988), *Public Administration in Developed Democracies,* Marcel Dekker, New York.

SAUNDERS, P. and F. KLAU (1985), "The Role of the Public Sector: Causes and Consequences of the Growth of Government", *OECD Economic Studies* No. 4, Spring, OECD, Paris.

SCHICK A. (1990), "Budgeting for Results: Recent Developments in Five Industrialized Countries", *Public Administration Review,* Vol. 50, No. 1, January/February 1990.

STRONCK, Gaston and Dietrich VAUBEL, eds. (1988), *Administrative Reform in Benelux and Germany,* European Institute of Public Administration, Maastricht, and Bundesakademie für öffentliche Verwaltung, Bonn.

THOENIG, Jean-Claude (1988), "La Modernisation de la fonction publique dans les États membres de la Communauté européenne", *Revue Politique et Management Public,* Vol. 6, No. 2, June 1988, pp. 69-79.

TREBILCOCK, M. J. (1993), *Can Government be Reinvented?,* University of Toronto, Toronto.

WALSH, K. and STEWART, J. (1992), "Change in the Management of Public Services", *Public Administration,* Vol. 70, No. 4, Winter 1992, pp. 499-518.

WILENSKI, Peter (1986), *Public Power and Public Administration,* Hale and Iremonger, Sydney.

WILLIAMSON O.E. (1990), "A comparison of Alternative Approaches to Economic Organization", *Journal of Institutional and Theoretical Economics.*

WINSTON C. (1993), "Economic Deregulation: Days of Reckoning for Microeconomists", *Journal of Economic Literature,* Vol. XXXI.

ZILLER, J. (1993), *Administrations comparées: les systèmes politico-administratifs de l'Europe des Douze,* Éditions Montchrestien, Paris.

AUSTRALIA

COMMONWEALTH OF AUSTRALIA (1981), *Review of Commonwealth Functions* (P. Lynch, Chair), Prime Minister's Statement to the Parliament, AGPS, Canberra.

COMMONWEALTH OF AUSTRALIA (1984), *Budget Reform,* AGPS, Canberra.

COMMONWEALTH OF AUSTRALIA (1986), *Reform of Commonwealth Primary Industry Statutory Marketing Authorities,* Canberra.

COMMONWEALTH OF AUSTRALIA (1987), *Policy Guidelines for Commonwealth Statutory Authorities and GBEs,* AGPS, Canberra.

DEPARTMENT OF FINANCE (1988), *FMIP Report December 1988,* AGPS, Canberra.

KEATING, M. (1989), "Quo Vadis: Challenges of the New Managerialism", address to the Royal Australian Institute of Public Administration, Perth.

KEATING, M. and M. HOLMES (1990), "Australia's Budgetary and Financial Management Reforms", *Governance,* Vol. 3, No. 2, April 1990, pp. 168-185.

MANAGEMENT ADVISORY BOARD (1992), *The Australian Public Service Reformed: An Evaluation of a Decade of Management Reform,* AGPS, Canberra.

MANAGEMENT ADVISORY BOARD (MAB) and MANAGEMENT IMPROVEMENT ADVISORY COMMITTEE (MIAC): MAB-MIAC Publication Series, AGPS, Canberra:

   (1991*a*), No. 1, *Improving Asset Management in the Public Sector.*

   (1991*b*), No. 2, *Devolution and Regional Offices.*

   (1991*c*), No. 3, *Budget Flexibility: Carryover Provisions between Financial Periods.*

   (1991*d*), No. 4, *Resource Agreements.*

   (1991*e*), No. 5, *Accountability in the Commonwealth Public Sector: An Exposure Draft.*

   (1992*a*), No. 6, *Devolution of Corporate Services.*

   (1992*b*), No. 7, *The Management of Underperforming Officers in the Australian Public Service.*

   (1992*c*), No. 8, *Contracting for the Provision of Services in Commonwealth Agencies.*

   (1993*a*), No. 9, *Strategic Planning for Training and Development.*

   (1993*b*), No. 10, *Performance Information and the Management Cycle.*

   (1993*c*), No. 11, *Accountability in the Commonwealth Public Sector.*

   (1993*d*), No. 12, *Building a Better Public Service.*

PARLIAMENT OF THE COMMONWEALTH OF AUSTRALIA (1990*a*), *Not Dollars Alone: Review of the Financial Management Improvement Program,* Report of the House of Representatives Standing Committee on Finance and Public Administration, AGPS, Canberra.

PARLIAMENT OF THE COMMONWEALTH OF AUSTRALIA (1990*b*), *The Development of the Senior Executive Service,* Report of the Senate Standing Committee on Finance and Public Administration, AGPS, Canberra.

PARLIAMENT OF THE COMMONWEALTH OF AUSTRALIA (1992), *Managing People in the Australian Public Service: Dilemmas of Devolution and Diversity,* Report 323 of the Joint Committee of Public Accounts, AGPS, Canberra.

PUBLIC SERVICE COMMISSION (1989), "APS 2000: The Australian Public Service Workforce of the Future", Canberra.

PUBLIC SERVICE COMMISSION (1992a), "Submission by the Public Service Commission to the Joint Committee of Public Accounts Inquiry into the efficiency and effectiveness of the management of Human Resources in the Australian Public Service", Canberra.

PUBLIC SERVICE COMMISSION (1992b), "A Framework for Human Resource Management in the Australian Public Service", Canberra.

REVIEW OF COMMONWEALTH ADMINISTRATION (1983), (J.B. Reid, Chair) Report, AGPS, Canberra.

SEDGWICK, Stephen (1993), "The State of the Service", Department of Finance, Canberra.

AUSTRIA

FEDERAL CHANCELLERY (1992), "Public Administration in Austria", Vienna

BELGIUM

FRANÇOIS, A. (1987), "The Modernization of Administration in Belgium", International Review of Administrative Sciences, Vol. 53, No. 3, September 1987, pp. 299-341.

LEGRAND, J.J. (1990), "L'Approche belge de la modernisation des administrations publiques: les cellules de modernisation comme outil stratégique de changement", Administration publique, revue du droit public et de science administrative, T2-3/1990.

MOTTOUL, J. M. (1987), "Instruments de gestion à la disposition des services publics", Bulletin de documentation, No. 9, Service d'études et de documentation du Ministère des Finances, September 1987, Brussels.

CANADA

AUDITOR GENERAL OF CANADA (1990), Values, Service and Performance (Extract from the 1990 Annual Report), Minister of Supply and Services, Ottawa.

AUDITOR GENERAL OF CANADA (1992), The Learning Organization (Extract from the 1992 Annual Report), Minister of Supply and Services, Ottawa.

AUDITOR GENERAL OF CANADA (1993a), Canada's Public Service Reform, and Lessons Learned from Selected Jurisdictions (Extract from the 1993 Annual Report), Minister of Supply and Services, Ottawa.

AUDITOR GENERAL OF CANADA (1993b), Revitalizing Public Services, Office of the Auditor General of Canada, Ottawa.

AUDITOR GENERAL OF CANADA (1989), Attributes of Well-Performing Organizations, Office of the Auditor General of Canada, Ottawa.

GOVERNMENT OF CANADA (1990), Public Service 2000. The Renewal of the Public Service of Canada, Minister of Supply and Services, Ottawa.

HOUSE OF COMMONS (1993), "Regulations and Competitiveness", First report of the Sub-committee on Regulations and Competitiveness, Standing Committee on Finance, Queen's Printer for Canada, Ottawa.

JABES, J. and ZUSSMAN, D. (1989), The Vertical Solitude: Managing in the Public Sector, The Institute for Research on Public Policy, Halifax.

MASSÉ, Marcel (1993), "Partners in the management of Canada: The changing roles of government and the public service", Optimum, Vol. 24-1, Summer 1993, pp. 56-62.

TELLIER, P.M. (1992), Public Service 2000. First Annual Report to the Prime Minister on the Public Service of Canada, Minister of Supply and Services, Ottawa.

TREASURY BOARD OF CANADA (1989), Enterprising Management: a Progress Report on IMAA, Minister of Supply and Services, Ottawa.

TREASURY BOARD OF CANADA (1992), "Notes for a Statement on Regulation and Competitiveness by the President of the Treasury Board and Minister responsible for Regulatory Affairs to the Sub-Committee on Regulation and Competitiveness of the Standing Committee on Finance, May 12, 1992, Ottawa.

DENMARK

DALGAARD, J.V. (1992), *Do we get the Benefits from the Use of Information Technology in the Government?*, Ministry of Finance, Copenhagen.

MINISTRY OF FINANCE (1988), "Review of the Public Sector 1988" (translation of *Redegørelse om den offentlige sektor 1988, Sammenfatning*), Public Management Service, OECD, Paris.

MINISTRY OF FINANCE (1990), *Modernization of the Public Sector in Denmark,* Copenhagen.

MINISTRY OF FINANCE (1991), *The Public Sector in the Year 2000. Report on the Danish Modernization Programme 1991,* Copenhagen.

MINISTRY OF FINANCE (1992a), *Choice of Welfare: Competition and the Citizen's Right to Choose,* "White Paper on Modernisation 1992: The Public Sector in 2000", Copenhagen.

MINISTRY OF FINANCE (1992b), *Effective IT in Government: Summary of Report by the EDP Policy Committee on the Use by Government of Information Technology in the 1990s,* Copenhagen.

MINISTRY OF FINANCE (1993), *Fresh Approach to the Public Sector: Summary,* Copenhagen.

FINLAND

GOVERNMENT OF FINLAND (1993), *Government decision-in-principle on reforms in central and regional government,* Helsinki.

KIVINIEMI, M. (1988), *The Improvement of the Public Services,* Government Printing Centre, Helsinki.

MINISTRY OF FINANCE (1992), *Public Sector Management Reforms, Government Decision on Public Sector Management Reform,* Helsinki.

MINISTRY OF FINANCE (1993), *The World's Best Public Sector?,* final report, shortened version, Helsinki.

STATE EMPLOYER'S OFFICE (1992), "The State Employer's Salary and Wage Policy Programme", Helsinki.

FRANCE

BAROUCH, G. and H. CHAVAS (1993), *Où va la modernisation? Dix années de modernisation de l'administration d'État en France,* L'Harmattan, Paris.

COMMISSARIAT GÉNÉRAL DU PLAN (1989), *Rapport de la Commission "Efficacité de l'État": Le Pari de la responsabilité,* La Documentation Française, Paris.

COMMISSARIAT GÉNÉRAL DU PLAN (1992), *L'Informatique de l'État: évaluation du développement de l'informatique et de son impact sur l'efficacité de l'administration,* La Documentation française, Paris.

COMMISSARIAT GÉNÉRAL DU PLAN (1993), *Pour un État stratège, garant de l'intérêt général,* La Documentation française, Paris.

CONSEIL D'ÉTAT (1992), "Rapport Public 1991", La Documentation Française, Paris.

CONSEIL SCIENTIFIQUE DE L'ÉVALUATION (1992), *L'Évaluation de l'expertise à la responsabilité: Rapport 1991,* La Documentation française, Paris.

CROZIER M. and S. TROSA (1992), "La Décentralisation, réforme de l'État", Pouvoirs Locaux, Paris.

DE CLAUSADE, J. (1989), "L'Adaptation de l'administration française à l'Europe", Conseil d'État, Paris.

GIBERT P. and THOENIG J.-C. (1993), "La Gestion publique: entre l'apprentissage et l'amnésie", *Revue Politique et Management Public,* Vol. 11, No. 1.

INSTITUT DE MANAGEMENT PUBLIC (1990), "Innovations et développements dans le management des organisations publiques", *Politiques et management public,* off-print, Vol. 8, No. 1, March 1990, pp. 80-124.

INSTITUT INTERNATIONAL D'ADMINISTRATION PUBLIQUE (1989), "Fonction publique: les statuts à l'épreuve de la gestion", *Revue française d'administration publique,* No. 49, January-March 1989.

MINISTÈRE DE LA FONCTION PUBLIQUE ET DES RÉFORMES ADMINISTRATIVES (1990a), *Les Projets de service,* La Documentation française, Paris.

MINISTÈRE DE LA FONCTION PUBLIQUE ET DES RÉFORMES ADMINISTRATIVES (1990b), *Renouveau du service public: Les rencontres 1990,* Paris.

MINISTÈRE DE LA FONCTION PUBLIQUE ET DES RÉFORMES ADMINISTRATIVES (1992), *La Charte des services publics. Bilan 1992,* Paris.

MINISTÈRE DE LA FONCTION PUBLIQUE (1991), *Les Outils de gestion,* ''Cahiers du Renouveau'', Paris, La Documentation française.

MINISTÈRE DE LA RÉFORME ADMINISTRATIVE (1987), *L'Administration partenaire,* Livre blanc, Paris.

ROCARD, M. (1989), ''Le Renouveau du service public'', circulaire du Premier ministre, Paris.

THOENIG, J.C., ''La Décentralisation, dix ans après'', *Pouvoirs,* No. 60.

VIVERET, P. (1989), ''L'Évaluation des politiques et des actions publiques. Rapport au Premier ministre'', Report to the Prime Minister, Paris.

GERMANY

KONIG, Klaus, Hans Joachim VON OERTZEN and Frido WAGENER, eds. (1983), *Public Administration in the Federal Republic of Germany,* Kluwer-Deventer, Netherlands.

FEDERAL MINISTRY OF THE INTERIOR (1988), ''Simplifying Law and Administration: An Important Policy Objective of the Federal Government. A Brief Review of 1983-1987'', Bonn.

GREECE

MINISTRY TO THE PRESIDENCY OF GOVERNMENT (1993), *Programme of Administrative Modernisation 1993-1995,* Athens.

VERNARDAKIS, G., and C.D. PAPASTATHOPOULOS (1989), ''The Higher Civil Service in Greece'', *International Review of Administrative Sciences,* Vol. 55, No. 4, December 1989, pp. 603-629.

IRELAND

BOYLE, Richard (1992), *Administrative Budgets in the Irish Civil Service,* Institute of Public Administration, Dublin.

CLINCE, Seamus, Evelyn BLENNERHASSET and Niamh CAMPBELL (1992), *Achieving the Benefits of Information Technology in the Irish Civil Service,* Institute of Public Administration, Dublin.

GOVERNMENT OF IRELAND (1985), *Serving the Country Better: A White Paper on Public Service,* Dublin.

MOORE, P. J. (1991), ''Administrative Budgets: A New Era for Civil Service Managers'', *Seirbhís Phoiblí,* Vol. 12, No. 1, April 1991, pp. 24-28.

MURPHY, Kevin (1993), ''Managing the Irish Public Service in the 1990s'', *Seirbhís Phoiblí,* Vol. 14, No. 2, October 1993, pp. 7-26.

REYNOLDS, Albert (1994), ''Developing Strategic Management in the Irish Public Service'', speech by the *Taoiseach,* Mr. Albert Reynolds, T.D., 22 February 1994, Government Buildings, Dublin.

ITALY

SEPE, O. (1988), ''Les Réformes de l'administration publique'', Chapter 5 in *L'Année administrative 87,* Institut international d'administration publique, Paris.

JAPAN

MANAGEMENT AND COORDINATION AGENCY, *Organization of the Government of Japan,* periodic report, Tokyo.

MANAGEMENT AND COORDINATION AGENCY (1990), ''Privatization and Deregulation: The Japanese Experience'', Tokyo.

MASUJIMA, Toshiyuki and Minoru O'UCHI, eds. (1993), *The Management and Reform of Japanese Government,* The Institute of Administrative Management, Tokyo.

PROVISIONAL COUNCIL FOR THE PROMOTION OF ADMINISTRATIVE REFORM (1993), ''Final Report of the Provisional Council for the Promotion of Administrative Reform'', Tokyo.

SAKURAI, Y. and D.S. WRIGHT (1987), ''Administrative Reform in Japan: Politics, Policy and Public Administration in a Deliberative Society'', *Public Administration Review,* Vol. 47, No. 2, March 1987, pp. 121-133.

LUXEMBOURG

BACKES, V. (1987), "Reform of the Public Administration in the Grand-Duchy of Luxembourg", European Institute of Public Administration, Maastricht.

NETHERLANDS

BREUNESE, J.N. (1987), "Administrative Reforms in the Netherlands", European Institute of Public Administration, Maastricht.

COX, R.M., "Can Welfare States Grow in Leaps or Bounds? Non-Incremental Policymaking in the Netherlands", *Governance*, Vol. 5, No. 1, January 1992.

NETHERLANDS SCIENTIFIC COUNCIL FOR GOVERNMENT POLICY (1993), *Report and Evaluation of the Fourth Term of Office 1988-1992,* The Hague.

ROSENTHAL, U., R. ROBORGH and F. VAN DER MEER (1990), "Memorandum on Dutch Government Organization", International Institute of Administrative Sciences, Brussels.

NEW ZEALAND

BALL, Ian (1989), "Changes in Accounting and Auditing Practices: The New Zealand Experience", Centre for Australian Public Sector Management, Brisbane.

BOSTON, J., J. MARTIN, J. PALLOT, P. WALSH, eds. (1991), *Reshaping the State: New Zealand's Bureaucratic Revolution,* Oxford University Press, Oxford.

CLARK, Margaret and Elizabeth SINCLAIR, eds. (1986), *Purpose, Performance and Profit: Redefining the Public Sector. Proceedings of the 1986 Convention of the Nez Zealand Institute of Public Administration,* Government Printing Office, Wellington.

KELSEY, J. (1993), *Rolling Back the State,* Bridget Williams, Wellington.

MASCARENHAS, R.C. (1991), "State-Owned Enterprises", Chapter 2 in Boston, *et al.,* eds. (1991), *Reshaping the State: New Zealand's Bureaucratic Revolution,* Oxford University Press, Oxford.

MARTIN, John (1992), "Transformation of a Bureaucracy: The New Zealand Experience", Victoria University of Wellington, Wellington.

McCULLOCH, B.W. (1992), "Output Specification", New Zealand Society of Accountants, Wellington.

SCOTT, Graham, Peter BUSHNELL and Nikitin SALLEE (1990), "Reform of the Core Public Sector: New Zealand Experience", *Governance,* Vol. 3, No. 2, April 1990, pp. 138-167.

STATE SERVICES COMMISSION (1988), *Managing Change: A Personnel View,* Wellington.

STATE SERVICES COMMISSION (1991), *Review of State Sector Reforms: Report of Steering Group (Logan Review),* Wellington.

STATE SERVICES COMMISSION (1992), *The Policy Advice Initiative: Opportunities for Management,* Wellington.

STATE SERVICES COMMISSION (1993), *Public Sector Reform in New Zealand: A Senior Management Perspective,* Wellington.

STATE SERVICES COMMISSION (1994), *New Zealand's Reformed State Sector,* Wellington.

TREASURY (1984), *Economic Management,* Government Printer, Wellington.

TREASURY (1987), *Government Management,* Government Printer, Wellington.

TREASURY (1989), "Financial Management Reform", Wellington.

NORWAY

GOVERNMENT OF NORWAY (1992), *Improving the Structure of Legislation in Norway,* Law Structure Committee, Norwegian Official Reports (NOR 1992:32E), (Summary in English), p. 8.

NYMO, Synnove and Jan PERSSON (1990), "Organizational Approaches to Improve Efficiency in the Public Sector in Norway", Ministry of Finance, Oslo.

OLSEN, J.P. (1988), *The Modernisation of Public Administration in the Nordic Countries,* Norwegian Research Centre in Organization and Management, Bergen.

ROYAL NORWEGIAN MINISTRY OF CONSUMER AFFAIRS AND GOVERNMENT ADMINISTRATION (1988), "The Government's Renewal Program", Oslo.

ROYAL NORWEGIAN MINISTRY OF LABOUR AND GOVERNMENT ADMINISTRATION (1992a), "Plan for the Readjustment of Central Government Administration in the 1990s: Administration Policy Guidelines and Measures", Oslo.

ROYAL NORWEGIAN MINISTRY OF LABOUR AND GOVERNMENT ADMINISTRATION (1992b), "The Central Government's Administration and Personnel Policies", Oslo.

PORTUGAL

SECRETARIAT FOR ADMINISTRATIVE MODERNIZATION (1989), "Interdepartmental Programme for Debureaucratization", Lisbon.

SECRETARIAT FOR ADMINISTRATIVE MODERNIZATION (1992), "Deontological Charter for Civil Servants", Lisbon.

SWEDEN

ASPEGREN, L. (1988), *Responsiveness in the Swedish Public Service,* Statens Institut för Personalutveckling, Stockholm-Solna.

BLOMQVIST, Å., Y. BOURDET and I. PERSSON (1993), *Reforming the Welfare State: The Swedish Experience,* School of Policy Studies (Queen's University), Ottawa.

FUDGE, C. and L. GUSTAFSSON (1989), "Administrative Reform and Public Management in Sweden and the United Kingdom", *Public Money and Management,* Vol. 9, No. 2, Summer 1989, pp. 29-34.

GOVERNMENT COMMISSION ON CENTRAL GOVERNMENT-STATE AGENCY RELATIONS (1985), *The Central Government, the State Agencies and their Management and the Public Service Corporations and their Companies; A Summary of Two Swedish Official Reports (SOU 1985:40 and SOU 1985:41),* Ministry of Public Administration, Stockholm.

MINISTRY OF FINANCE (1987), *Public Services – A Searchlight on Productivity and Users: Report to the Expert Group on Public Finance,* Stockholm.

MINISTRY OF FINANCE (1988), "Renewing the Public Sector: Excerpts from the 1988 Revised Budget Statement", Stockholm.

MINISTRY OF FINANCE (1992), *Regulation and Management in the Central Government Administration and Financial Preconditions for Government Agencies,* Stockholm.

MINISTRY OF FINANCE (1993a), *Management by Objectives and Results: Excerpts from the 1993 Economic Policy Statement,* Stockholm.

MINISTRY OF FINANCE (1993b), *Management of Government Administration and Financial Conditions for State Agencies,* Stockholm.

MINISTRY OF FINANCE (1994), *In search of results and financial incentives: recent advancements in the Swedish Central Government budget processes,* "Papers on Public Sector Budgeting and Management, Vol. 1, Stockholm.

MINISTRY OF PUBLIC ADMINISTRATION (1988), "Simplification of Rules in Sweden: Three Examples", Stockholm.

NATIONAL AUDIT BUREAU (1993), "Results Analysis: For use in Reviews and Measures to Improve Efficiency and Effectiveness", Stockholm.

SWITZERLAND

CHANCELLERIE FÉDÉRALE (1988), *L'administration... au service du public,* Berne.

OFFICE FÉDÉRAL DE L'ORGANISATION (1988), "Projet EFFI: Rapport sur l'état de sa réalisation (Rapport final)", Berne.

TURKEY

DIRECTORATE OF ADMINISTRATIVE DEVELOPMENT (1989), *Reducing Bureaucracy in Public Administration, 1984-1989,* Ankara.

PRIME MINISTRY (1989), "A Manual on Administration System of Turkey", Foreign Affairs Department, Ankara.

UNITED KINGDOM

BUTLER, Sir Robin (1993), "The Evolution of the Civil Service: A Progress Report", *Public Administration*, Vol. 71, No. 3, September 1993, pp. 395-406.

DEPARTMENT OF TRADE AND INDUSTRY (1991), *Cutting Red Tape for Business*, London.

HER MAJESTY'S TREASURY (1991), *Competing for Quality: Buying Better Public Services*, HMSO, London.

JENKINS, K., G. OATES and A. STOTT (1985), *Making Things Happen: A Report on the Implementation of Government Efficiency Scrutinies*, HMSO, London.

NATIONAL AUDIT OFFICE (1989), *The Next Steps Initiative*, HMSO, London.

OFFICE OF PUBLIC SERVICE AND SCIENCE (1993a), *The Government's Guide to Market Testing*, HMSO, London.

OFFICE OF PUBLIC SERVICE AND SCIENCE (1993b), *Next Steps Review 1993*, HMSO, London.

OFFICE OF THE MINISTER FOR THE CIVIL SERVICE (1991), *Setting up Next Steps: A Short Account of the Origins, Launch and Implementation of the Next Steps Project in the British Civil Service*, HMSO, London.

PRIME MINISTER (1988), *Improving Management in Government: The Next Steps*, HMSO, London.

PRIME MINISTER (1991), *Making the Most of Next Steps: The Management of Ministers' Departments and their Executive Agencies*, HMSO, London.

PRIME MINISTER (1991), *The Citizen's Charter: Raising the Standard*, HMSO, London.

PRIME MINISTER (1994), *Next Steps: Moving On*, HMSO, London.

PRIME MINISTER (1994), *The Civil Service: Continuity and Change*, HMSO, London.

RICHARDS, Sue and Jeff RODRIGUES (1993), "Strategies for Management in the Civil Service: Change of Direction", *Public Money and Management*, Vol. 13, No. 2, April-June 1993, pp. 33-38.

SECRETARY OF STATE FOR EMPLOYMENT (1986), *Building Businesses... Not Barriers*, White Paper presented to Parliament, HMSO, London.

UNITED STATES

BOWSHER, Charles A. (1993), "Reinventing Government: Do It Now, Do It Right!", address by Charles A. Bowsher, Comptroller General of the United States, General Accounting Office, October 1993.

CONGRESS OF THE UNITED STATES (1993), "Using Performance Measures in the Federal Budget Process, A Congressional Budget Office Study", Washington DC.

DiIULIO, John. J.Jr., Gerald GARVEY and Donald F. KETTL (1993), *Improving Government Performance: An Owner's Manual*, The Brookings Institution, Washington DC.

GENERAL ACCOUNTING OFFICE (1991), *Government Contractors: Are Contractors Performing Inherently Governmental Functions?*, Washington DC.

GENERAL ACCOUNTING OFFICE (1993), *GAO's Comments on the National Performance Review's Recommendations*, Washington DC.

GENERAL ACCOUNTING OFFICE (1994), *Examples of Public and Private Innovations to Improve Service Delivery*, Washington DC.

GORE, Al (1993), *From Red Tape to Results: Creating a Government that Works Better and Costs Less*, Report of the National Performance Review, Superintendent of Documents, Pittsburgh, PA.

GOVERNMENTAL ACCOUNTING STANDARDS BOARD (1992), *Preliminary Views of the Governmental Accounting Standards Board on Concepts related to Service Efforts and Accomplishments Reporting*, Norwalk, CT.

INK, Dwight (1993), "Are Federal Oversight and Agency Management Out of Sync?", Institute of Public Administration, New York.

MOE, R. C. (1990), "Public and Private Sector Relationships in the Age of Privatization", American Political Science Association, San Francisco.

NATIONAL ACADEMY OF PUBLIC ADMINISTRATION (1993), *Leading People in Change: Empowerment, Commitment, Accountability*, Washington DC.

OFFICE OF MANAGEMENT AND BUDGET (1993), *A Vision of Change for America*, US Government Printing Office, Washington DC.

OFFICE OF TECHNOLOGY ASSESSMENT (1993), ''Making Government Work: Electronic Delivery of Federal Services'', Washington DC.

OSBORNE, David and Ted GAEBLER (1992), *Reinventing Government: How the Entrepreneurial Spirit is Transforming the Public Sector,* Addison-Wesley, Reading, Mass.

PRESIDENT'S COMMISSION ON PRIVATIZATION (1988), *Privatization: Toward More Effective Government,* Washington DC.

SCHULTZE, Charles (1977), *The Public Use of Private Interest,* The Brookings Institution, Washington DC.

SENATE OF THE UNITED STATES (1992), *Government Performance and Results Act,* Report of the Committee on Governmental Affairs of the US Senate to accompany S.20, US Government Printing Office, Washington DC.

MAIN SALES OUTLETS OF OECD PUBLICATIONS
PRINCIPAUX POINTS DE VENTE DES PUBLICATIONS DE L'OCDE

ARGENTINA – ARGENTINE
Carlos Hirsch S.R.L.
Galería Güemes, Florida 165, 4° Piso
1333 Buenos Aires   Tel. (1) 331.1787 y 331.2391
Telefax: (1) 331.1787

AUSTRALIA – AUSTRALIE
D.A. Information Services
648 Whitehorse Road, P.O.B 163
Mitcham, Victoria 3132   Tel. (03) 873.4411
Telefax: (03) 873.5679

AUSTRIA – AUTRICHE
Gerold & Co.
Graben 31
Wien I   Tel. (0222) 533.50.14
Telefax: (0222) 512.47.31.29

BELGIUM – BELGIQUE
Jean De Lannoy
Avenue du Roi 202 Koningslaan
B-1060 Bruxelles   Tel. (02) 538.51.69/538.08.41
Telefax: (02) 538.08.41

CANADA
Renouf Publishing Company Ltd.
1294 Algoma Road
Ottawa, ON K1B 3W8   Tel. (613) 741.4333
Telefax: (613) 741.5439
Stores:
61 Sparks Street
Ottawa, ON K1P 5R1   Tel. (613) 238.8985
211 Yonge Street
Toronto, ON M5B 1M4   Tel. (416) 363.3171
Telefax: (416)363.59.63

Les Éditions La Liberté Inc.
3020 Chemin Sainte-Foy
Sainte-Foy, PQ G1X 3V6   Tel. (418) 658.3763
Telefax: (418) 658.3763

Federal Publications Inc.
165 University Avenue, Suite 701
Toronto, ON M5H 3B8   Tel. (416) 860.1611
Telefax: (416) 860.1608

Les Publications Fédérales
1185 Université
Montréal, QC H3B 3A7   Tel. (514) 954.1633
Telefax: (514) 954.1635

CHINA – CHINE
China National Publications Import
Export Corporation (CNPIEC)
16 Gongti E. Road, Chaoyang District
P.O. Box 88 or 50
Beijing 100704 PR   Tel. (01) 506.6688
Telefax: (01) 506.3101

CHINESE TAIPEI – TAIPEI CHINOIS
Good Faith Worldwide Int'l. Co. Ltd.
9th Floor, No. 118, Sec. 2
Chung Hsiao E. Road
Taipei   Tel. (02) 391.7396/391.7397
Telefax: (02) 394.9176

CZECH REPUBLIC – RÉPUBLIQUE TCHÈQUE
Artia Pegas Press Ltd.
Narodni Trida 25
POB 825
111 21 Praha 1   Tel. 26.65.68
Telefax: 26.20.81

DENMARK – DANEMARK
Munksgaard Book and Subscription Service
35, Nørre Søgade, P.O. Box 2148
DK-1016 København K   Tel. (33) 12.85.70
Telefax: (33) 12.93.87

EGYPT – ÉGYPTE
Middle East Observer
41 Sherif Street
Cairo   Tel. 392.6919
Telefax: 360-6804

FINLAND – FINLANDE
Akateeminen Kirjakauppa
Keskuskatu 1, P.O. Box 128
00100 Helsinki
Subscription Services/Agence d'abonnements :
P.O. Box 23
00371 Helsinki   Tel. (358 0) 121 4416
Telefax: (358 0) 121.4450

FRANCE
OECD/OCDE
Mail Orders/Commandes par correspondance:
2, rue André-Pascal
75775 Paris Cedex 16   Tel. (33-1) 45.24.82.00
Telefax: (33-1) 49.10.42.76
Telex: 640048 OCDE
Internet: Compte.PUBSINQ @ oecd.org

Orders via Minitel, France only/
Commandes par Minitel, France exclusivement :
36 15 OCDE

OECD Bookshop/Librairie de l'OCDE :
33, rue Octave-Feuillet
75016 Paris   Tel. (33-1) 45.24.81.81
(33-1) 45.24.81.67

Documentation Française
29, quai Voltaire
75007 Paris   Tel. 40.15.70.00
Gibert Jeune (Droit-Économie)
6, place Saint-Michel
75006 Paris   Tel. 43.25.91.19
Librairie du Commerce International
10, avenue d'Iéna
75016 Paris   Tel. 40.73.34.60
Librairie Dunod
Université Paris-Dauphine
Place du Maréchal de Lattre de Tassigny
75016 Paris   Tel. (1) 44.05.40.13
Librairie Lavoisier
11, rue Lavoisier
75008 Paris   Tel. 42.65.39.95
Librairie L.G.D.J. - Montchrestien
20, rue Soufflot
75005 Paris   Tel. 46.33.89.85
Librairie des Sciences Politiques
30, rue Saint-Guillaume
75007 Paris   Tel. 45.48.36.02
P.U.F.
49, boulevard Saint-Michel
75005 Paris   Tel. 43.25.83.40
Librairie de l'Université
12a, rue Nazareth
13100 Aix-en-Provence   Tel. (16) 42.26.18.08
Documentation Française
165, rue Garibaldi
69003 Lyon   Tel. (16) 78.63.32.23
Librairie Decitre
29, place Bellecour
69002 Lyon   Tel. (16) 72.40.54.54
Librairie Sauramps
Le Triangle
34967 Montpellier Cedex 2   Tel. (16) 67.58.85.15
Tekefax: (16) 67.58.27.36

GERMANY – ALLEMAGNE
OECD Publications and Information Centre
August-Bebel-Allee 6
D-53175 Bonn   Tel. (0228) 959.120
Telefax: (0228) 959.12.17

GREECE – GRÈCE
Librairie Kauffmann
Mavrokordatou 9
106 78 Athens   Tel. (01) 32.55.321
Telefax: (01) 32.30.320

HONG-KONG
Swindon Book Co. Ltd.
Astoria Bldg. 3F
34 Ashley Road, Tsimshatsui
Kowloon, Hong Kong   Tel. 2376.2062
Telefax: 2376.0685

HUNGARY – HONGRIE
Euro Info Service
Margitsziget, Európa Ház
1138 Budapest   Tel. (1) 111.62.16
Telefax: (1) 111.60.61

ICELAND – ISLANDE
Mál Mog Menning
Laugavegi 18, Pósthólf 392
121 Reykjavik   Tel. (1) 552.4240
Telefax: (1) 562.3523

INDIA – INDE
Oxford Book and Stationery Co.
Scindia House
New Delhi 110001   Tel. (11) 331.5896/5308
Telefax: (11) 332.5993
17 Park Street
Calcutta 700016   Tel. 240832

INDONESIA – INDONÉSIE
Pdii-Lipi
P.O. Box 4298
Jakarta 12042   Tel. (21) 573.34.67
Telefax: (21) 573.34.67

IRELAND – IRLANDE
Government Supplies Agency
Publications Section
4/5 Harcourt Road
Dublin 2   Tel. 661.31.11
Telefax: 475.27.60

ISRAEL
Praedicta
5 Shatner Street
P.O. Box 34030
Jerusalem 91430   Tel. (2) 52.84.90/1/2
Telefax: (2) 52.84.93

R.O.Y. International
P.O. Box 13056
Tel Aviv 61130   Tel. (3) 546 1423
Telefax: (3) 546 1442

Palestinian Authority/Middle East:
INDEX Information Services
P.O.B. 19502
Jerusalem   Tel. (2) 27.12.19
Telefax: (2) 27.16.34

ITALY – ITALIE
Libreria Commissionaria Sansoni
Via Duca di Calabria 1/1
50125 Firenze   Tel. (055) 64.54.15
Telefax: (055) 64.12.57
Via Bartolini 29
20155 Milano   Tel. (02) 36.50.83
Editrice e Libreria Herder
Piazza Montecitorio 120
00186 Roma   Tel. 679.46.28
Telefax: 678.47.51
Libreria Hoepli
Via Hoepli 5
20121 Milano   Tel. (02) 86.54.46
Telefax: (02) 805.28.86
Libreria Scientifica
Dott. Lucio de Biasio 'Aeiou'
Via Coronelli, 6
20146 Milano   Tel. (02) 48.95.45.52
Telefax: (02) 48.95.45.48

JAPAN – JAPON
OECD Publications and Information Centre
Landic Akasaka Building
2-3-4 Akasaka, Minato-ku
Tokyo 107   Tel. (81.3) 3586.2016
Telefax: (81.3) 3584.7929

KOREA – CORÉE
Kyobo Book Centre Co. Ltd.
P.O. Box 1658, Kwang Hwa Moon
Seoul   Tel. 730.78.91
Telefax: 735.00.30

MALAYSIA – MALAISIE
University of Malaya Bookshop
University of Malaya
P.O. Box 1127, Jalan Pantai Baru
59700 Kuala Lumpur
Malaysia   Tel. 756.5000/756.5425
                             Telefax: 756.3246

MEXICO – MEXIQUE
Revistas y Periodicos Internacionales S.A. de C.V.
Florencia 57 - 1004
Mexico, D.F. 06600   Tel. 207.81.00
                             Telefax: 208.39.79

NETHERLANDS – PAYS-BAS
SDU Uitgeverij Plantijnstraat
Externe Fondsen
Postbus 20014
2500 EA's-Gravenhage   Tel. (070) 37.89.880
Voor bestellingen: Telefax: (070) 34.75.778

**NEW ZEALAND
NOUVELLE-ZÉLANDE**
GPLegislation Services
P.O. Box 12418
Thorndon, Wellington   Tel. (04) 496.5655
                             Telefax: (04) 496.5698

NORWAY – NORVÈGE
Narvesen Info Center – NIC
Bertrand Narvesens vei 2
P.O. Box 6125 Etterstad
0602 Oslo 6   Tel. (022) 57.33.00
                             Telefax: (022) 68.19.01

PAKISTAN
Mirza Book Agency
65 Shahrah Quaid-E-Azam
Lahore 54000   Tel. (42) 353.601
                             Telefax: (42) 231.730

PHILIPPINE – PHILIPPINES
International Book Center
5th Floor, Filipinas Life Bldg.
Ayala Avenue
Metro Manila   Tel. 81.96.76
                             Telex 23312 RHP PH

PORTUGAL
Livraria Portugal
Rua do Carmo 70-74
Apart. 2681
1200 Lisboa   Tel. (01) 347.49.82/5
                             Telefax: (01) 347.02.64

SINGAPORE – SINGAPOUR
Gower Asia Pacific Pte Ltd.
Golden Wheel Building
41, Kallang Pudding Road, No. 04-03
Singapore 1334   Tel. 741.5166
                             Telefax: 742.9356

SPAIN – ESPAGNE
Mundi-Prensa Libros S.A.
Castelló 37, Apartado 1223
Madrid 28001   Tel. (91) 431.33.99
                             Telefax: (91) 575.39.98

Libreria Internacional AEDOS
Consejo de Ciento 391
08009 – Barcelona   Tel. (93) 488.30.09
                             Telefax: (93) 487.76.59

Llibreria de la Generalitat
Palau Moja
Rambla dels Estudis, 118
08002 – Barcelona
            (Subscripcions) Tel. (93) 318.80.12
            (Publicacions) Tel. (93) 302.67.23
                             Telefax: (93) 412.18.54

SRI LANKA
Centre for Policy Research
c/o Colombo Agencies Ltd.
No. 300-304, Galle Road
Colombo 3   Tel. (1) 574240, 573551-2
                             Telefax: (1) 575394, 510711

SWEDEN – SUÈDE
Fritzes Customer Service
S–106 47 Stockholm   Tel. (08) 690.90.90
                             Telefax: (08) 20.50.21

Subscription Agency/Agence d'abonnements :
Wennergren-Williams Info AB
P.O. Box 1305
171 25 Solna   Tel. (08) 705.97.50
                             Telefax: (08) 27.00.71

SWITZERLAND – SUISSE
Maditec S.A. (Books and Periodicals - Livres
et périodiques)
Chemin des Palettes 4
Case postale 266
1020 Renens VD 1   Tel. (021) 635.08.65
                             Telefax: (021) 635.07.80

Librairie Payot S.A.
4, place Pépinet
CP 3212
1002 Lausanne   Tel. (021) 341.33.47
                             Telefax: (021) 341.33.45

Librairie Unilivres
6, rue de Candolle
1205 Genève   Tel. (022) 320.26.23
                             Telefax: (022) 329.73.18

Subscription Agency/Agence d'abonnements :
Dynapresse Marketing S.A.
38 avenue Vibert
1227 Carouge   Tel. (022) 308.07.89
                             Telefax: (022) 308.07.99

See also – Voir aussi :
OECD Publications and Information Centre
August-Bebel-Allee 6
D-53175 Bonn (Germany)   Tel. (0228) 959.120
                             Telefax: (0228) 959.12.17

THAILAND – THAÏLANDE
Suksit Siam Co. Ltd.
113, 115 Fuang Nakhon Rd.
Opp. Wat Rajbopith
Bangkok 10200   Tel. (662) 225.9531/2
                             Telefax: (662) 222.5188

TURKEY – TURQUIE
Kültür Yayinlari Is-Türk Ltd. Sti.
Atatürk Bulvari No. 191/Kat 13
Kavaklidere/Ankara   Tel. 428.11.40 Ext. 2458
Dolmabahce Cad. No. 29
Besiktas/Istanbul   Tel. (312) 260 7188
                             Telex: (312) 418 29 46

UNITED KINGDOM – ROYAUME-UNI
HMSO
Gen. enquiries   Tel. (171) 873 8496
Postal orders only:
P.O. Box 276, London SW8 5DT
Personal Callers HMSO Bookshop
49 High Holborn, London WC1V 6HB
                             Telefax: (171) 873 8416
Branches at: Belfast, Birmingham, Bristol,
Edinburgh, Manchester

UNITED STATES – ÉTATS-UNIS
OECD Publications and Information Center
2001 L Street N.W., Suite 650
Washington, D.C. 20036-4910 Tel. (202) 785.6323
                             Telefax: (202) 785.0350

VENEZUELA
Libreria del Este
Avda F. Miranda 52, Aptdo. 60337
Edificio Galipán
Caracas 106   Tel. 951.1705/951.2307/951.1297
                             Telegram: Libreste Caracas

Subscription to OECD periodicals may also be
placed through main subscription agencies.

Les abonnements aux publications périodiques de
l'OCDE peuvent être souscrits auprès des
principales agences d'abonnement.

Orders and inquiries from countries where Distribu-
tors have not yet been appointed should be sent to:
OECD Publications Service, 2 rue André-Pascal,
75775 Paris Cedex 16, France.

Les commandes provenant de pays où l'OCDE n'a
pas encore désigné de distributeur peuvent être
adressées à : OCDE, Service des Publications,
2, rue André-Pascal, 75775 Paris Cedex 16, France.

7-1995